David Hockney

My Window

David Hockney

My Window

Taschen

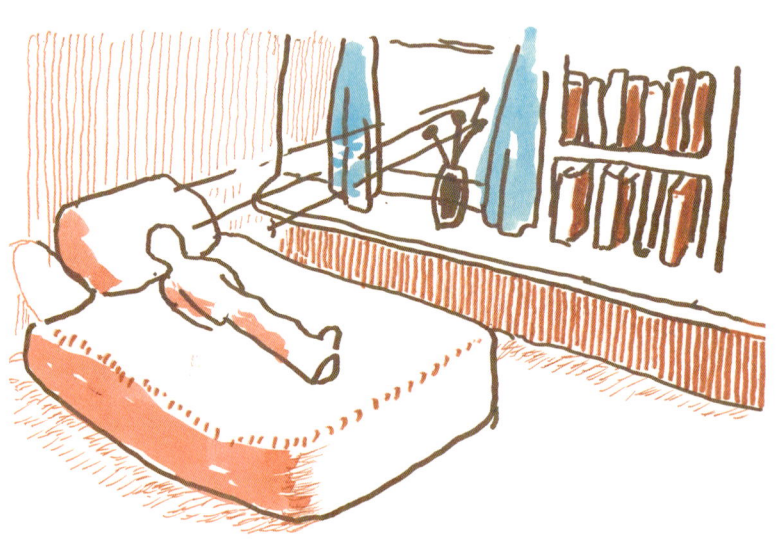

MY WINDOW describes flowers and the sunrise in Bridlington, East Yorkshire.

I started on the iPhone in 2009 (Twenty o'nine). There was great advantage in this medium because it's backlit and I could draw in the dark. I didn't ever have to get out of bed. Everything I needed was on the iPhone.

From about April to August when the sun is in the north, if I didn't pull the curtains or lower the venetian blind down, the sun would wake me up – at about 4h30 am on 21st June. I would never have thought to do a sunrise without the iPhone.

My friend John would put different flowers there every two or three days. I drew on the iPhone with my thumb, but when the iPad came out in 2010 I immediately got one from California, probably the first one in Bridlington. Ever since I've used the iPad, as I could draw with a stylus and get more details in.

DAVID HOCKNEY, 17th August 2019

'No. 183', 4th May 2009, iPhone drawing

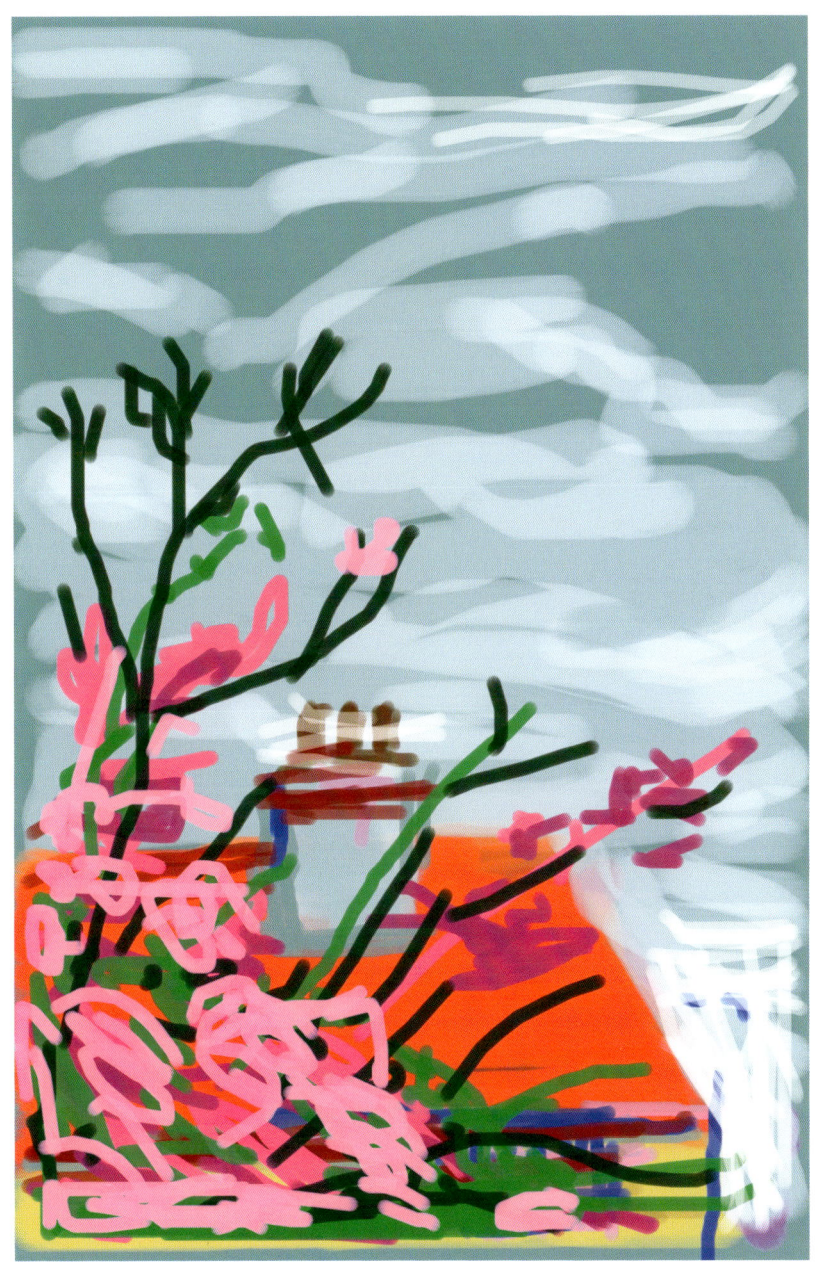

'No. 184', 4th May 2009, iPhone drawing
Page 10: 'No. 274', 23rd May 2009, iPhone drawing;
Page 11: 'No. 275', 23rd May 2009, iPhone drawing

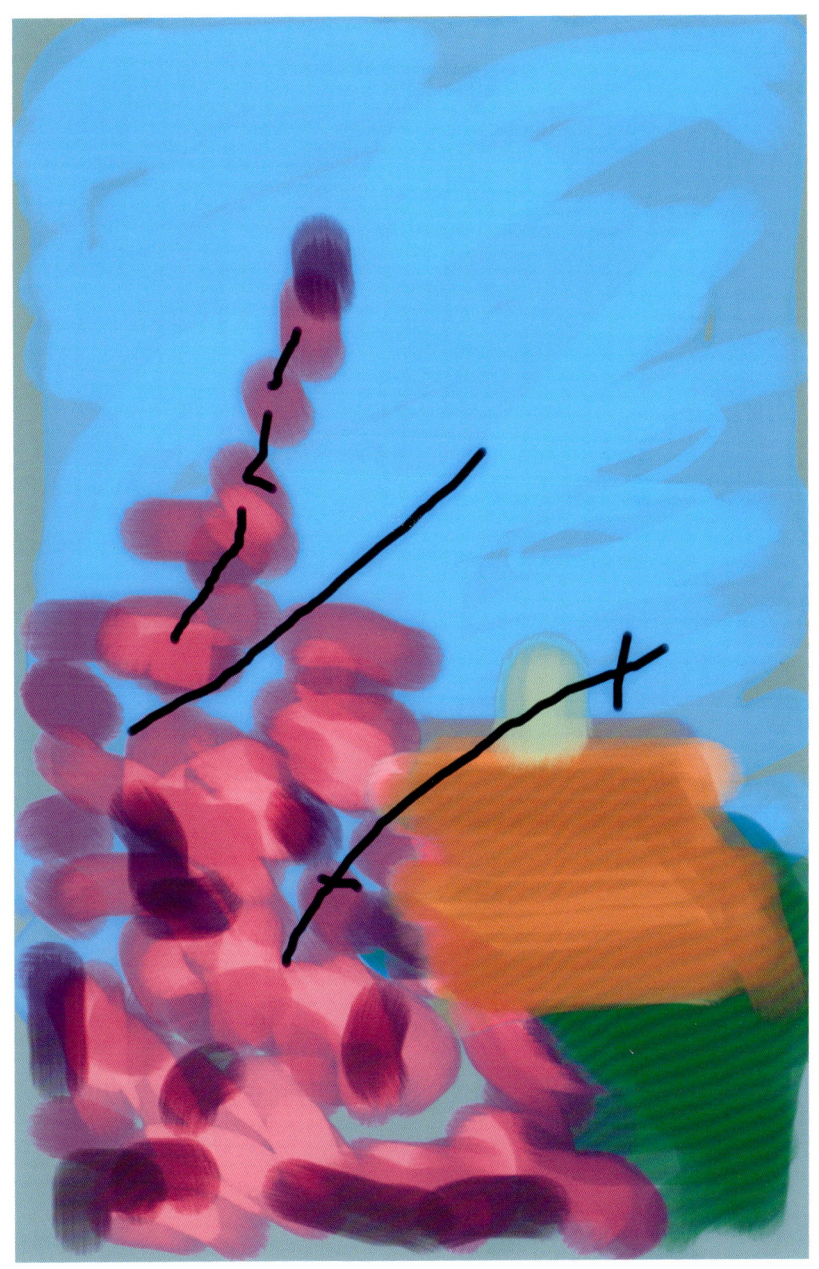

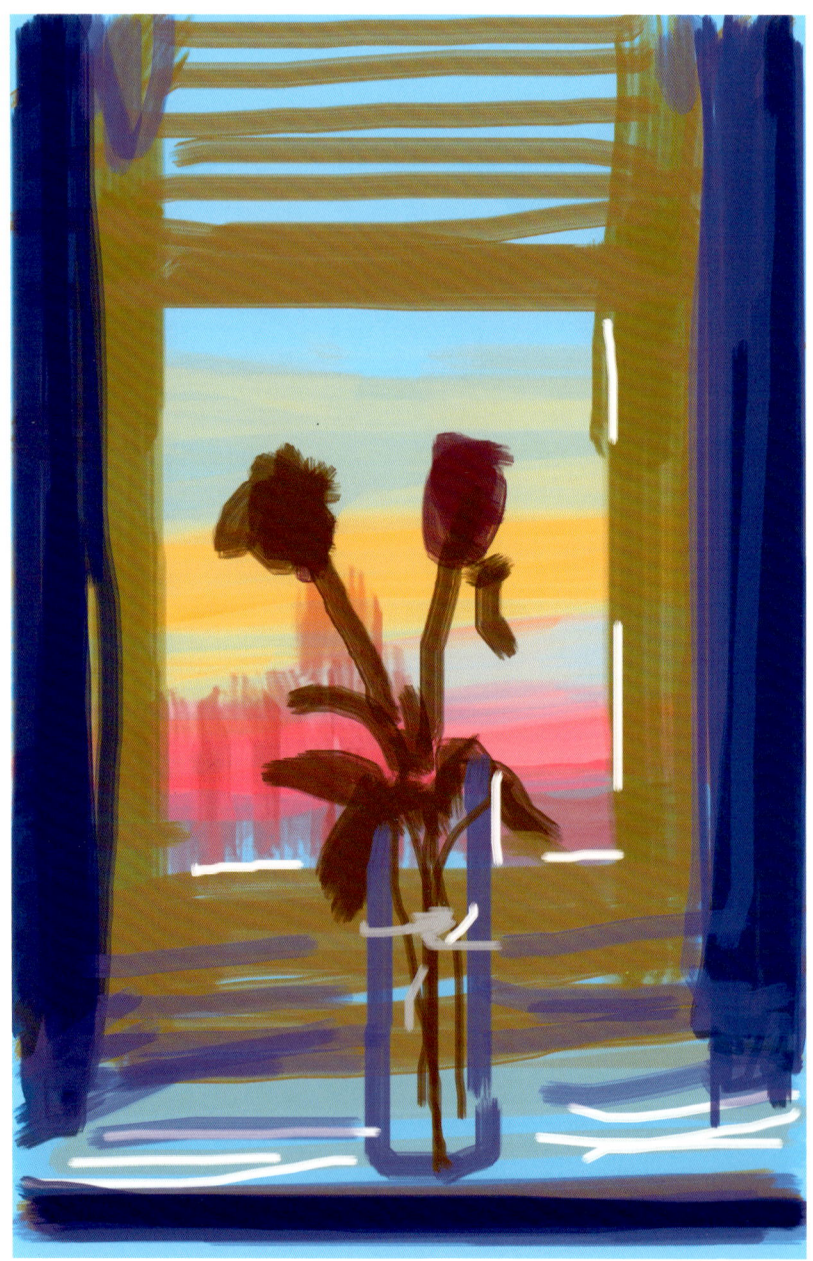

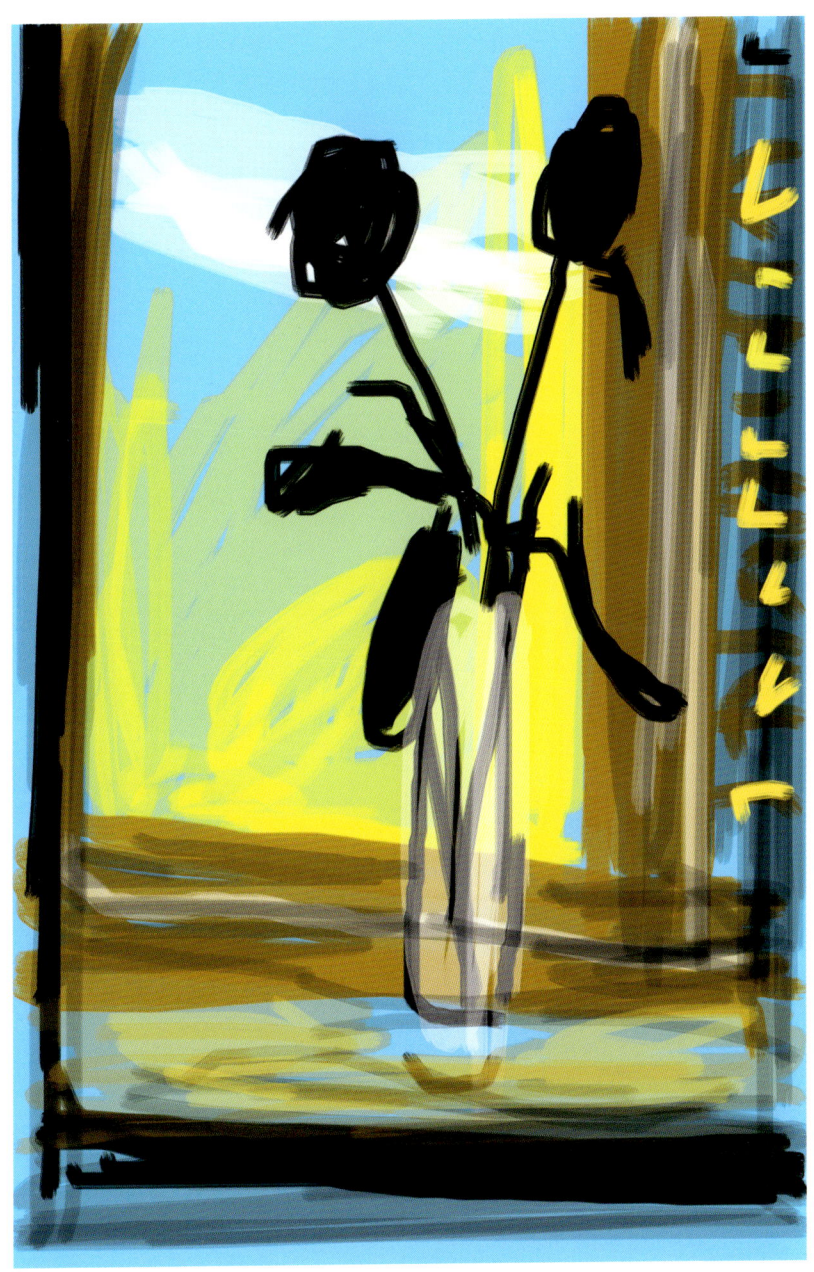

'No. 284', 23rd May 2009, iPhone drawing
Page 14: 'No. 286', 24th May 2009, iPhone drawing;
Page 15: 'No. 292', 25th May 2009, iPhone drawing

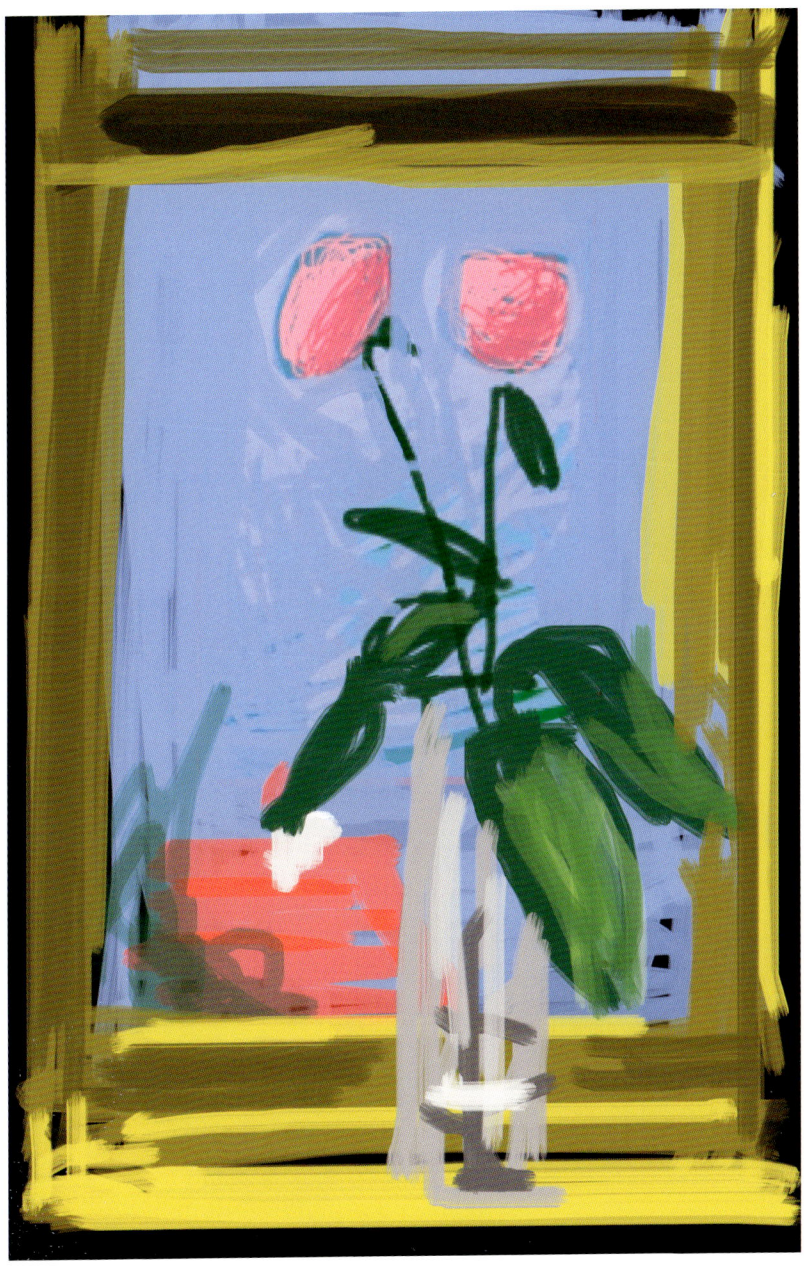

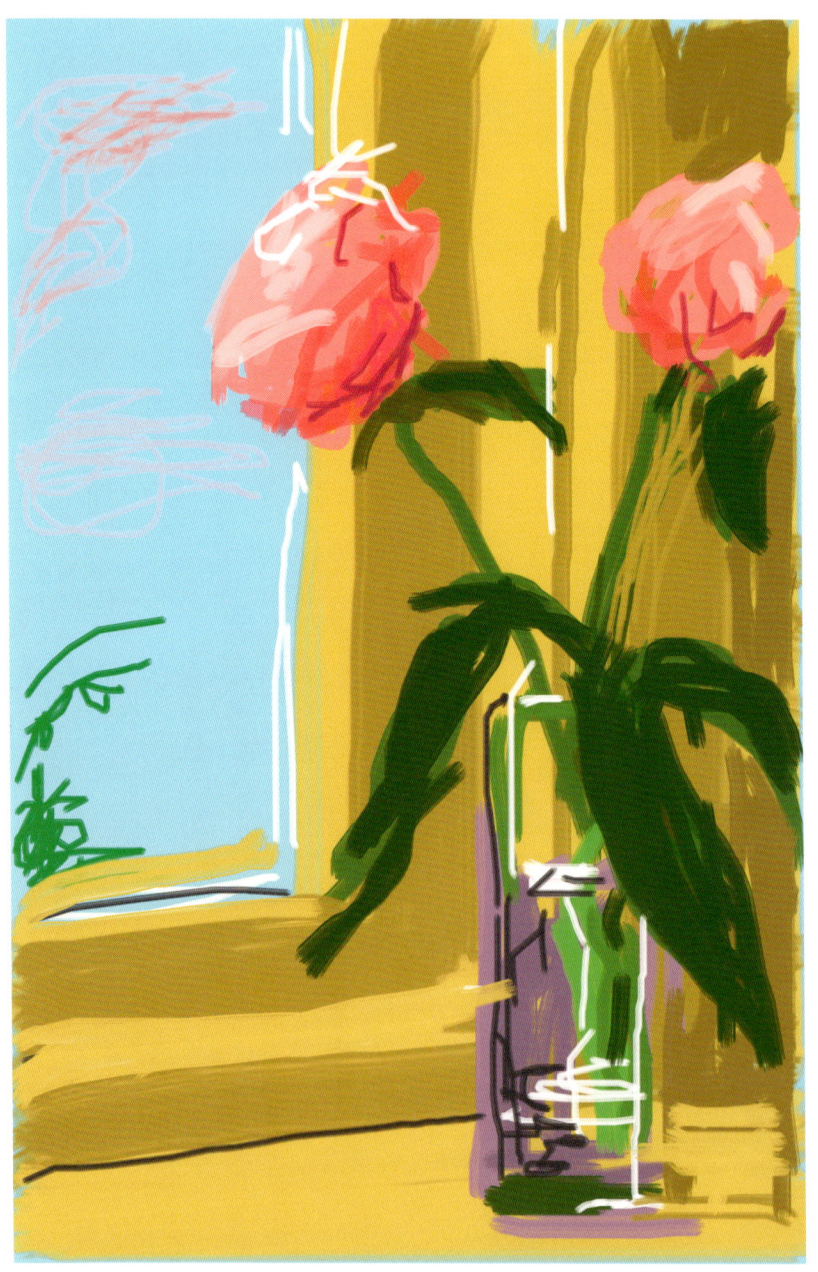

14

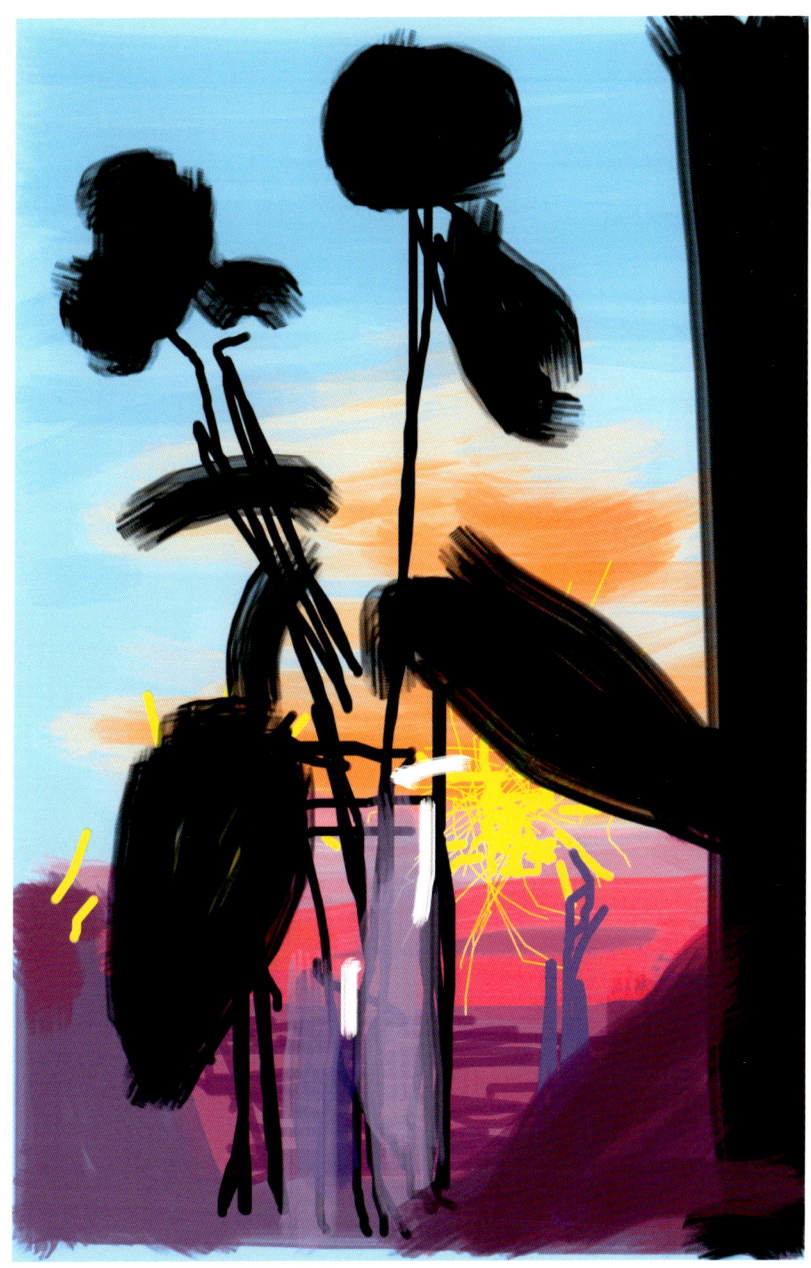

'No. 324', 27th May 2009, iPhone drawing

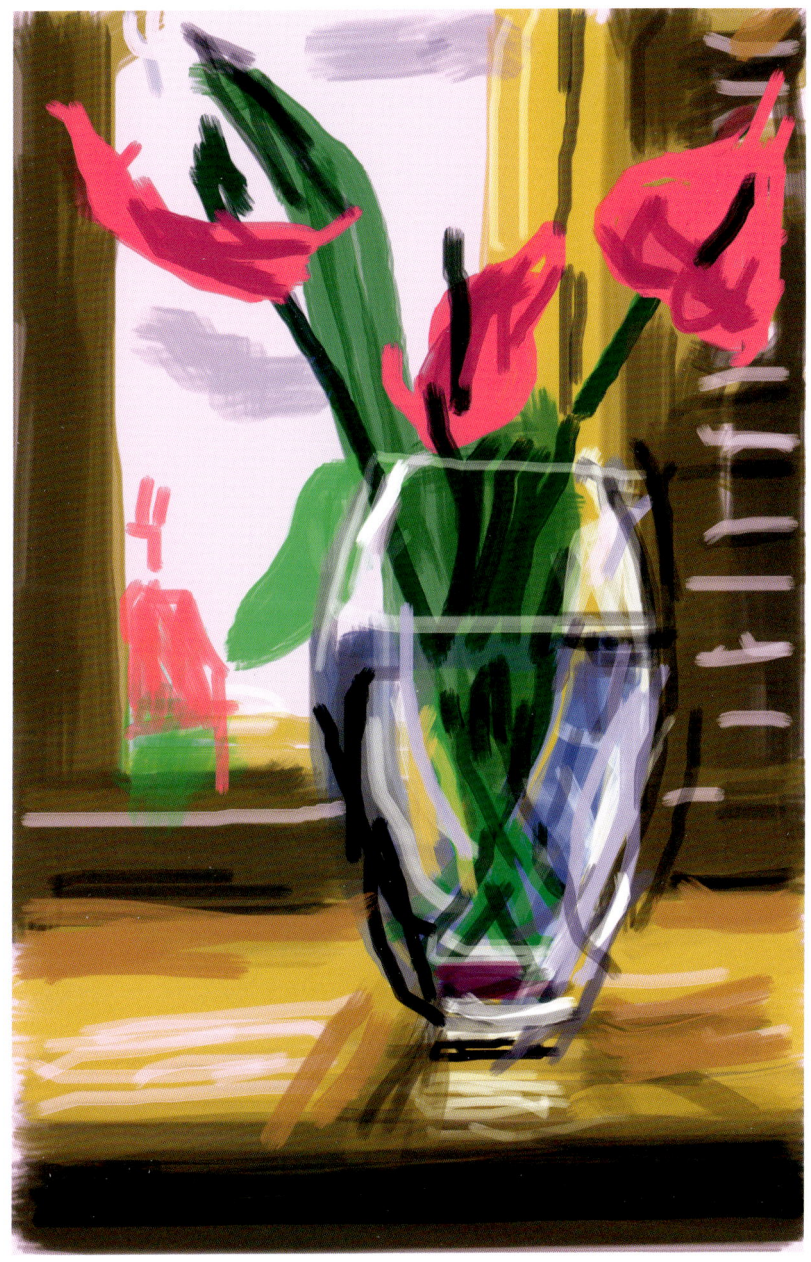

17

'No. 328', 27th May 2009, iPhone drawing

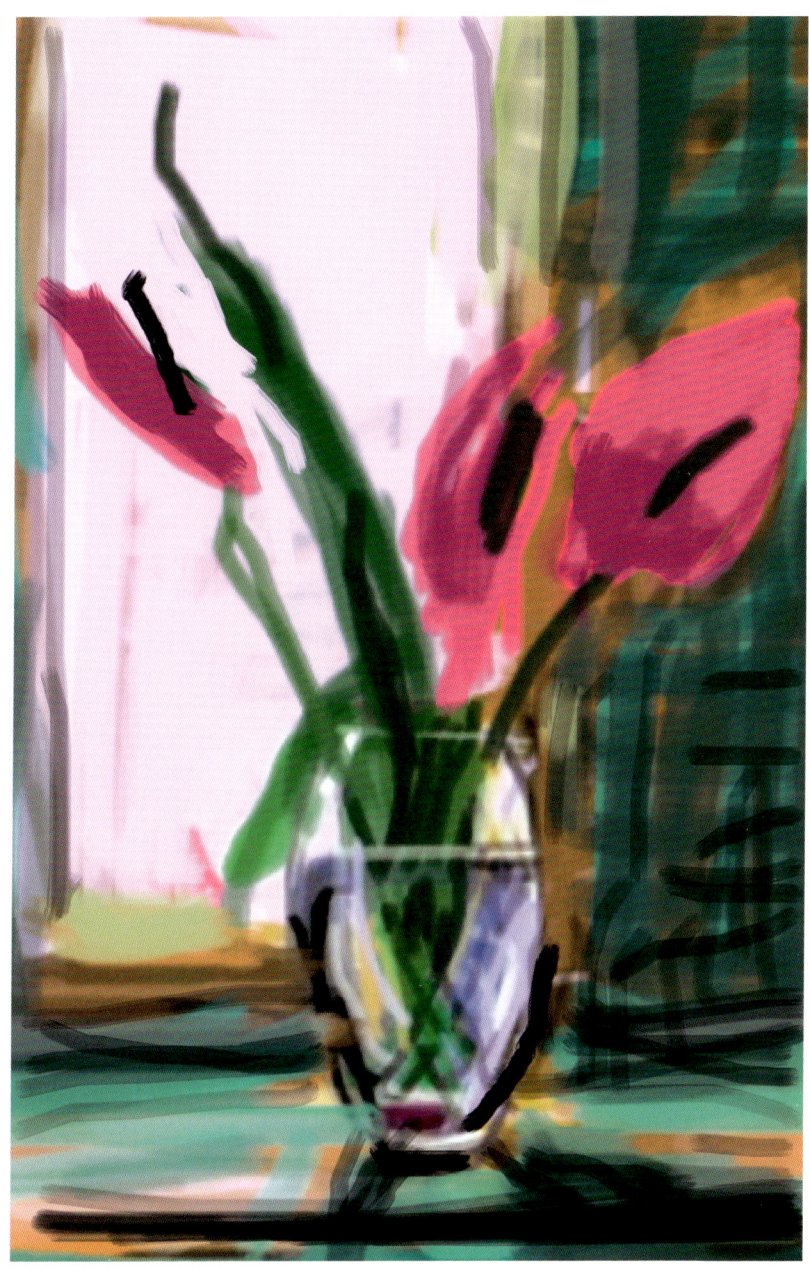

'No. 339', 28th May 2009, iPhone drawing
Page 22: 'No. 341', 29th May 2009, iPhone drawing;
Page 23: 'No. 344', 29th May 2009, iPhone drawing

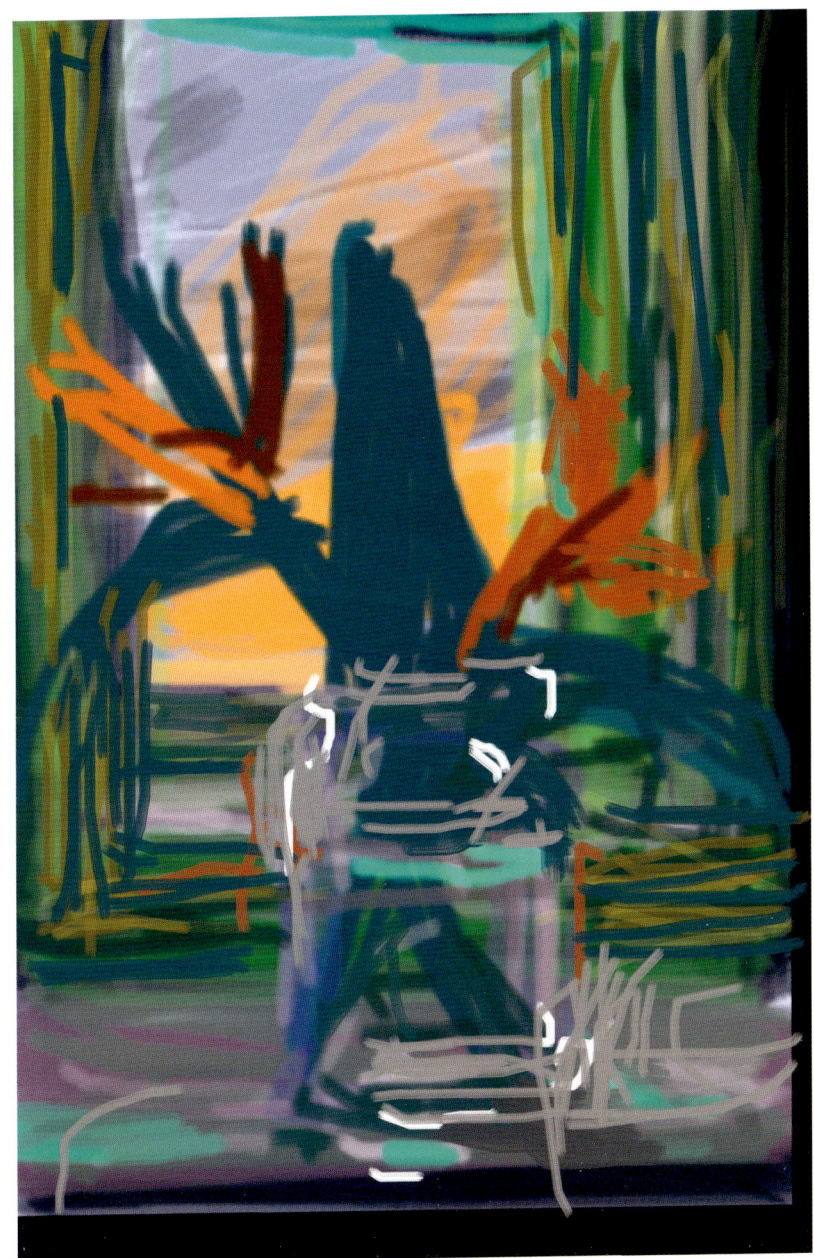

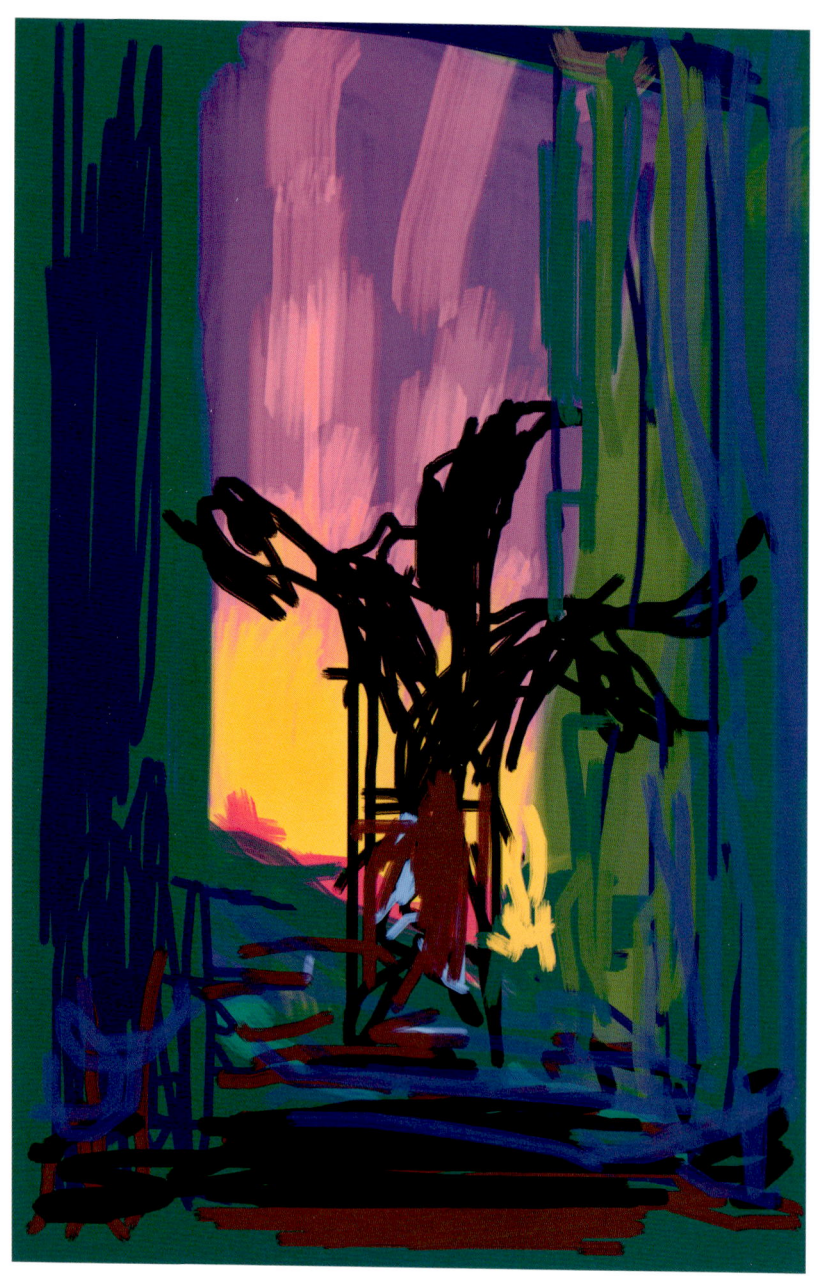

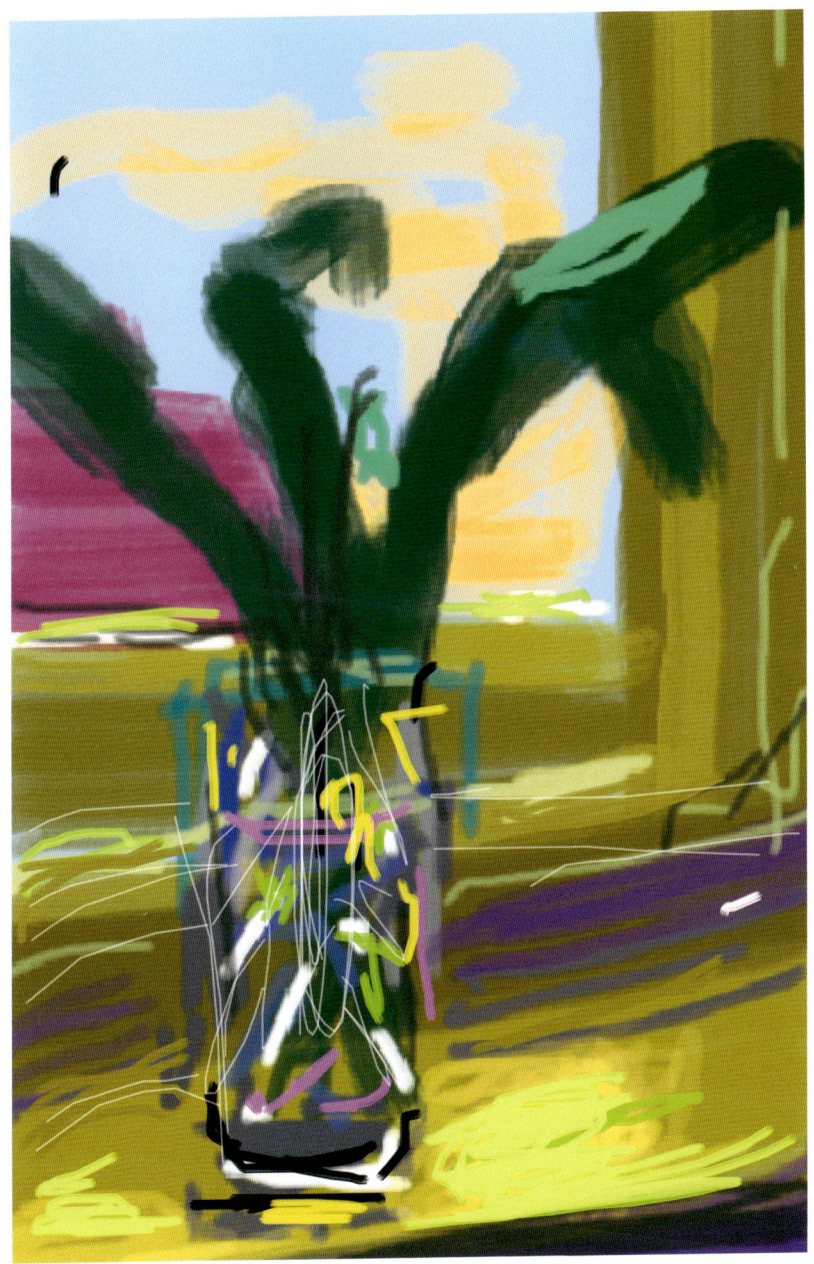

'No. 347', 30th May 2009, iPhone drawing

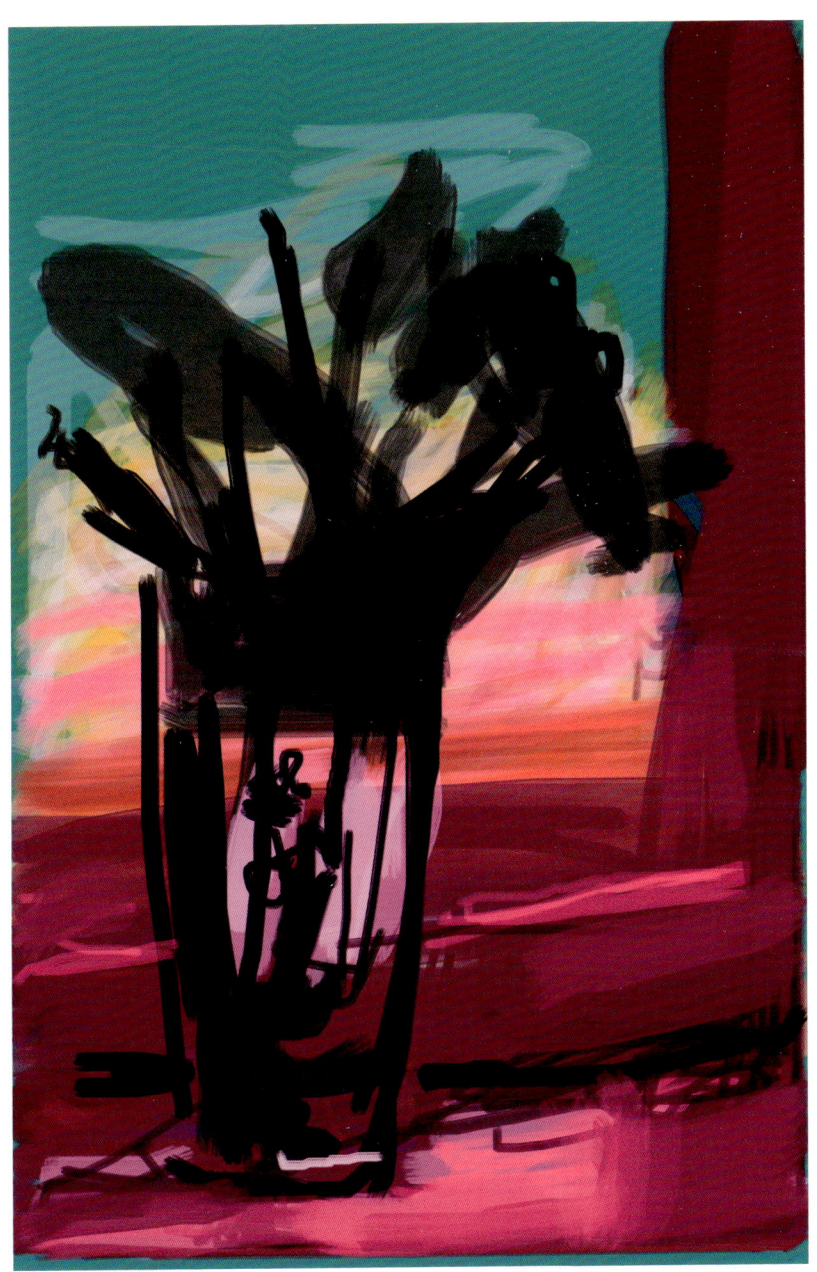

'No. 343', 30th May 2009, iPhone drawing
Page 28: 'No. 357', 1st June 2009, iPhone drawing;
Page 29: 'No. 359', 1st June 2009, iPhone drawing

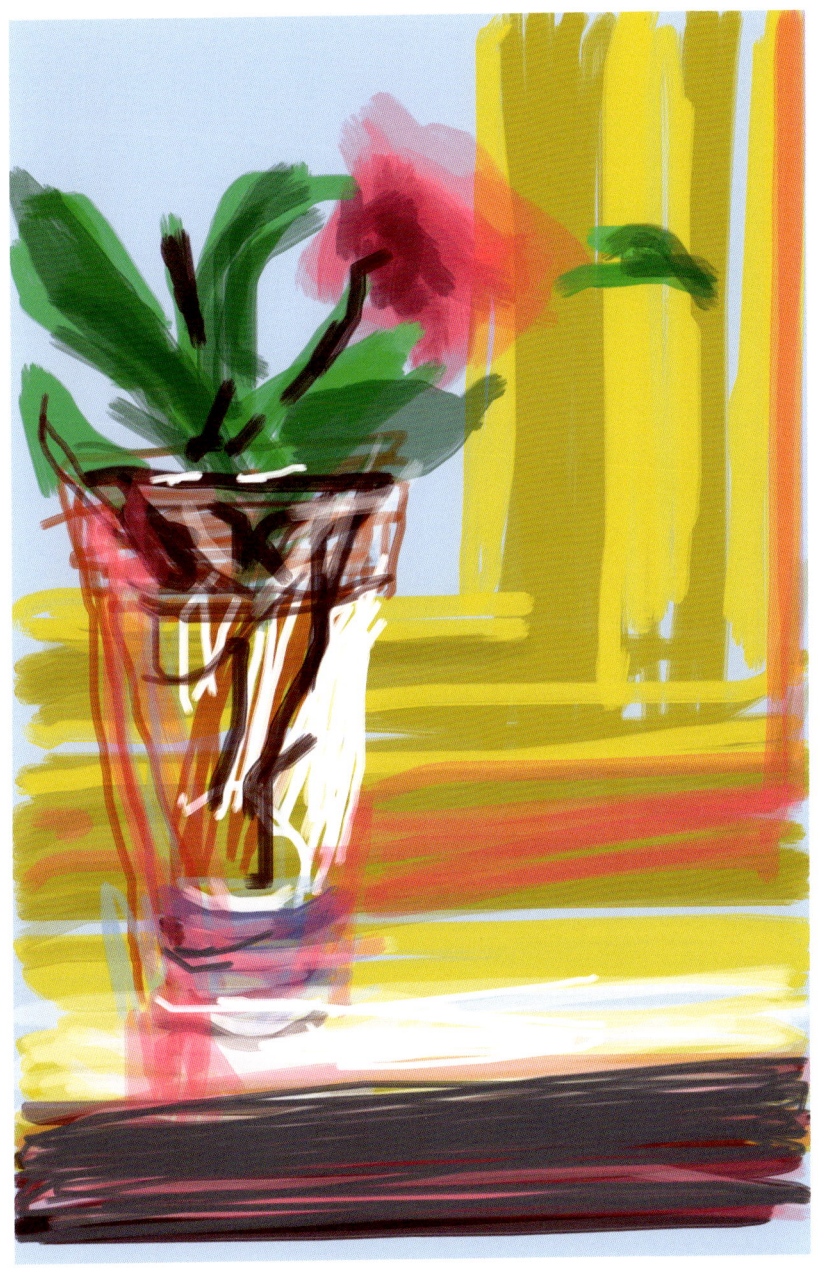

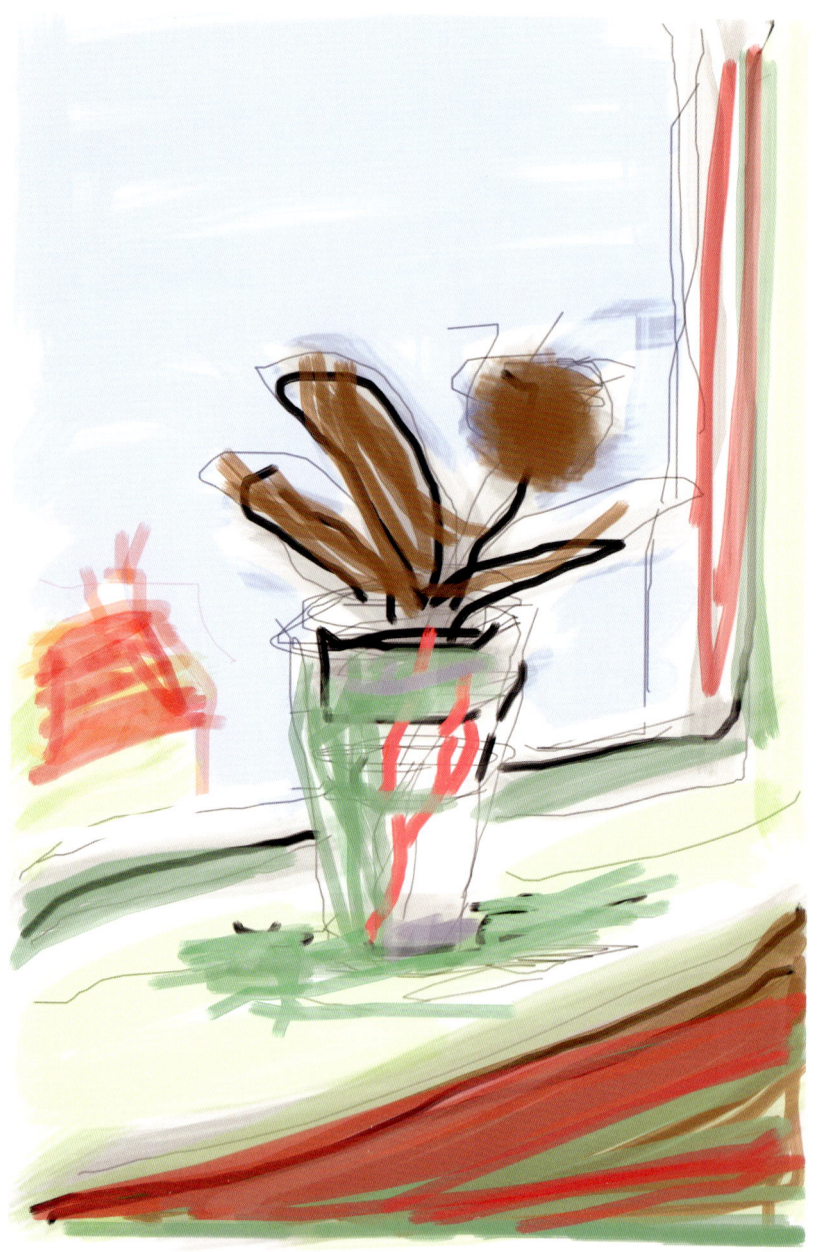

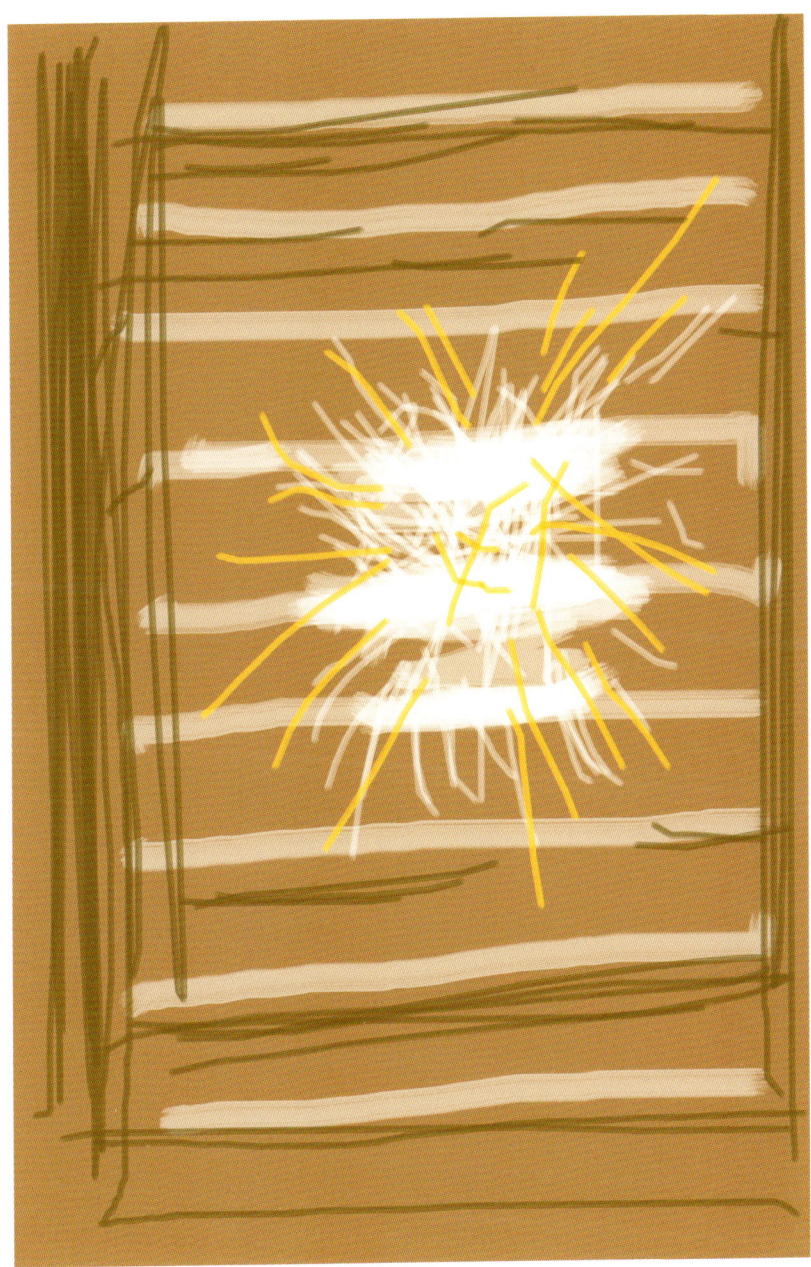

'No. 360', 2nd June 2009, iPhone drawing

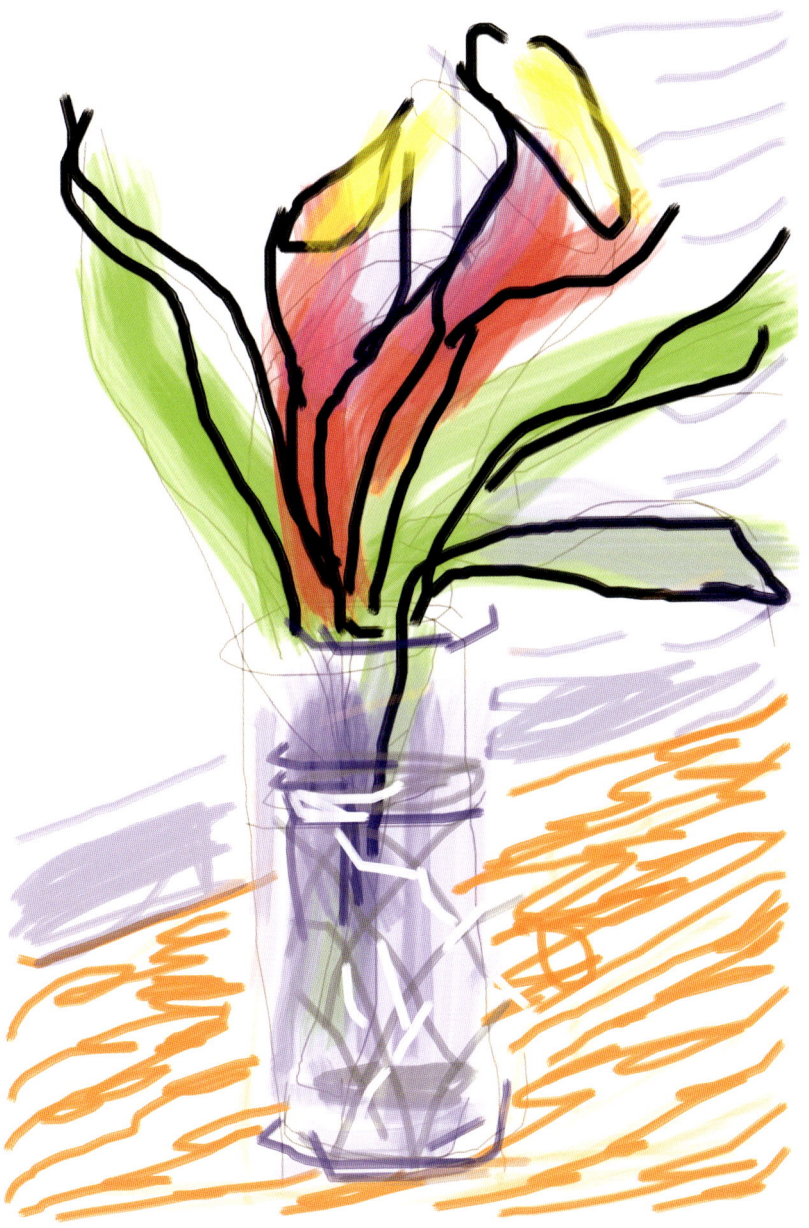

'No. 364', 2nd June 2009, iPhone drawing

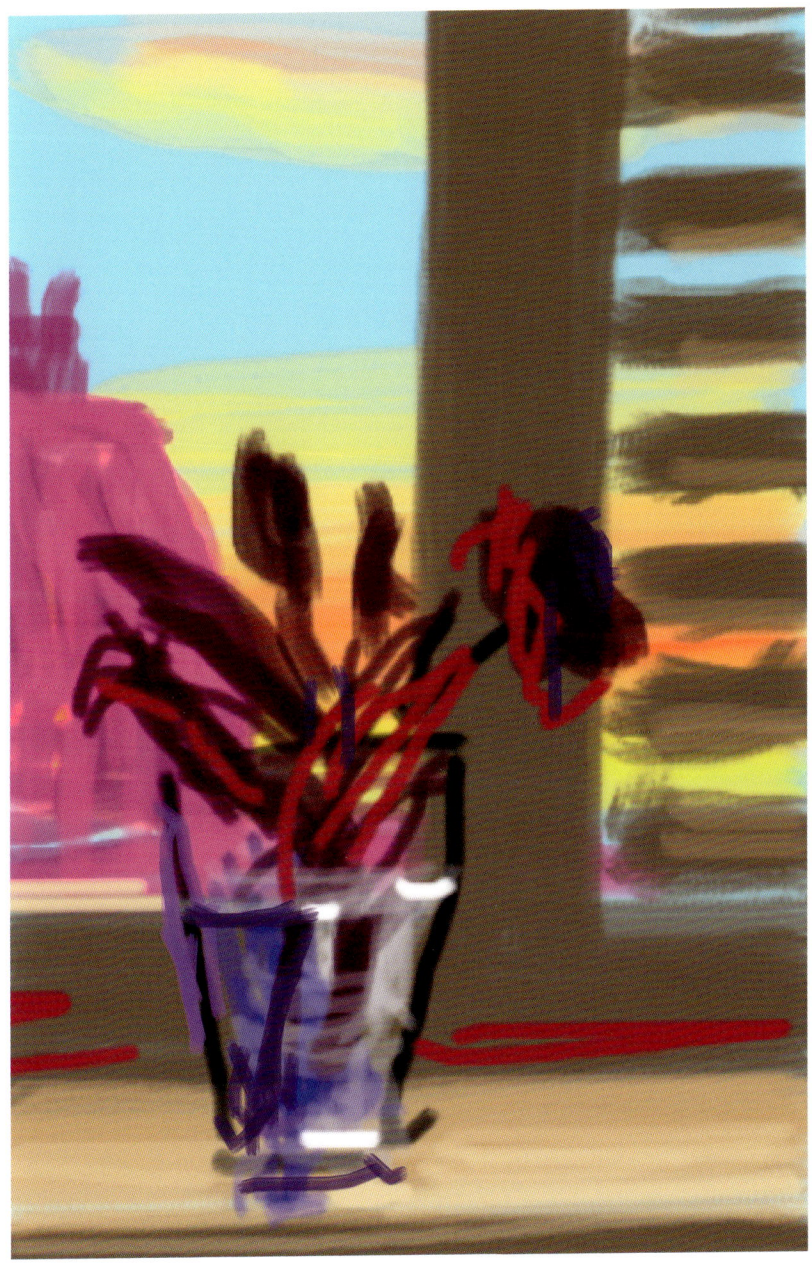

'No. 365', 2nd June 2009, iPhone drawing
Page 36: 'No. 381', 6th June 2009, iPhone drawing;
Page 37: 'No. 382', 6th June 2009, iPhone drawing

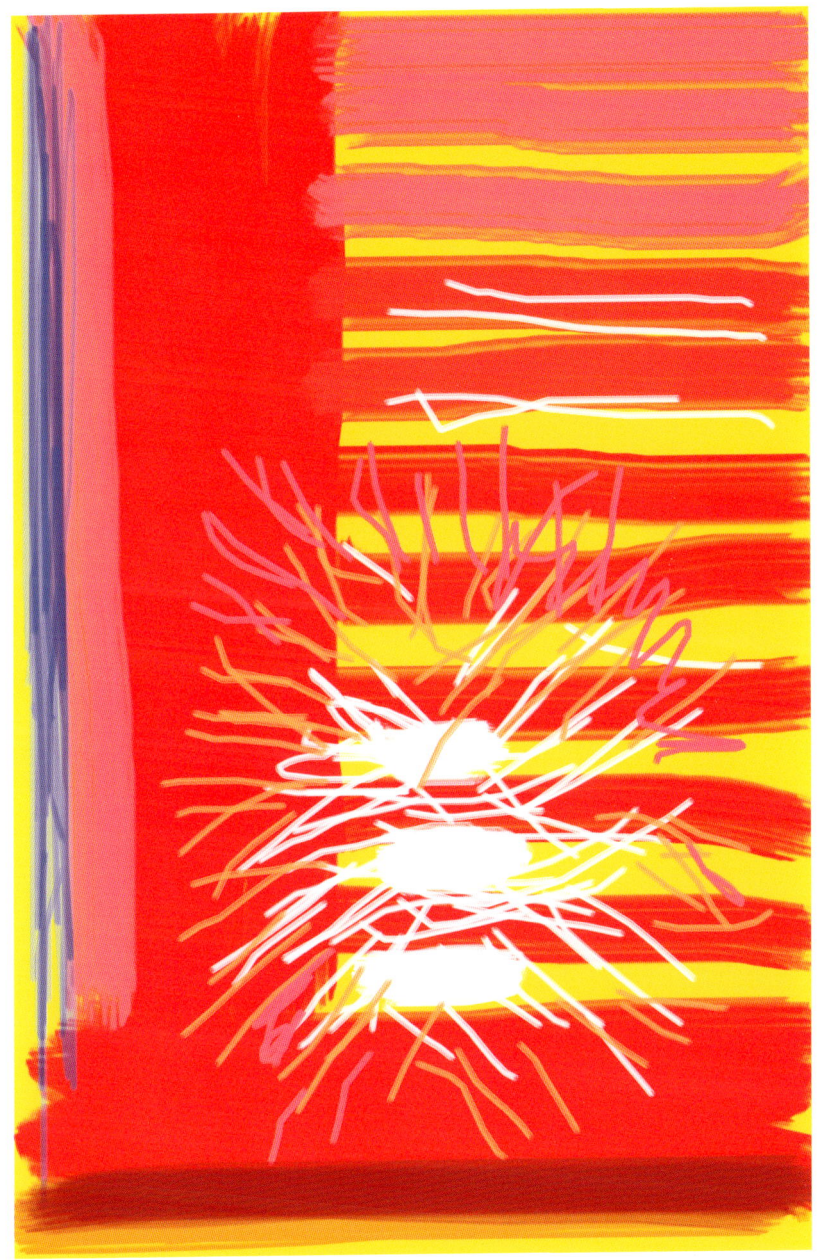

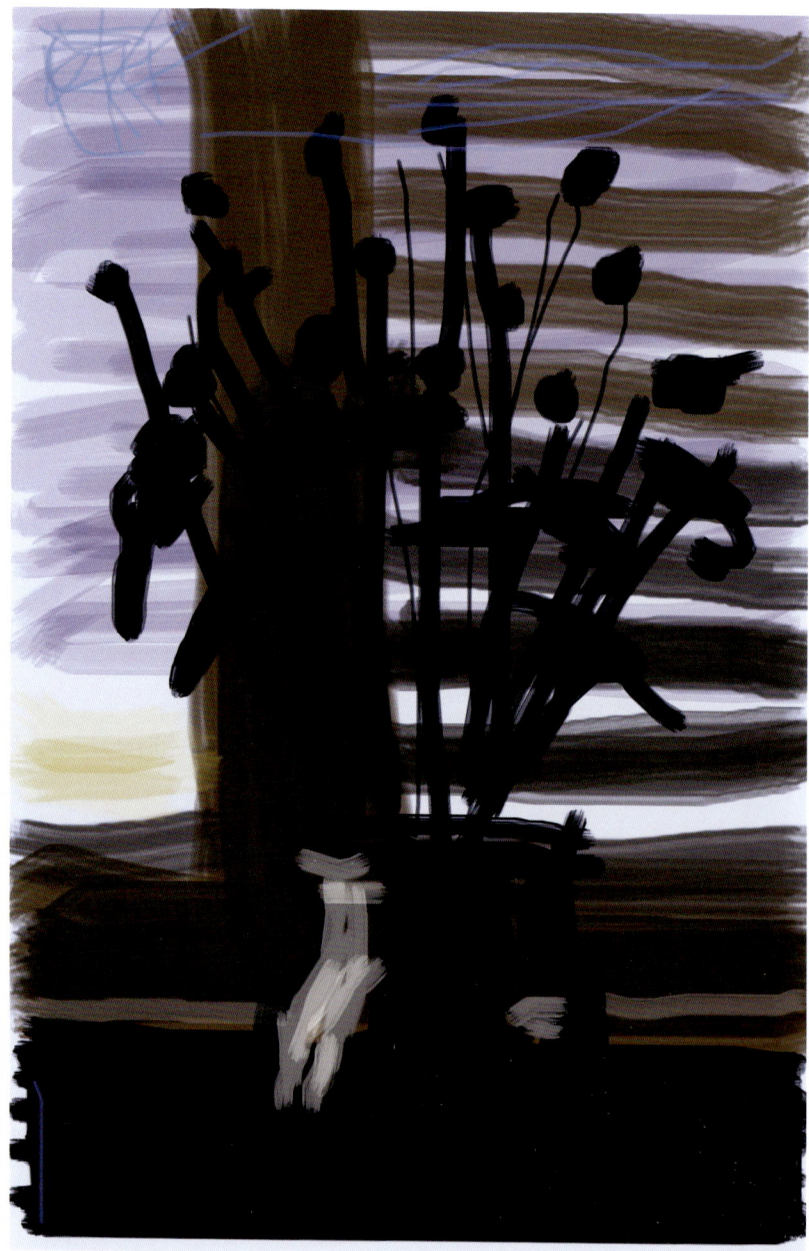

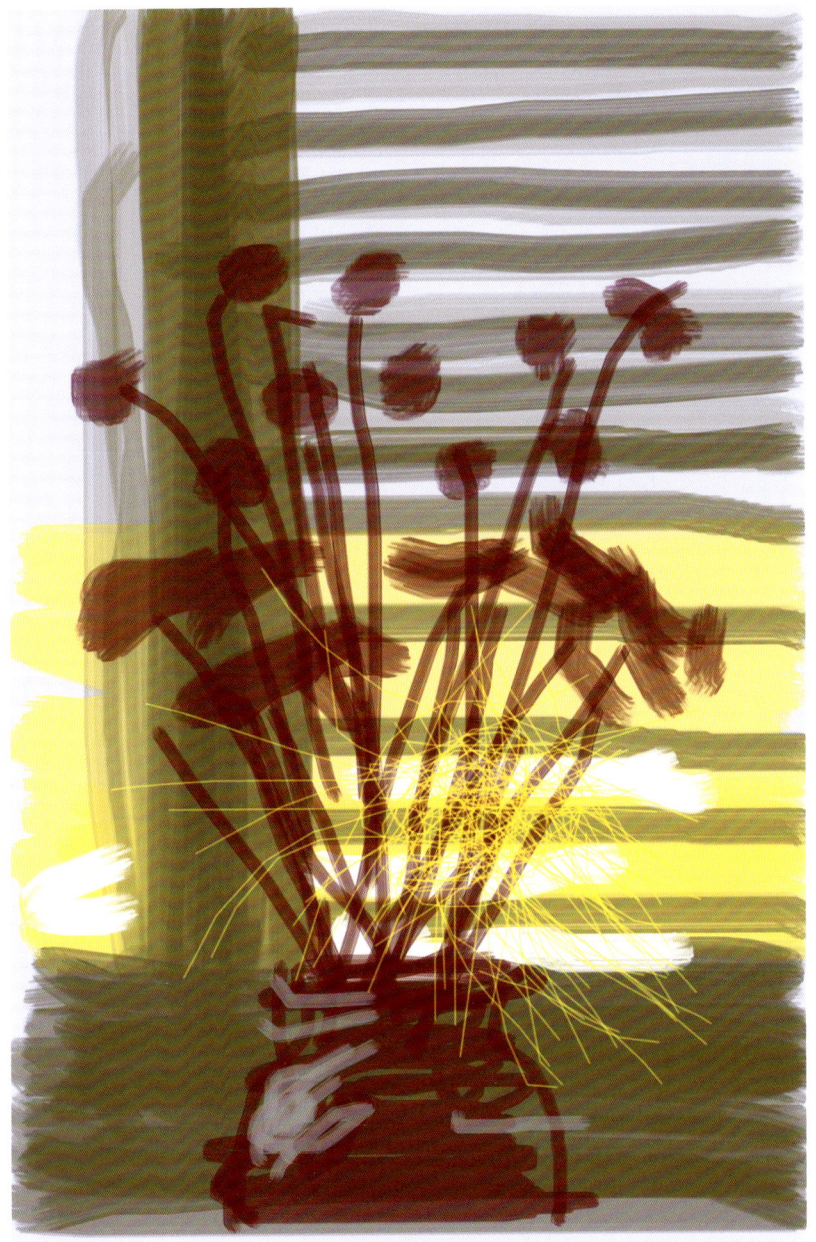

'No. 383', 6th June 2009, iPhone drawing

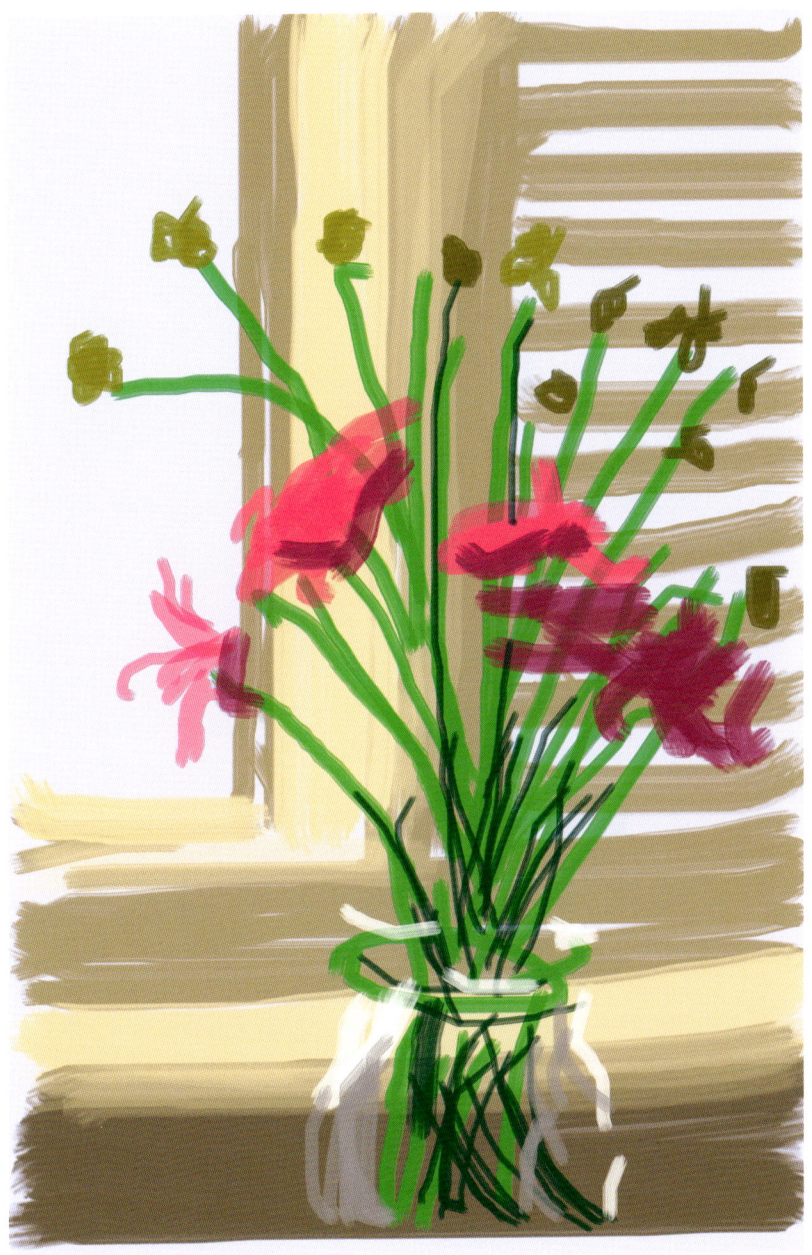

'No. 389', 7th June 2009, iPhone drawing
Page 42: 'No. 390', 7th June 2009, iPhone drawing;
40   Page 43: 'No. 391', 7th June 2009, iPhone drawing

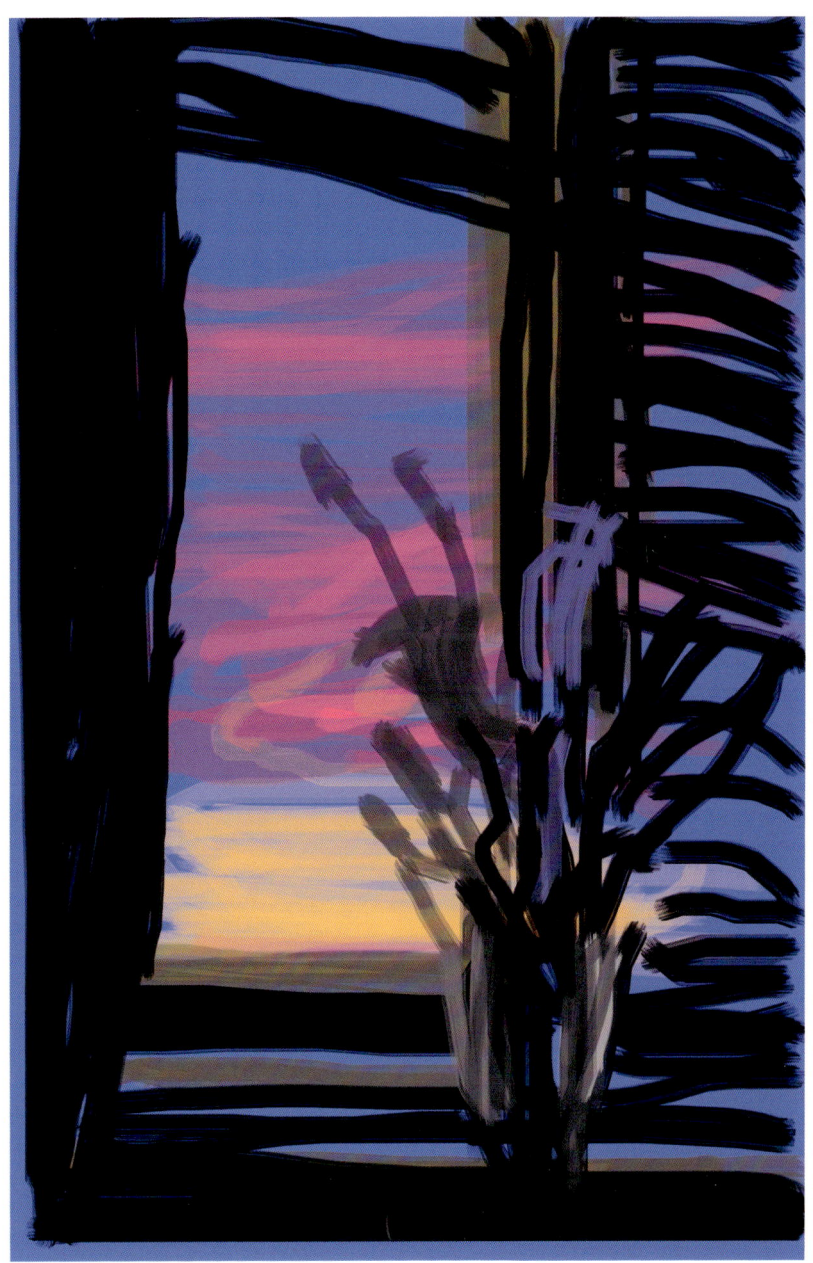

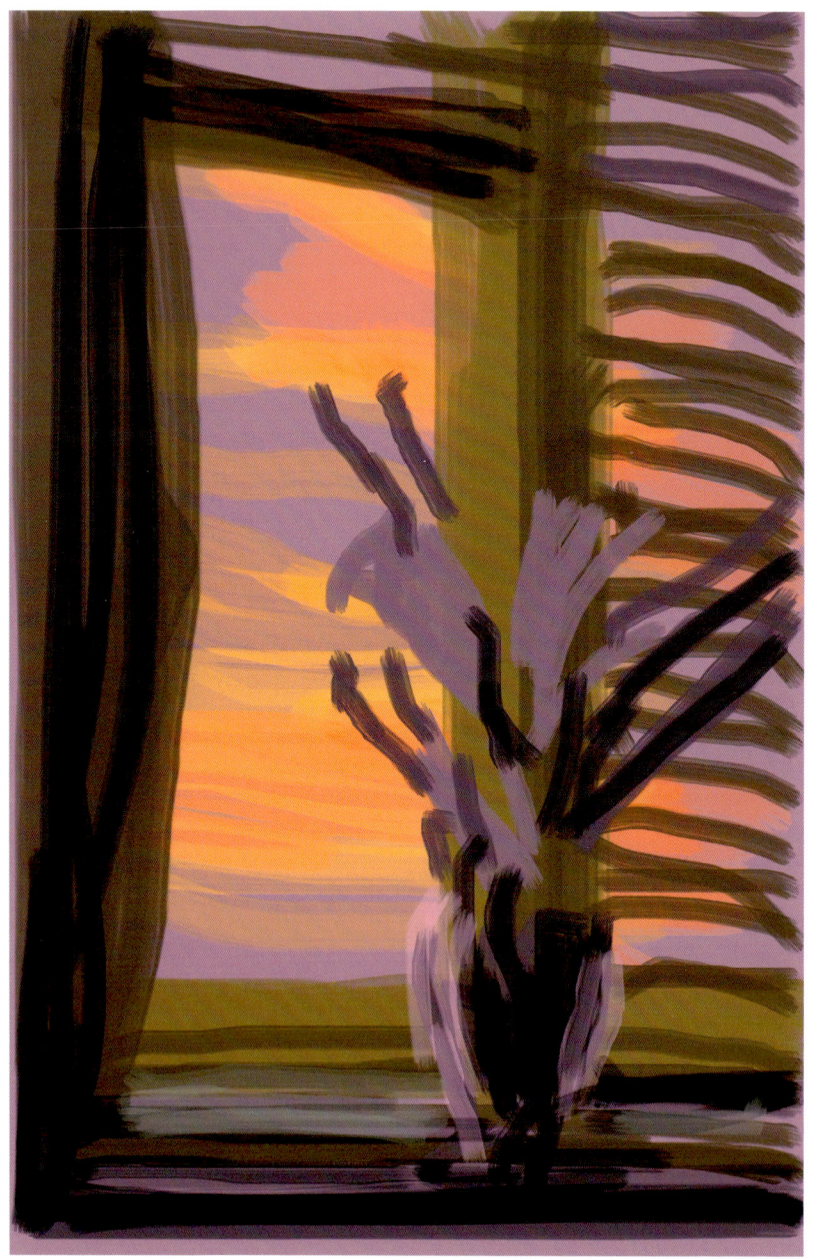

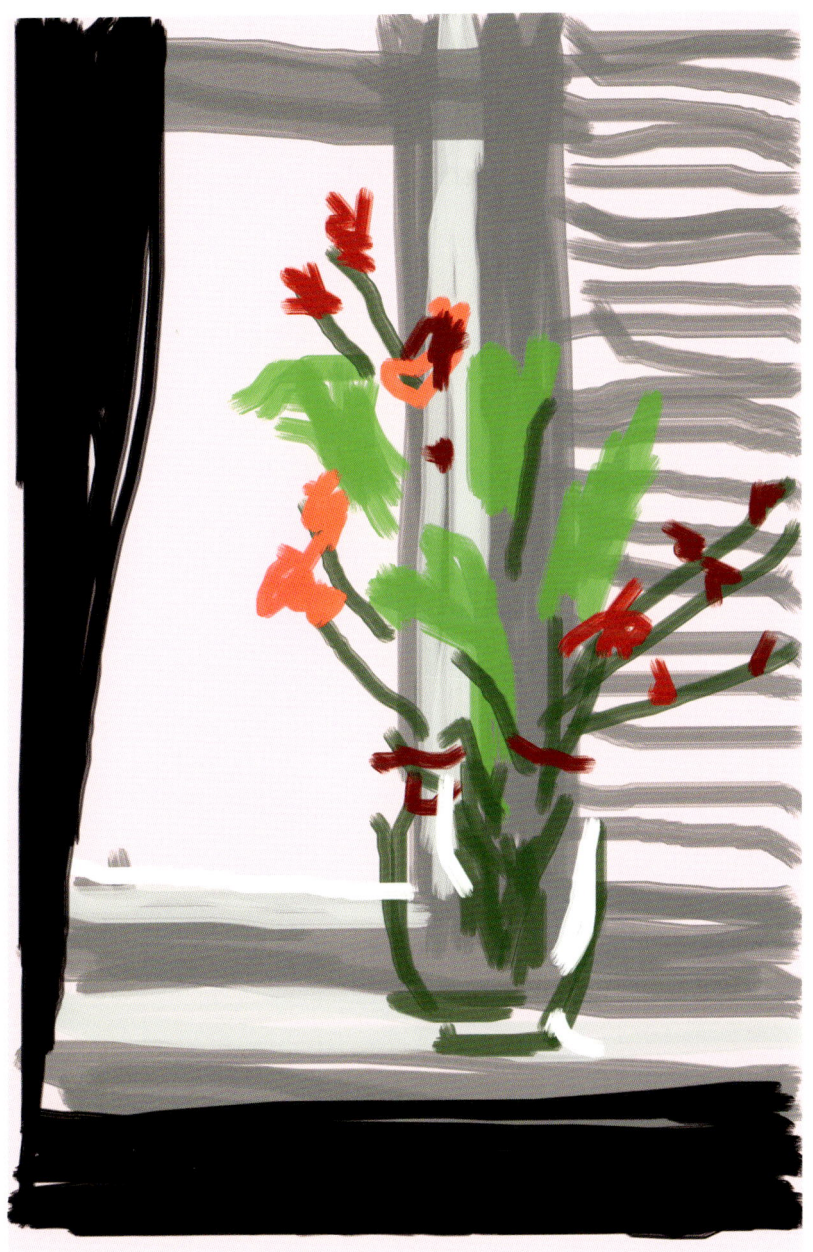

'No. 392', 7th June 2009, iPhone drawing

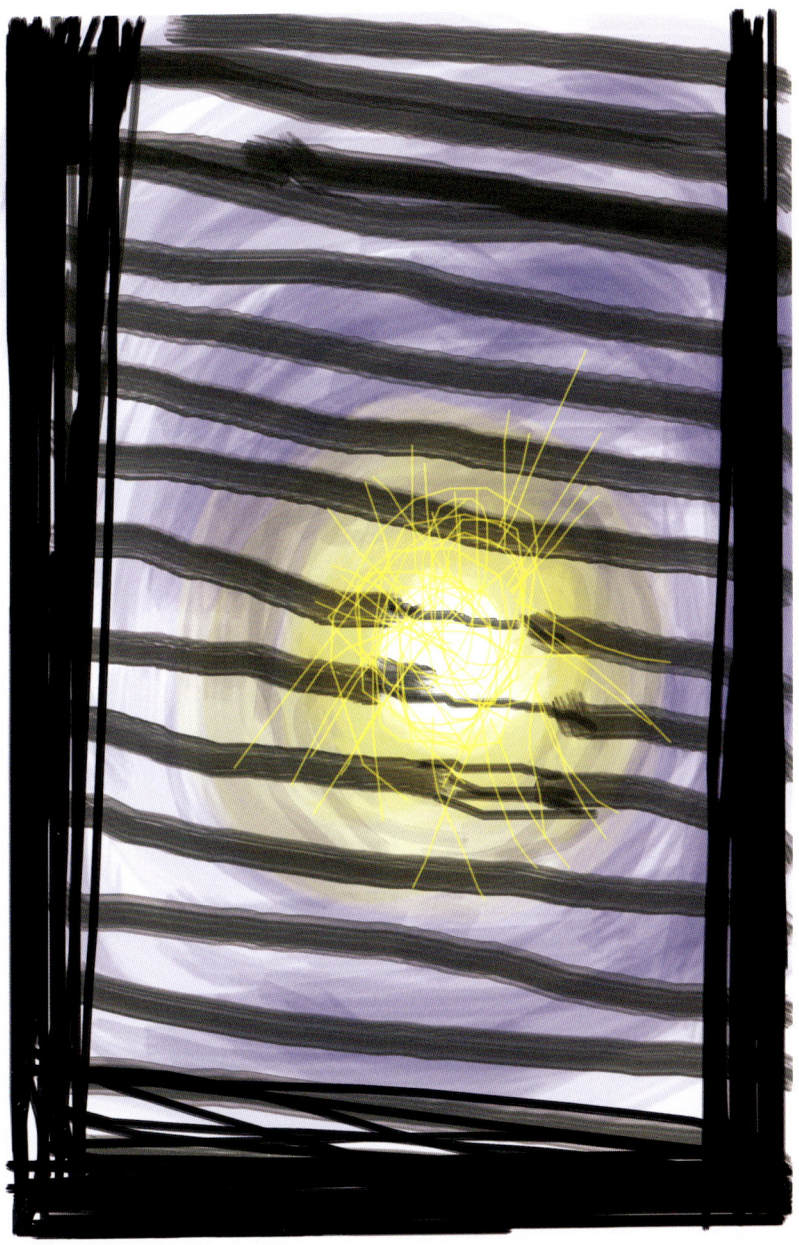

'No. 393', 7th June 2009, iPhone drawing

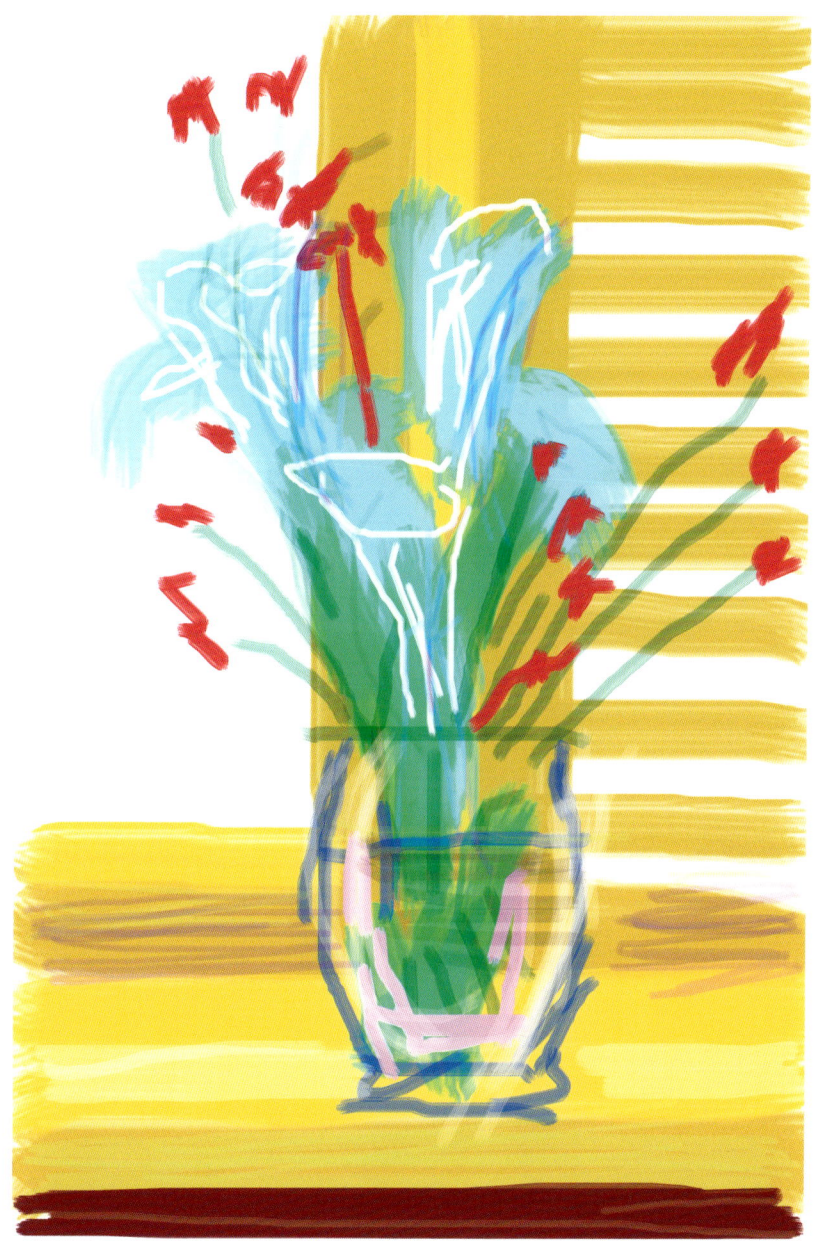

'No. 398', 8th June 2009, iPhone drawing

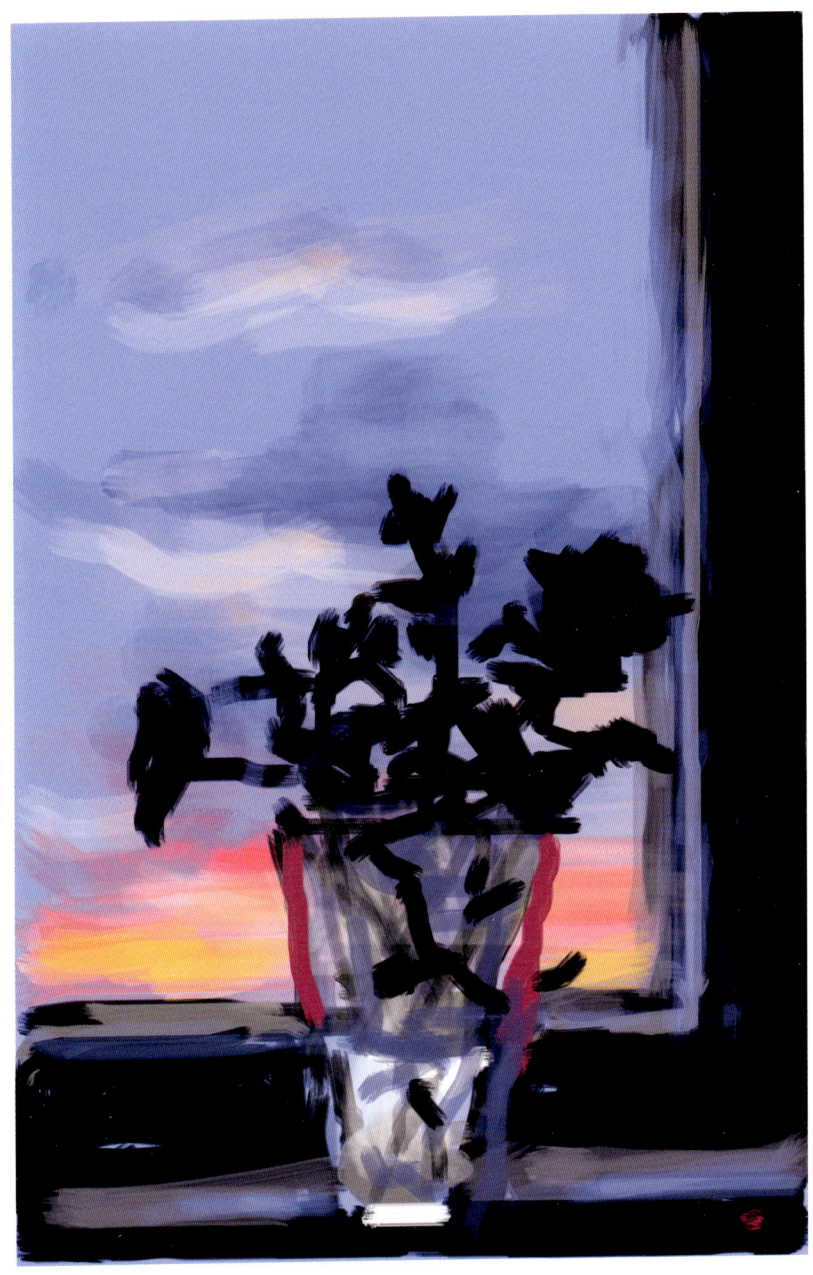

'No. 400', 8th June 2009, iPhone drawing
Page 52: 'No. 403', 9th June 2009, iPhone drawing;
50   Page 53: 'No. 404', 9th June 2009, iPhone drawing

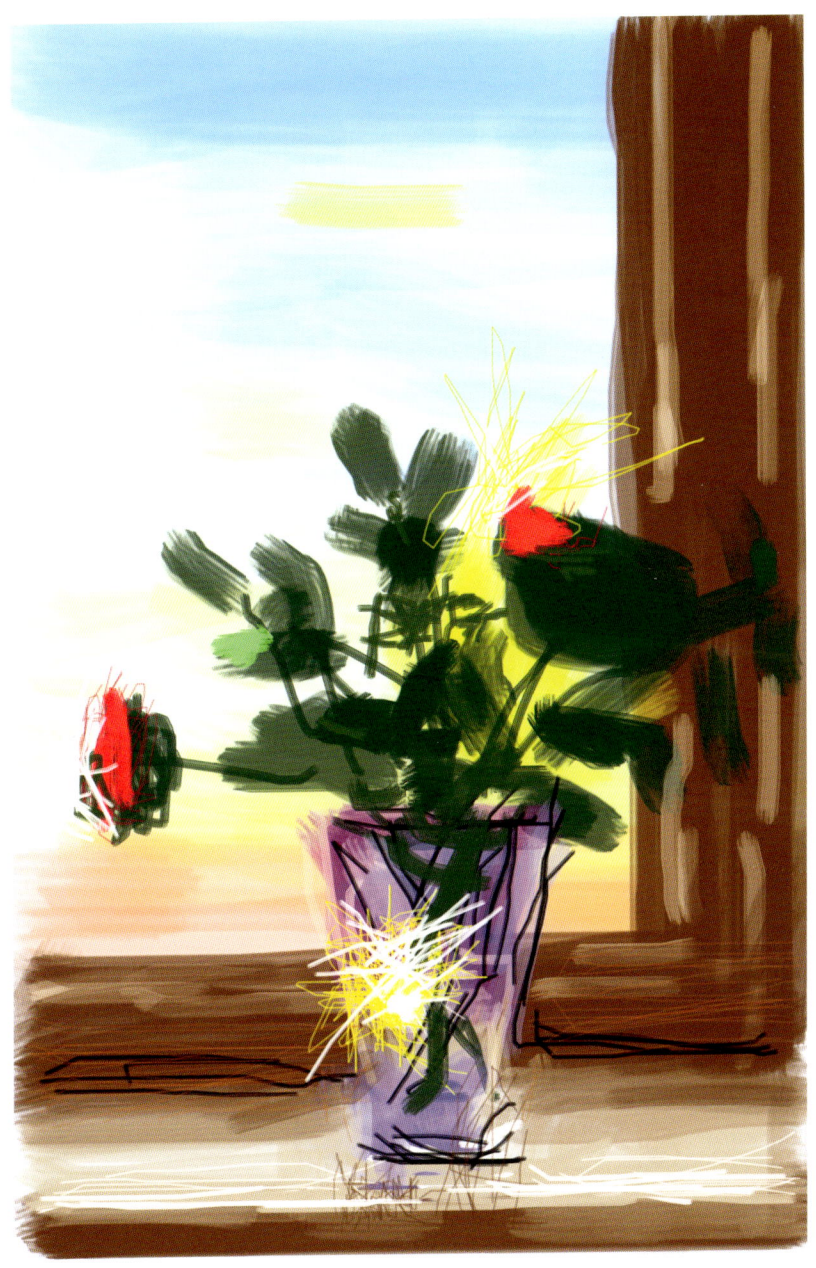

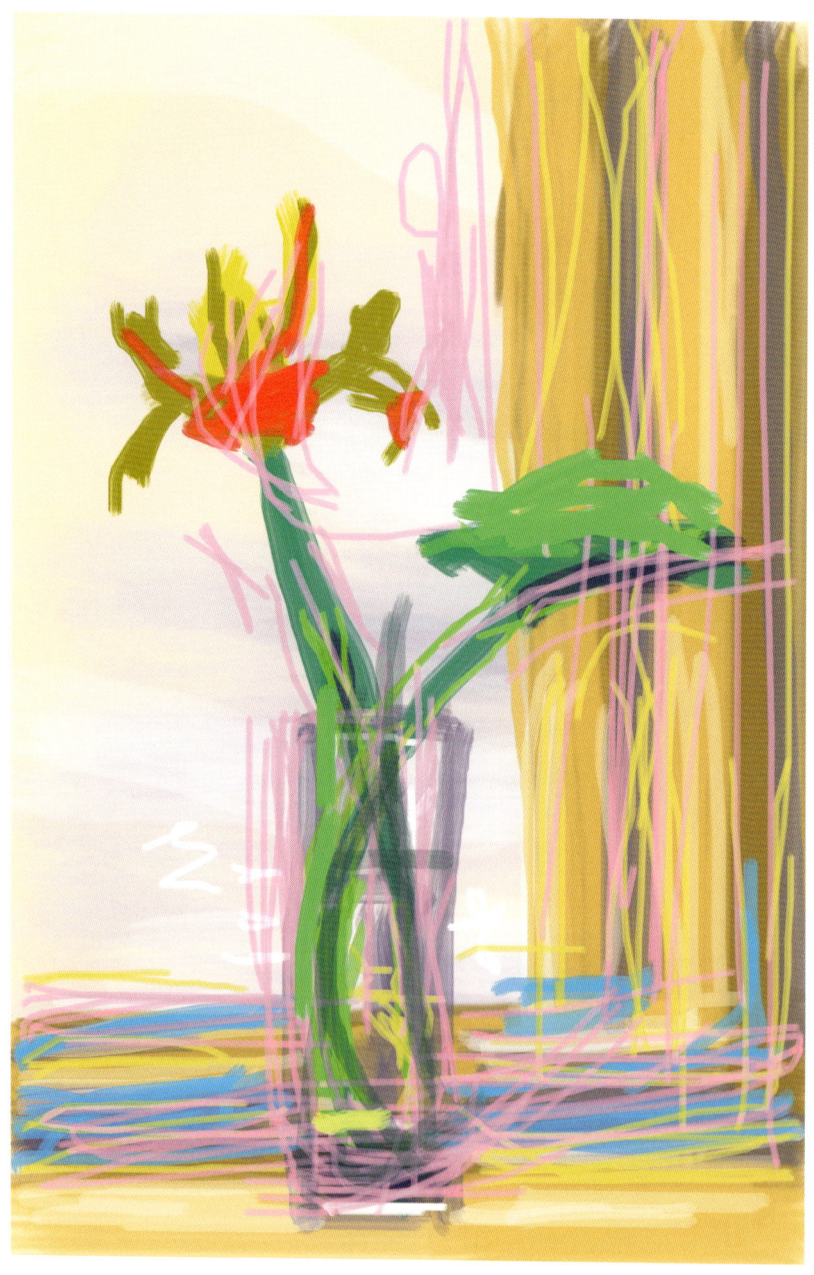

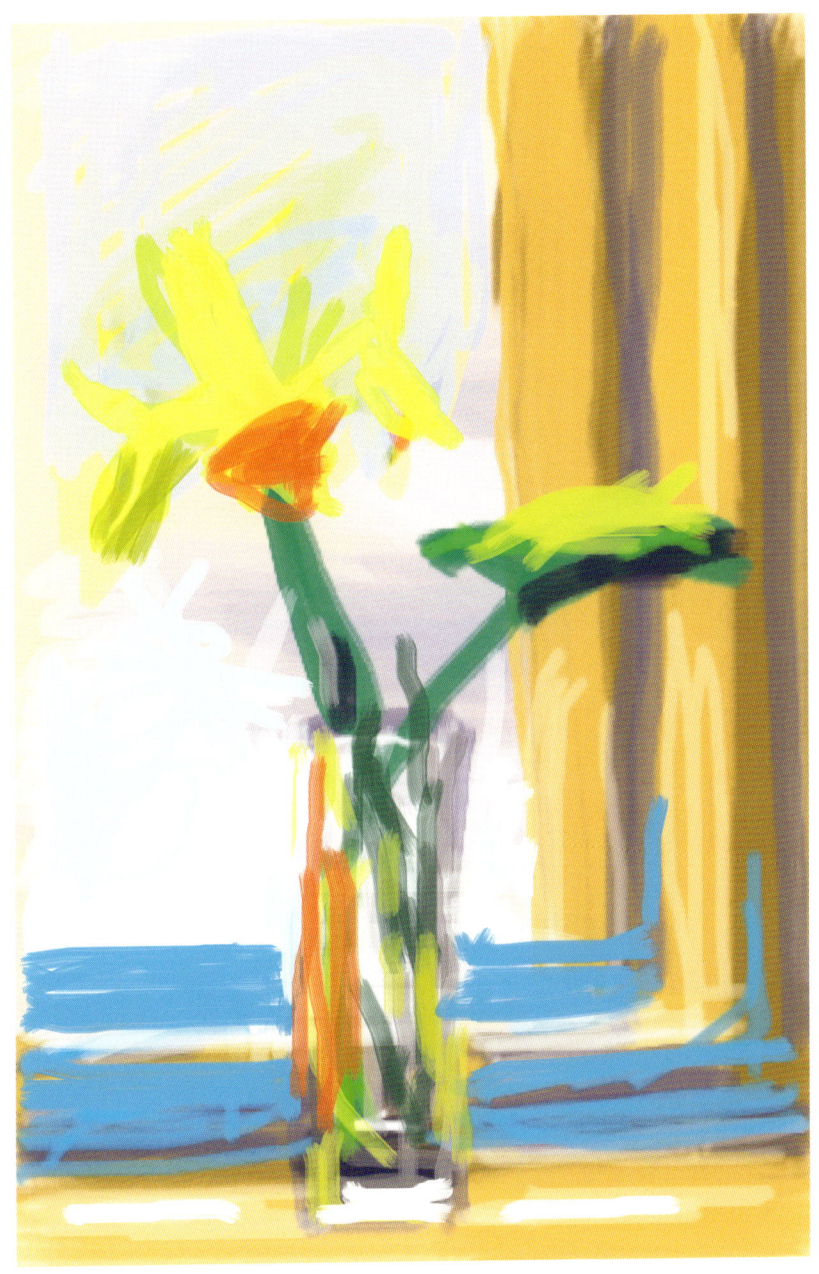

'No. 406', 9th June 2009, iPhone drawing

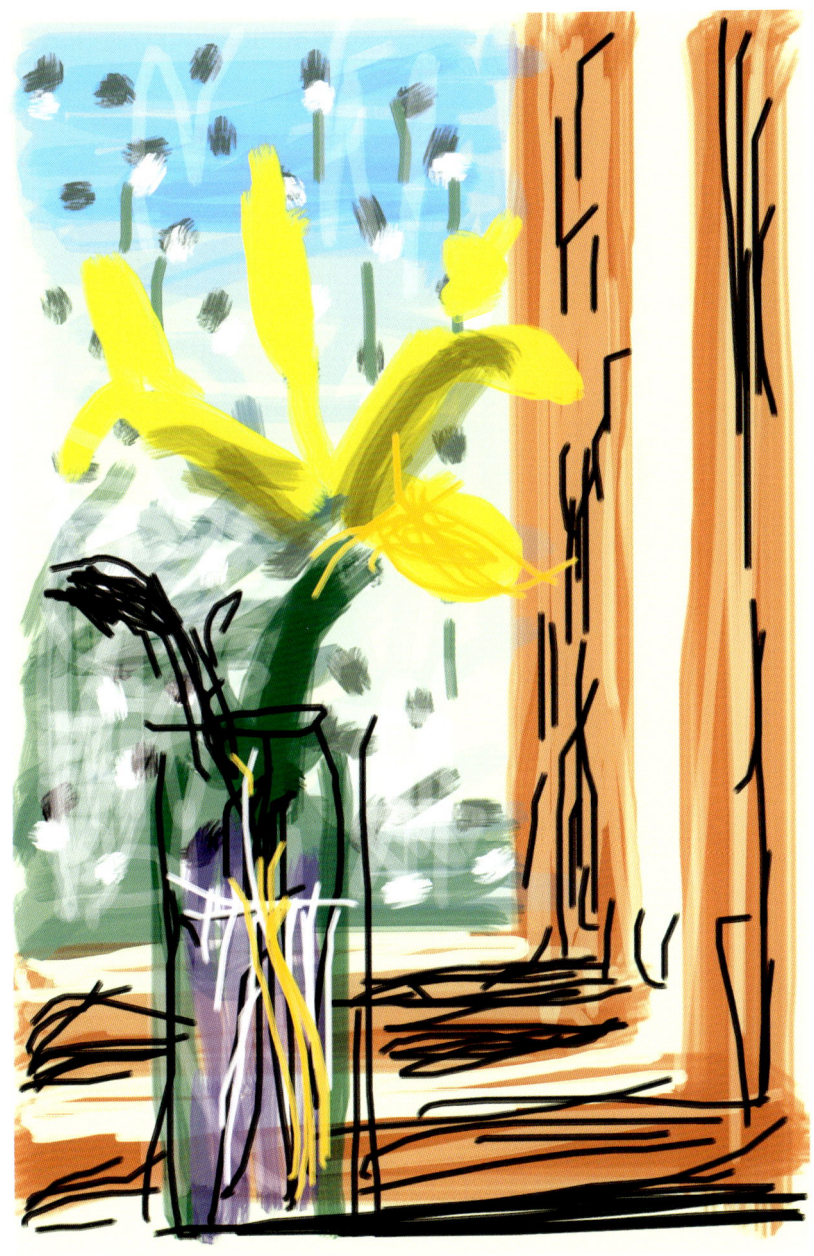

'No. 461', 16th June 2009, iPhone drawing
Page 58: 'No. 464', 16th June 2009, iPhone drawing;
Page 59: 'No. 465', 16th June 2009, iPhone drawing

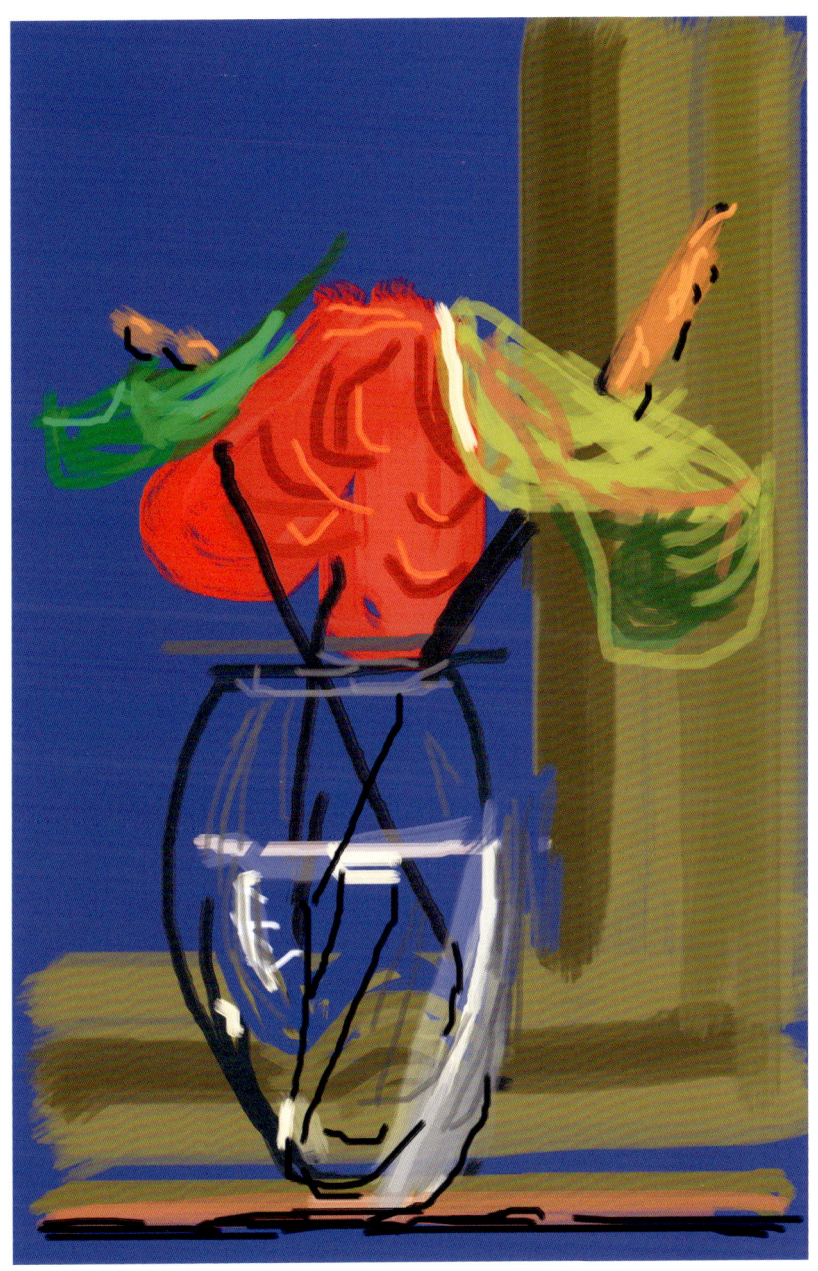

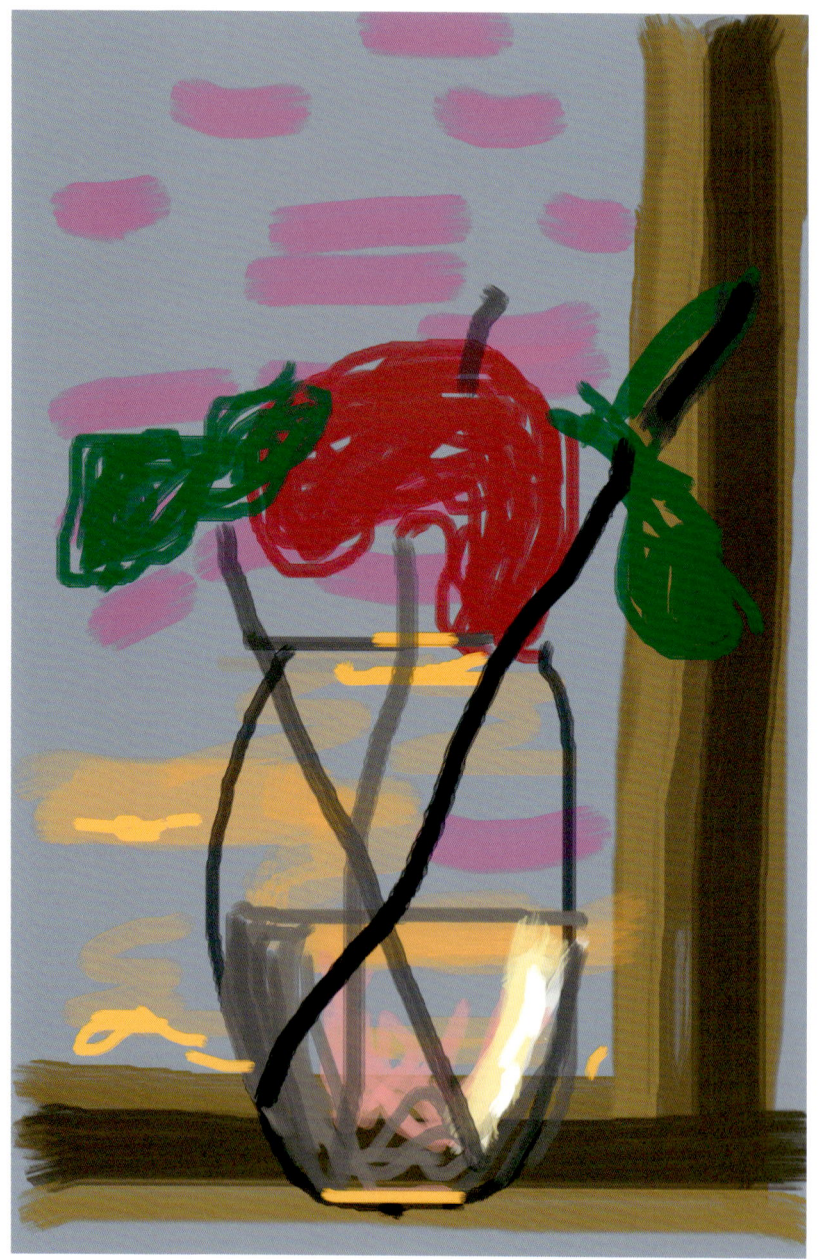

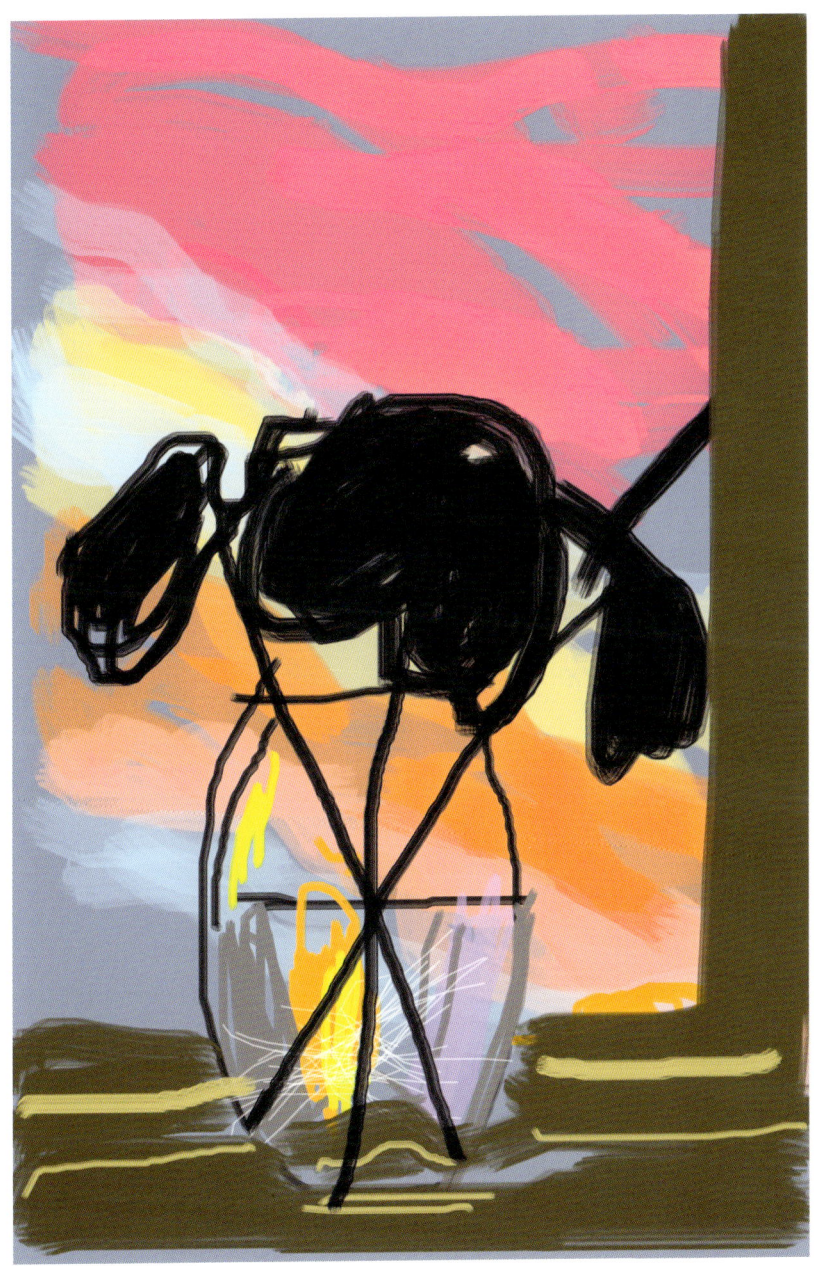

59

'No. 468', 17th June 2009, iPhone drawing
Page 62: 'No. 469', 17th June 2009, iPhone drawing;

Page 63: 'No. 470', 17th June 2009, iPhone drawing

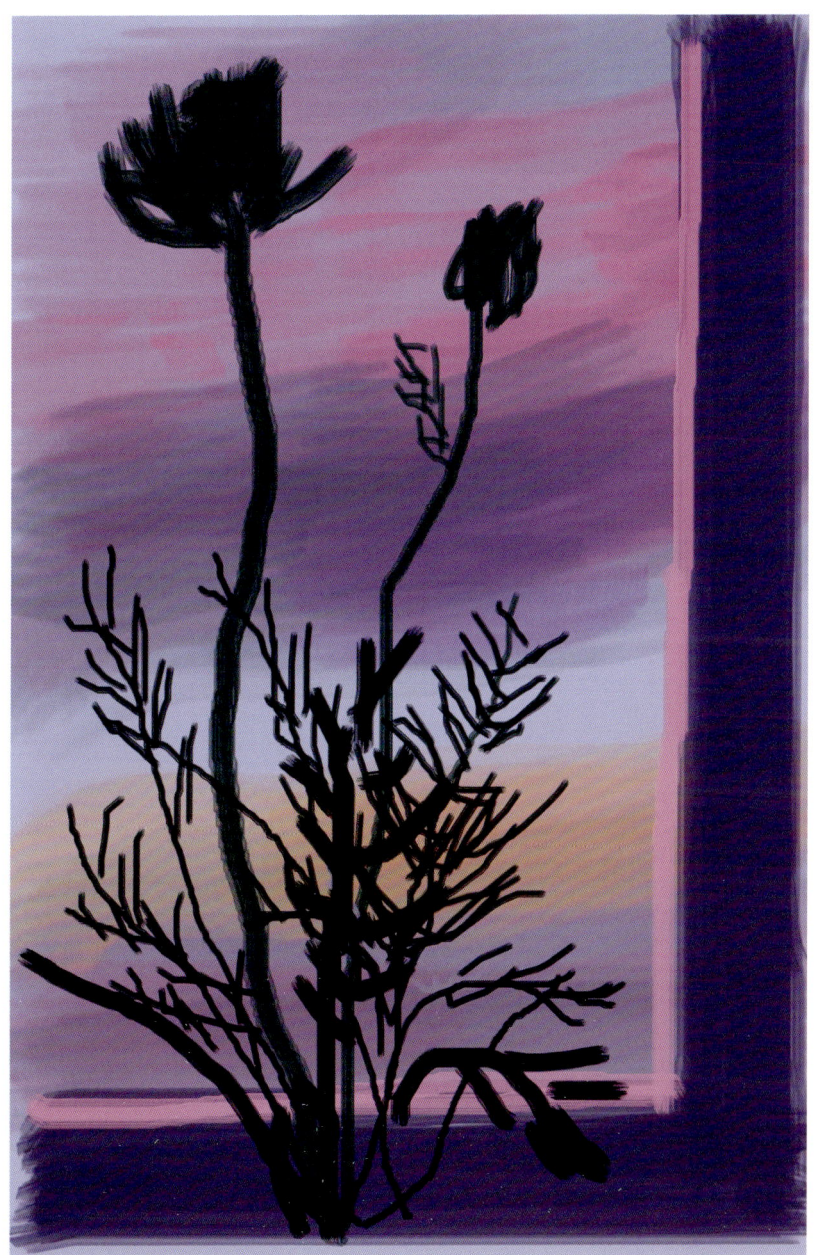

61

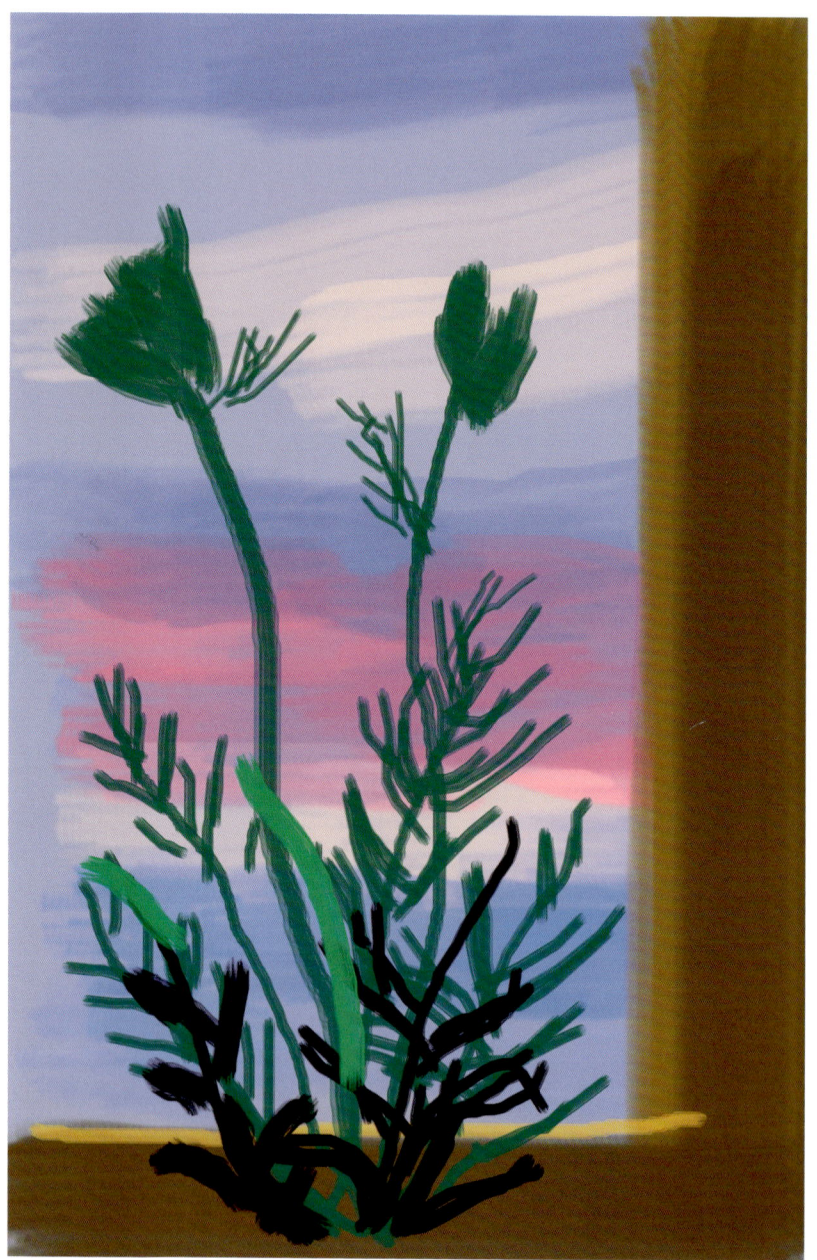

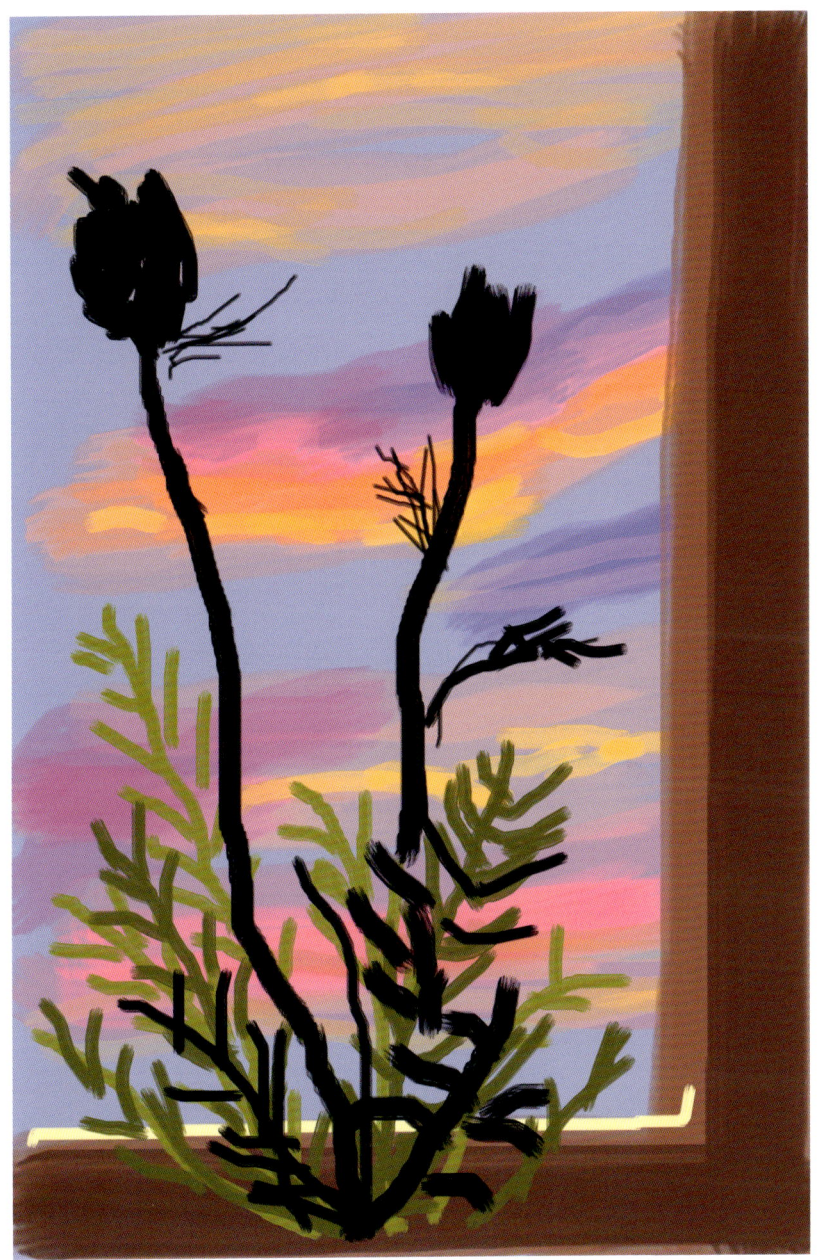

'No. 471', 17th June 2009, iPhone drawing

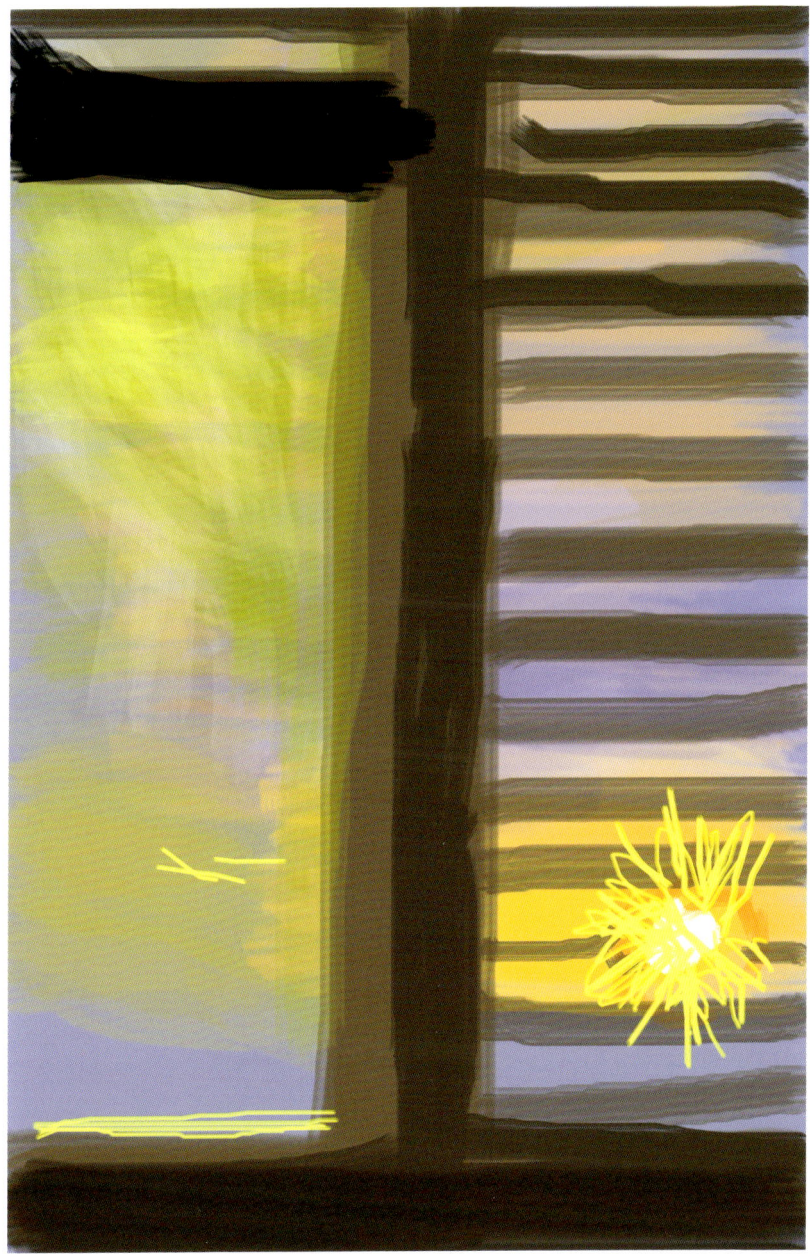

'No. 530', 27th June 2009, iPhone drawing

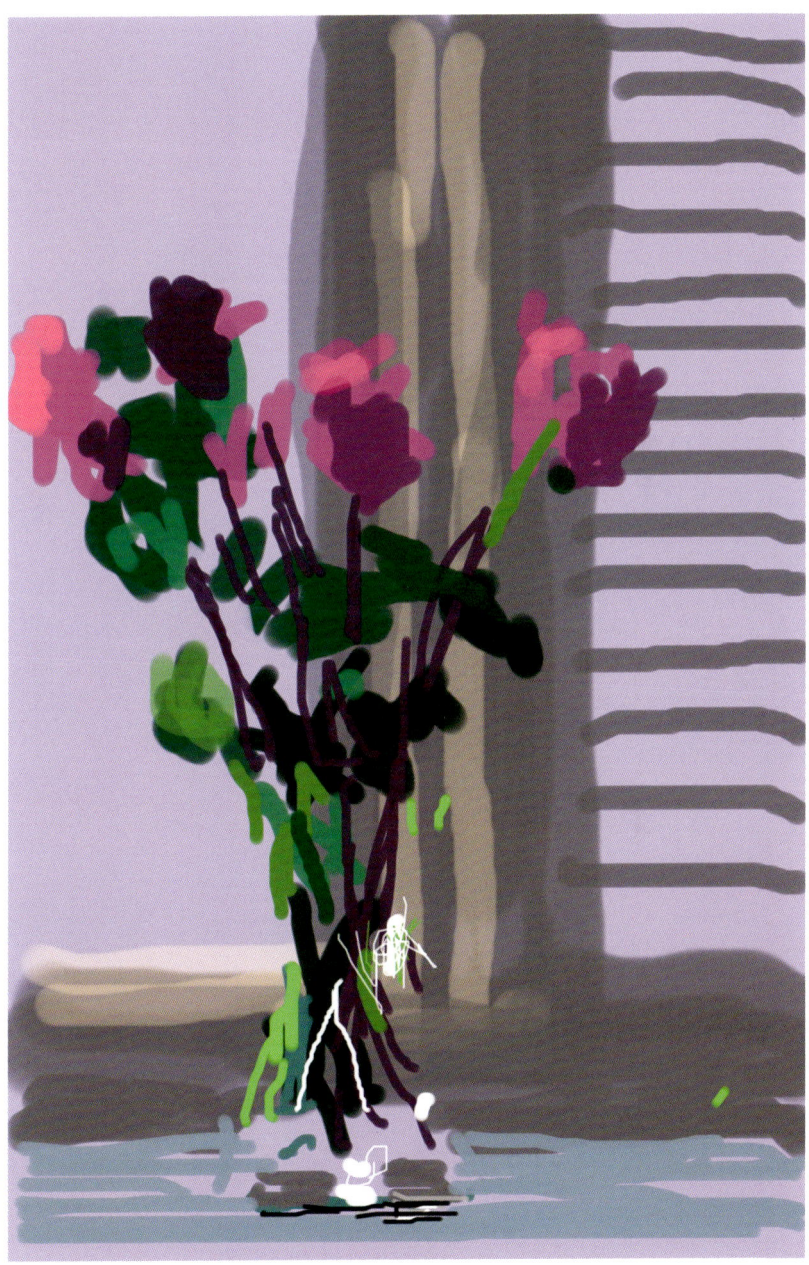

'No. 535', 28th June 2009, iPhone drawing
Page 70: 'No. 536', 30th June 2009, iPhone drawing;
Page 71: 'No. 539', 2nd July 2009, iPhone drawing

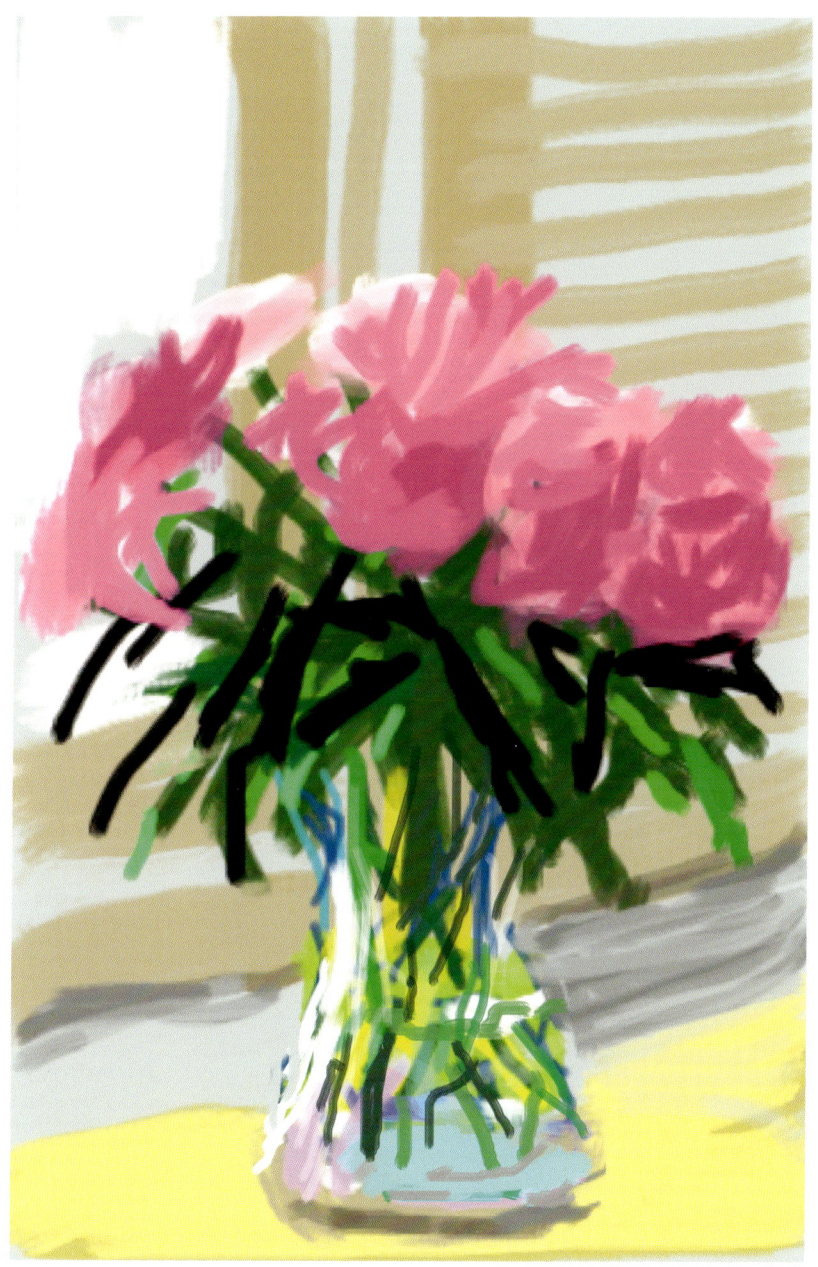

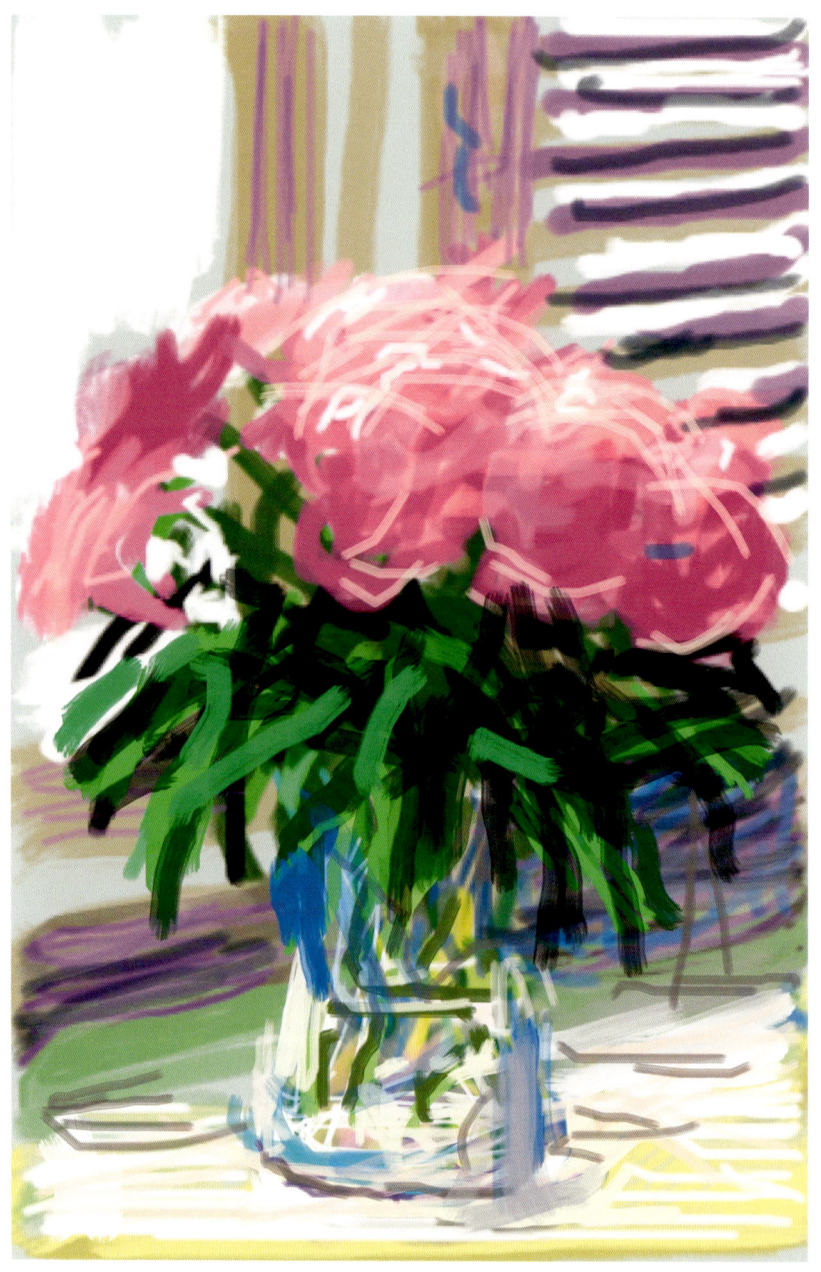

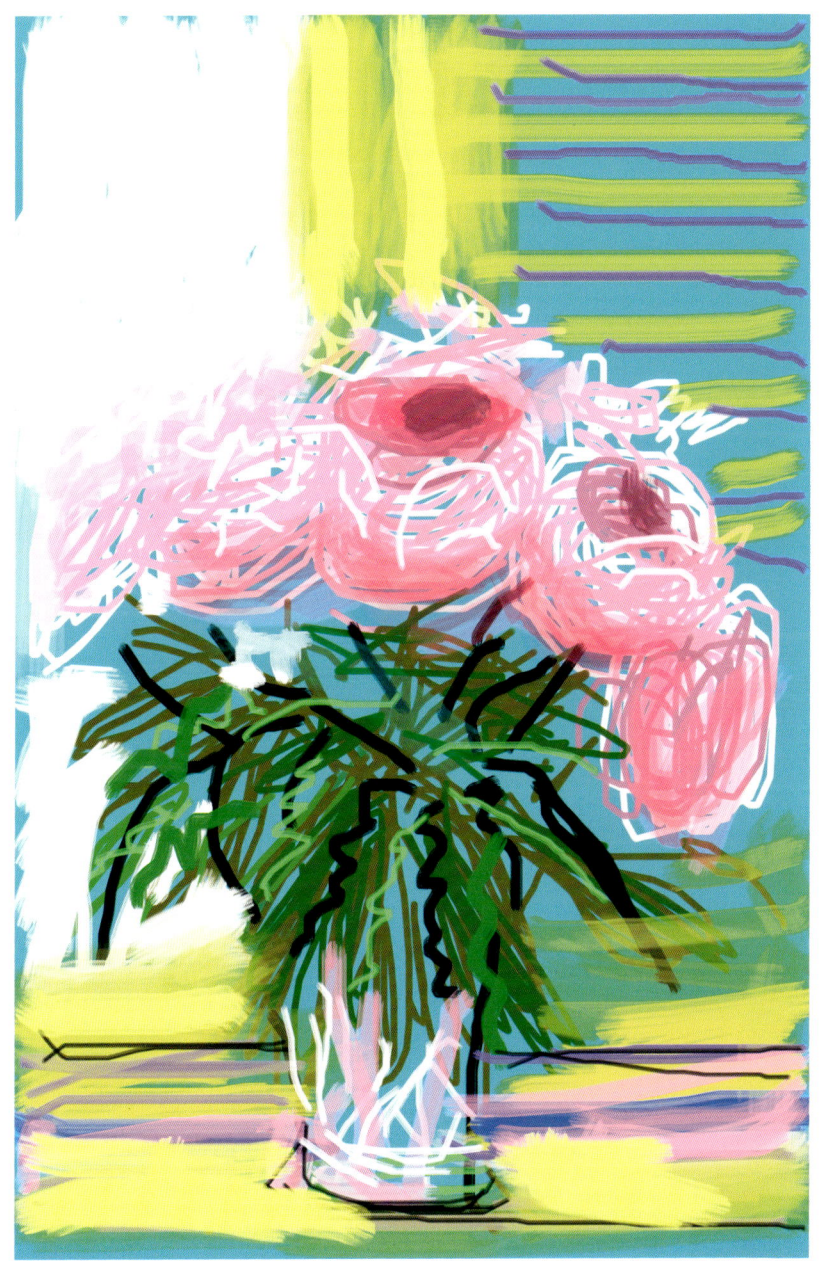

71

'No. 550', 15th September 2009, iPhone drawing

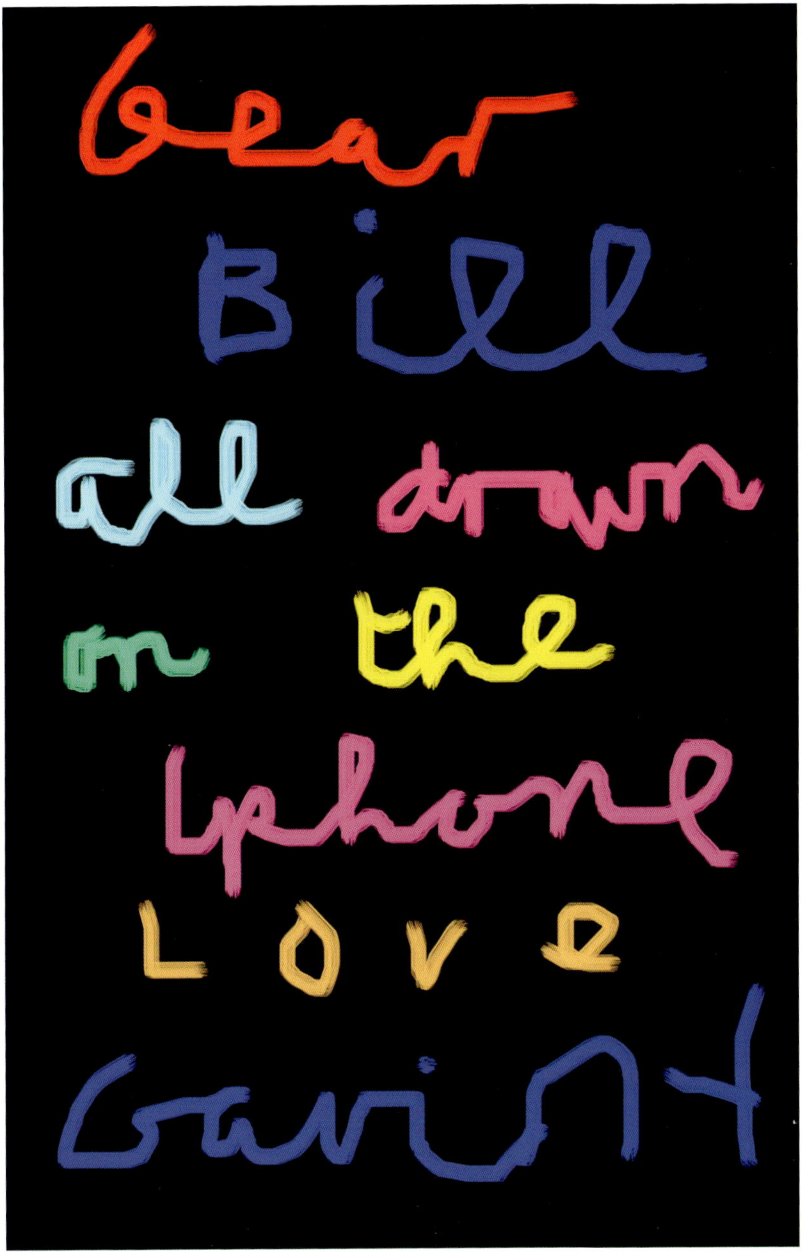

dear
Bill
all drawn
on the
iphone
LOVE
Gavin H

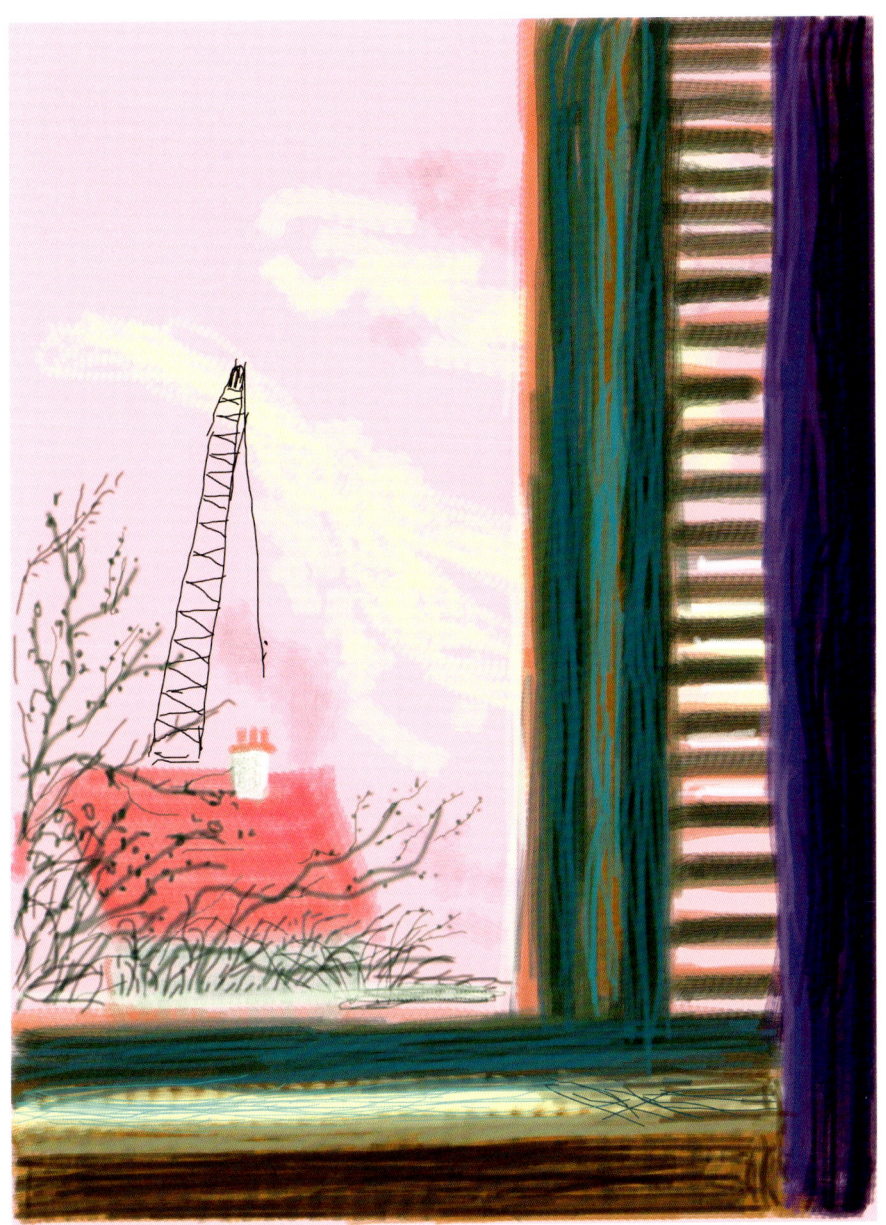

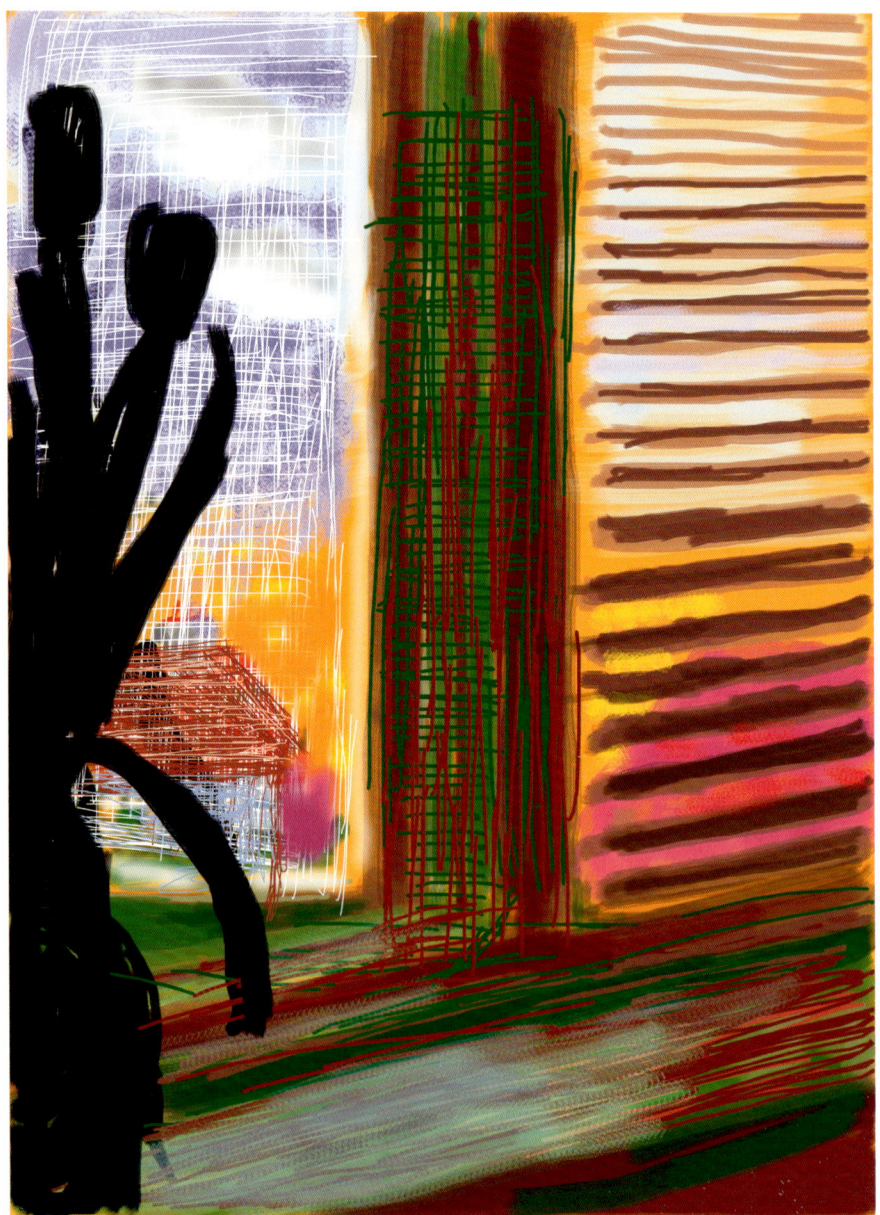

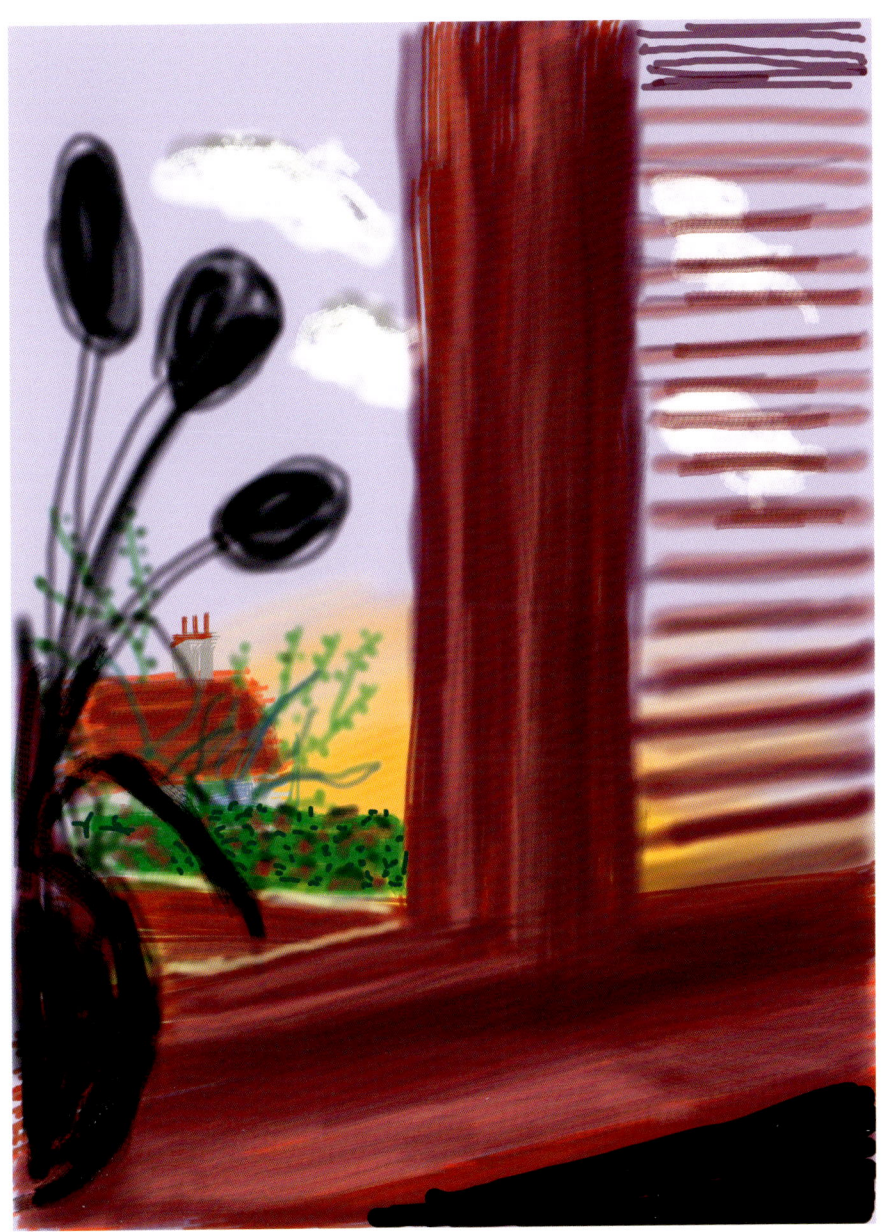

'No. 79', 1st May 2010, iPad drawing
Page 80: 'No. 86', 3rd May 2010, iPad drawing;
78   Page 81: 'No. 87', 3rd May 2010, iPad drawing

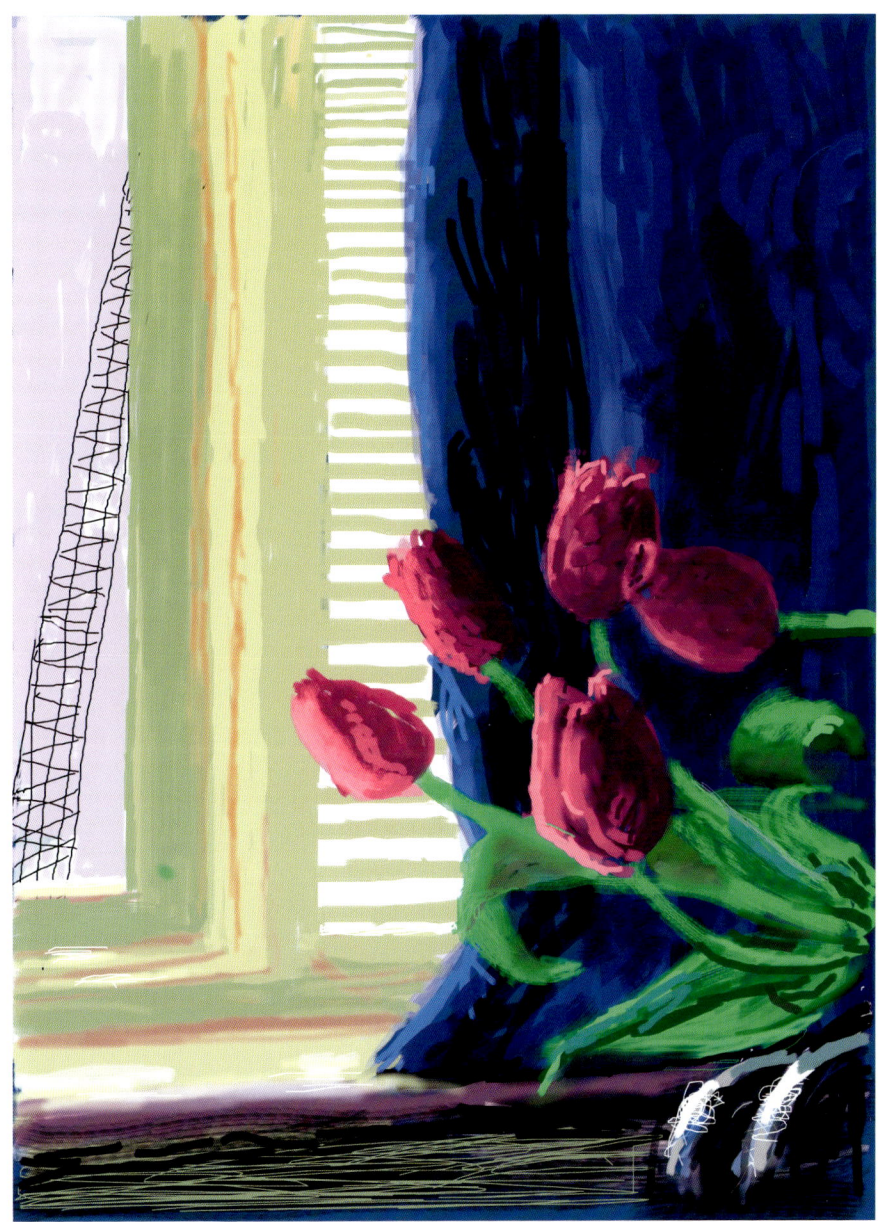

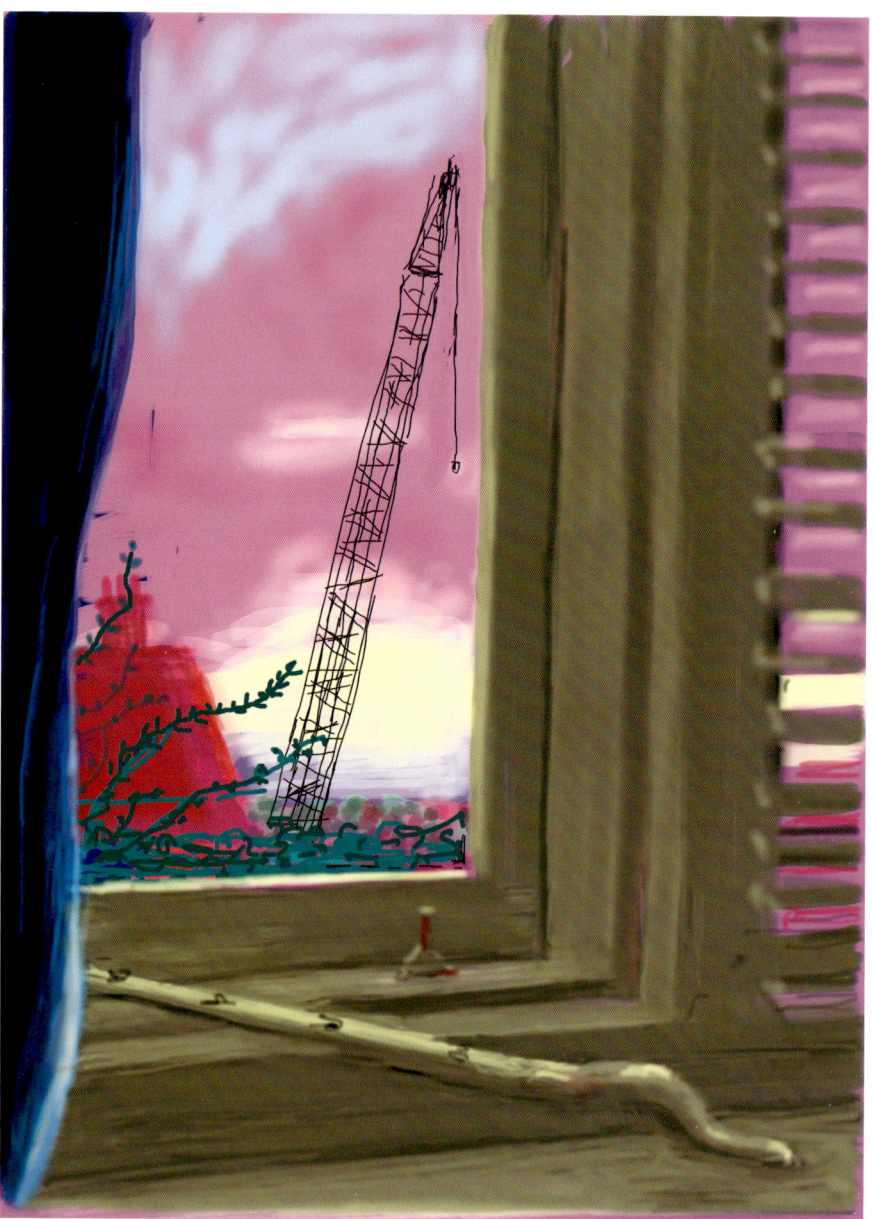

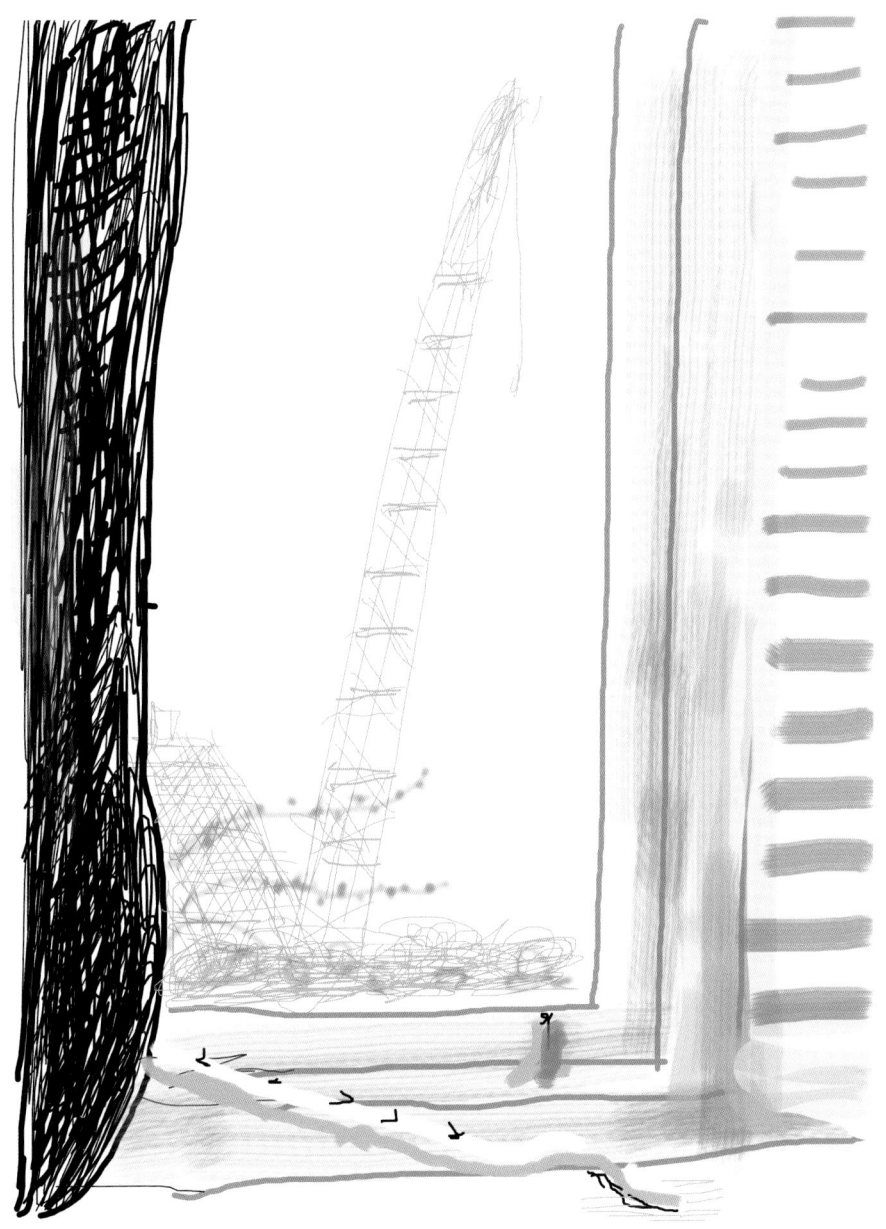

'No. 91', 4th May 2010, iPad drawing

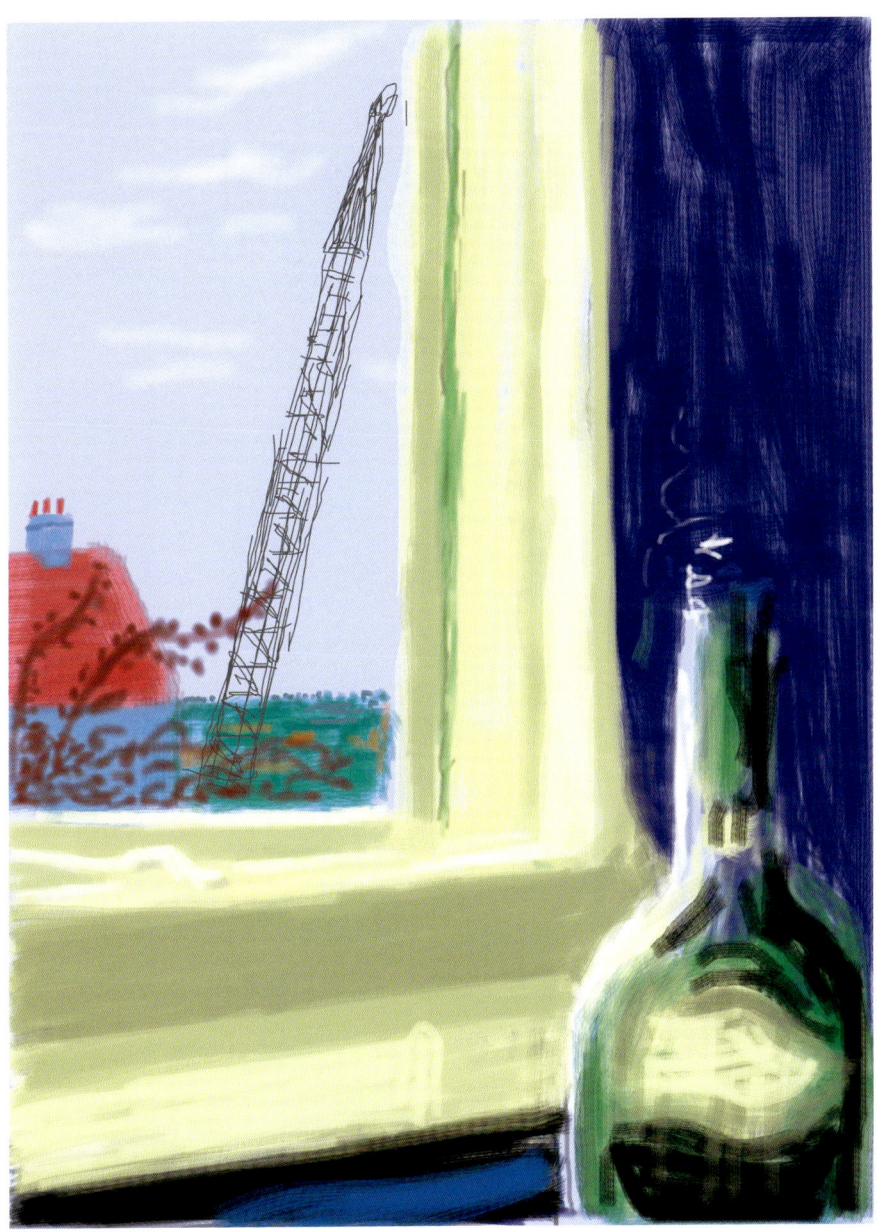

83

'No. 104', 10th May 2010, iPad drawing

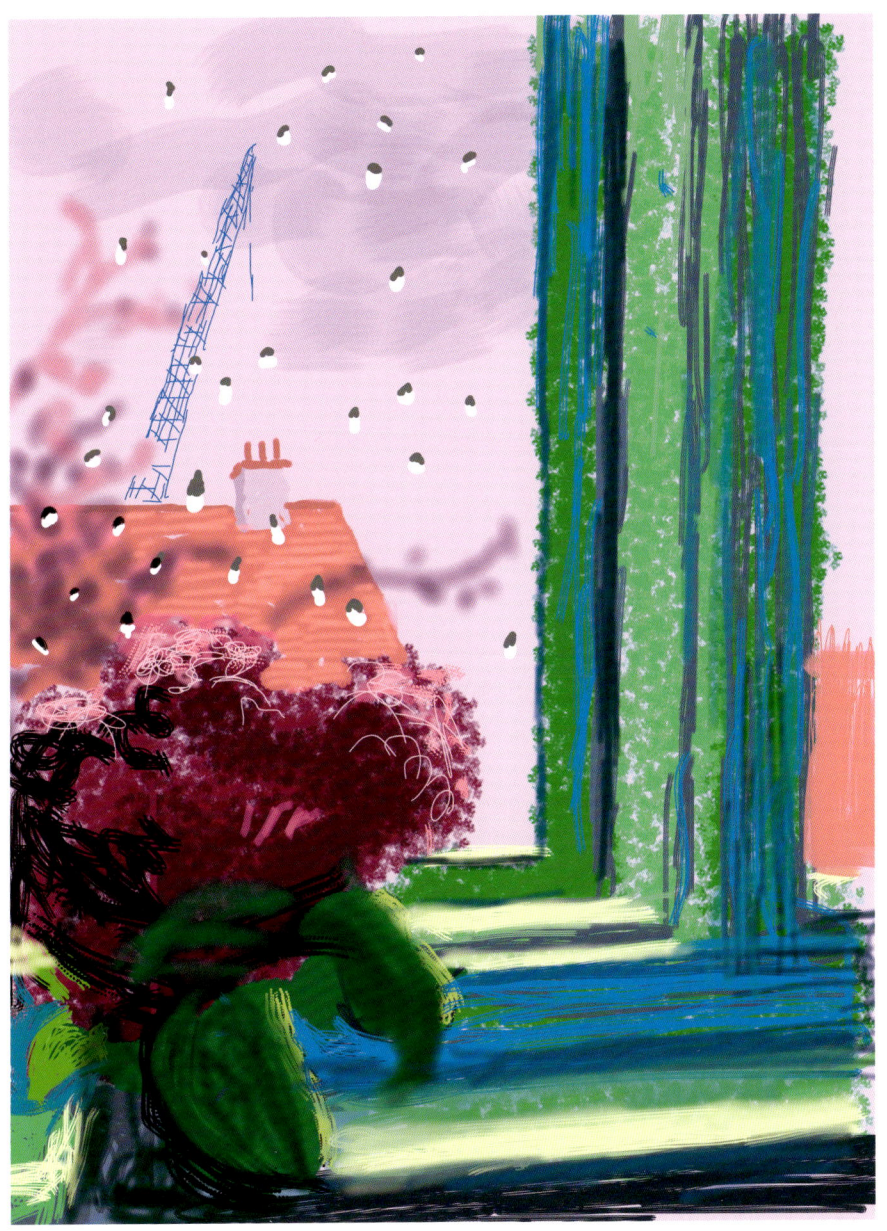

'No. 112', 10th May 2010, iPad drawing
Page 88: 'No. 117', 10th May 2010, iPad drawing;
Page 89: 'No. 120', 24th May 2010, iPad drawing

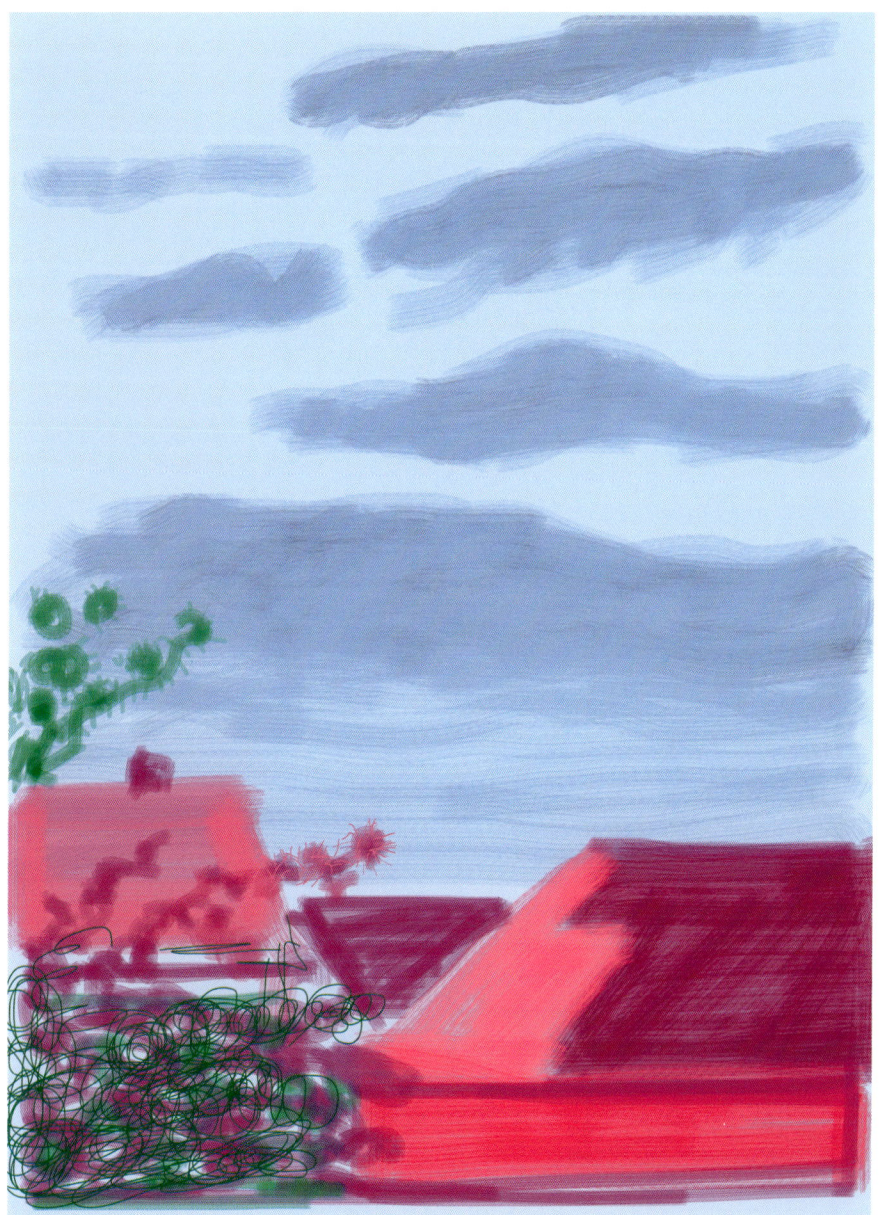

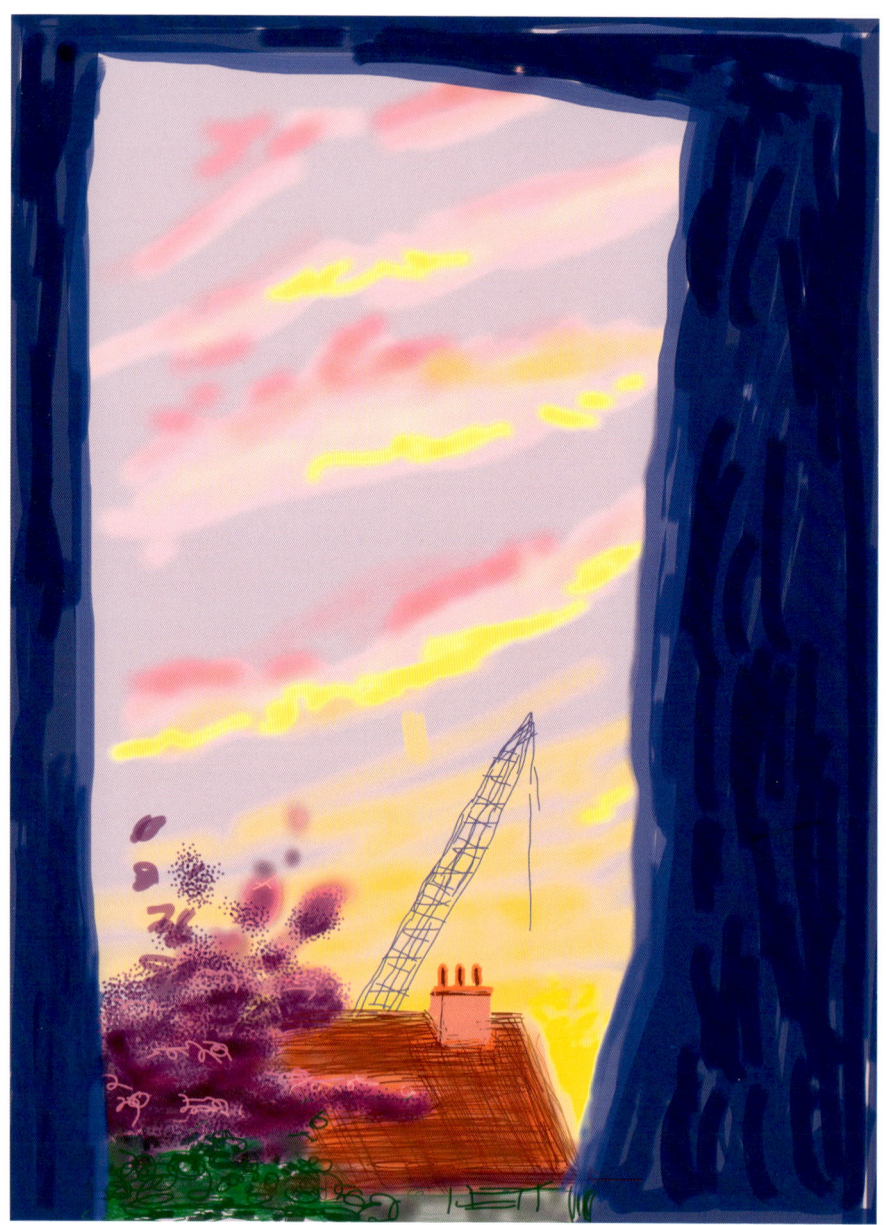

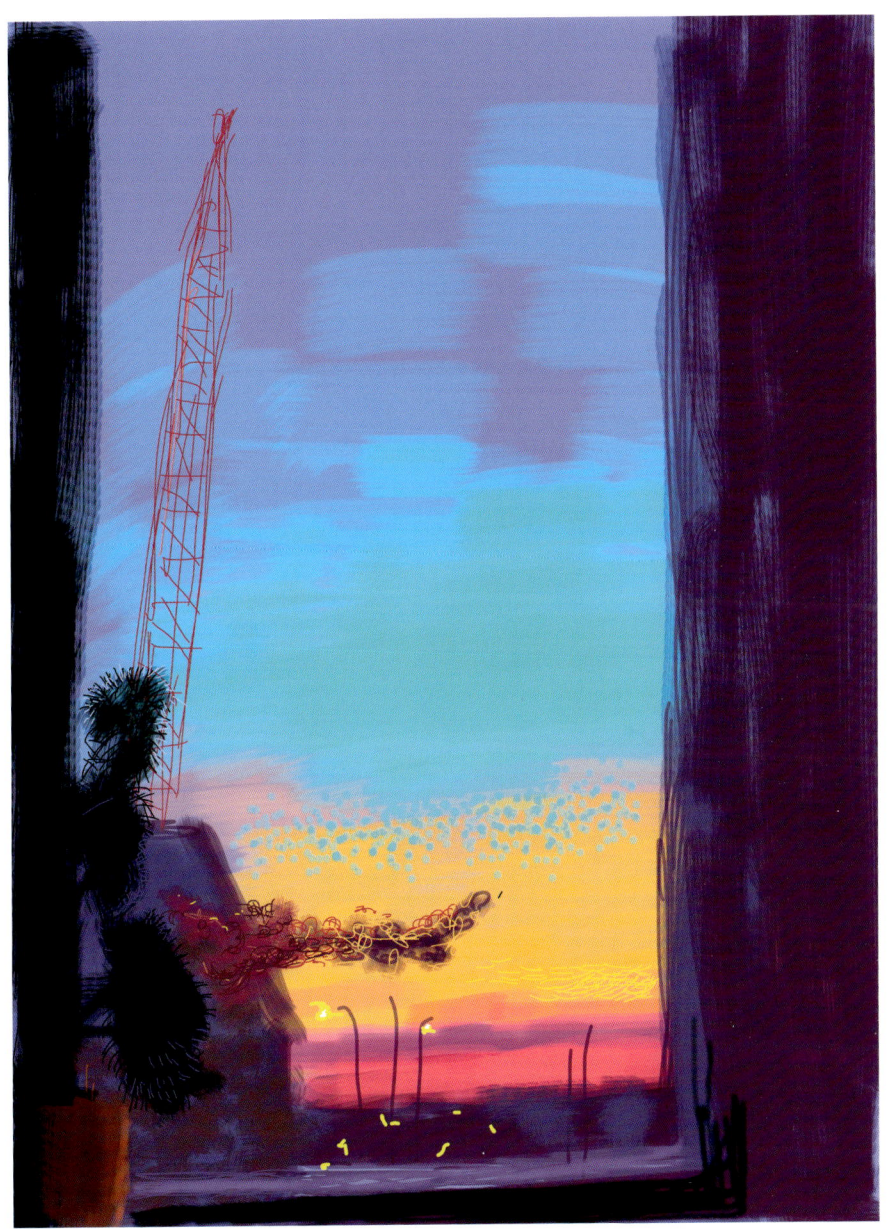

'No. 122', 24th May 2010, iPad drawing

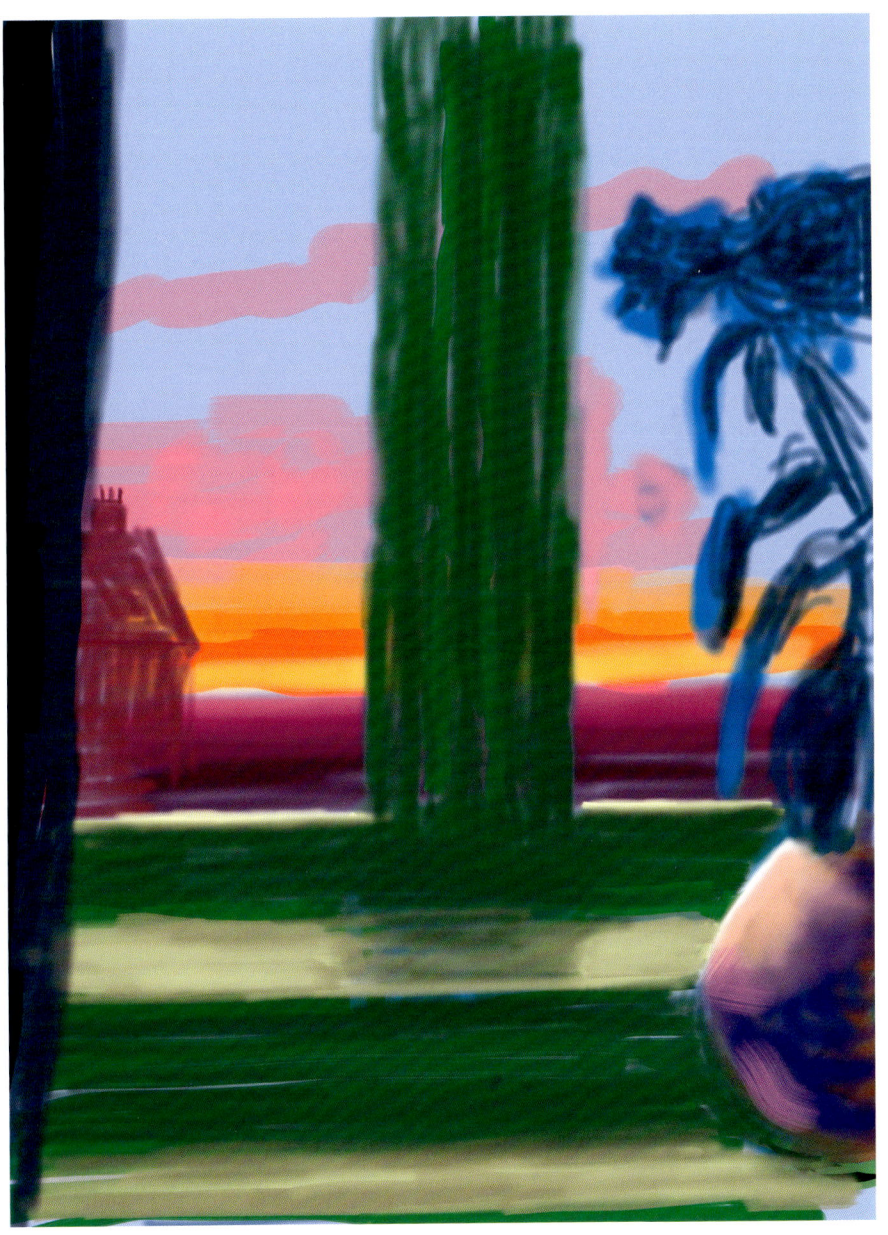

'No. 126', 26th May 2010, iPad drawing

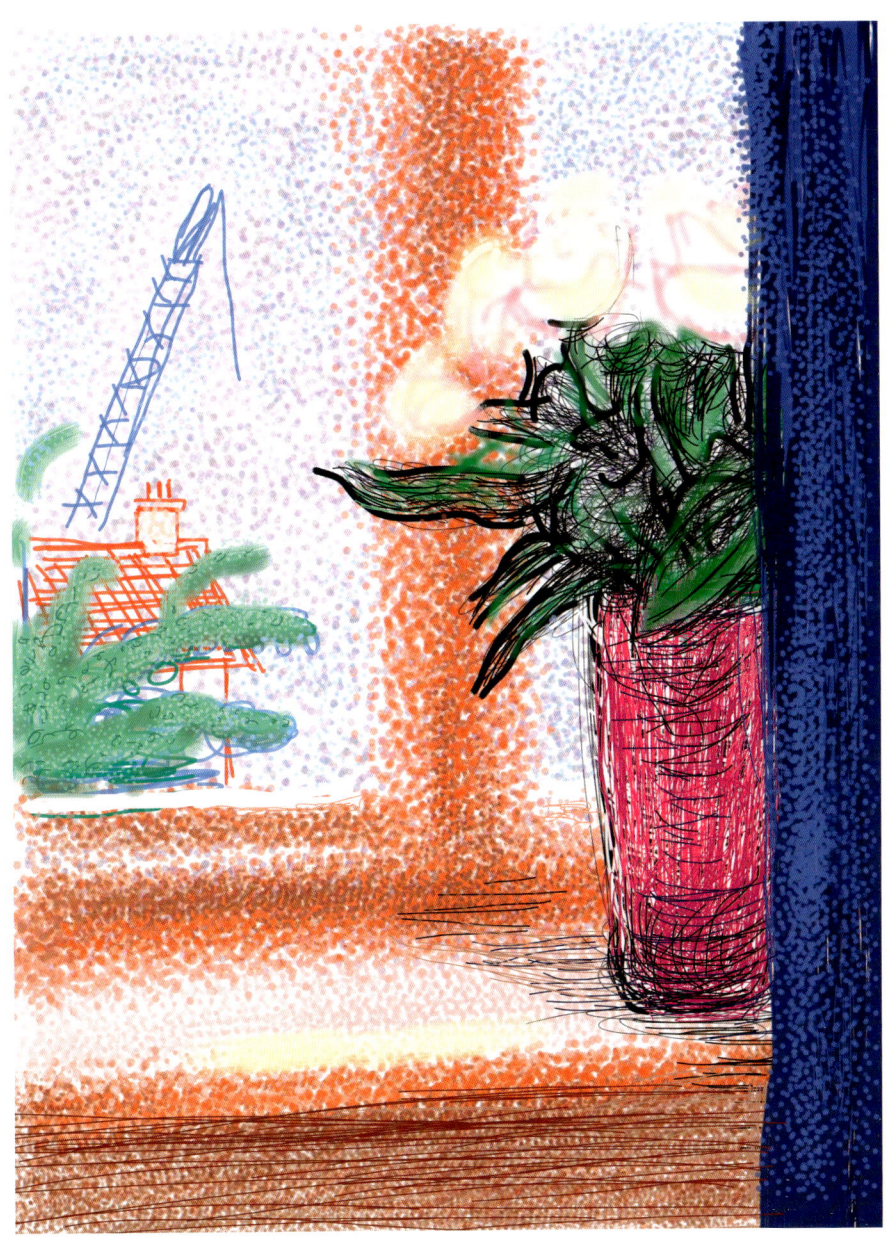

'No. 128', 27th May 2010, iPad drawing
Page 96: 'No. 133', 28th May 2010, iPad drawing;
Page 97: 'No. 136', 1st June 2010, iPad drawing

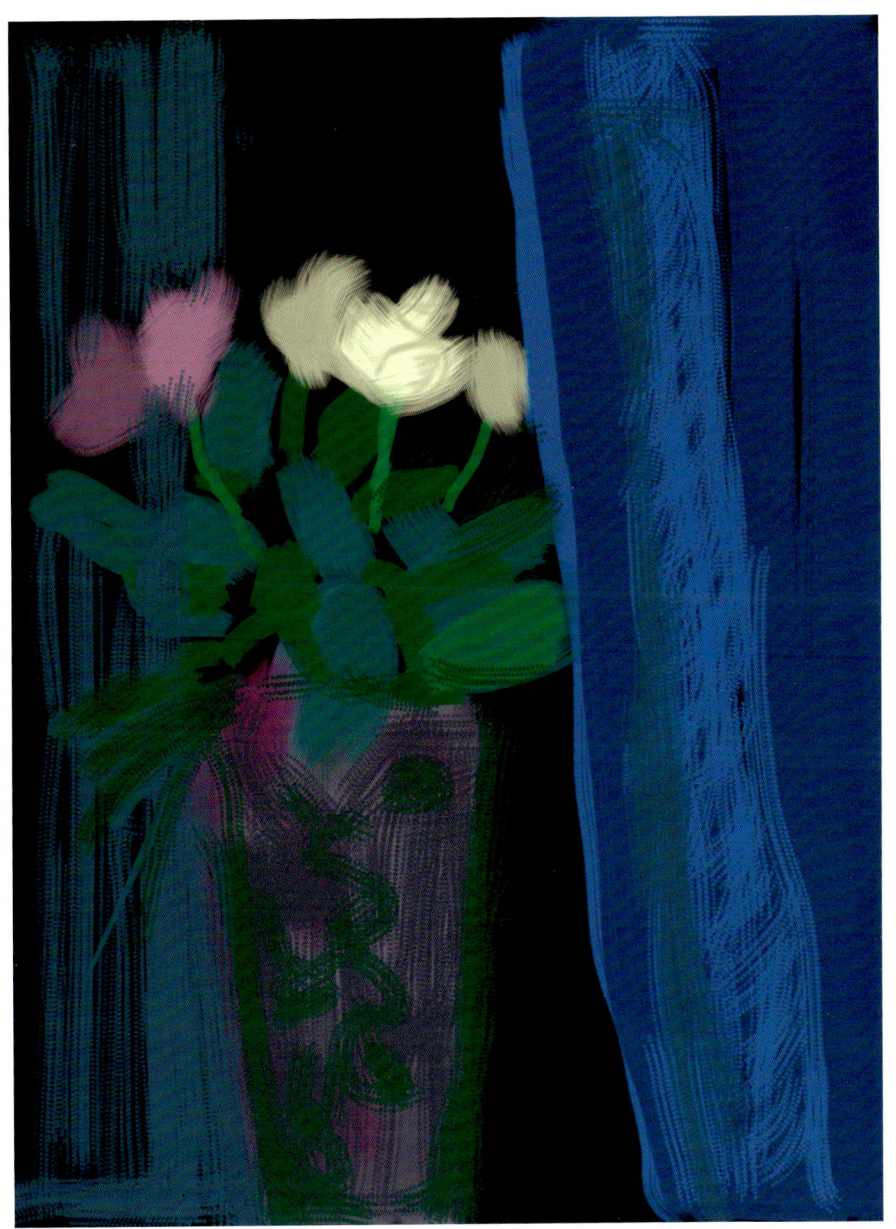

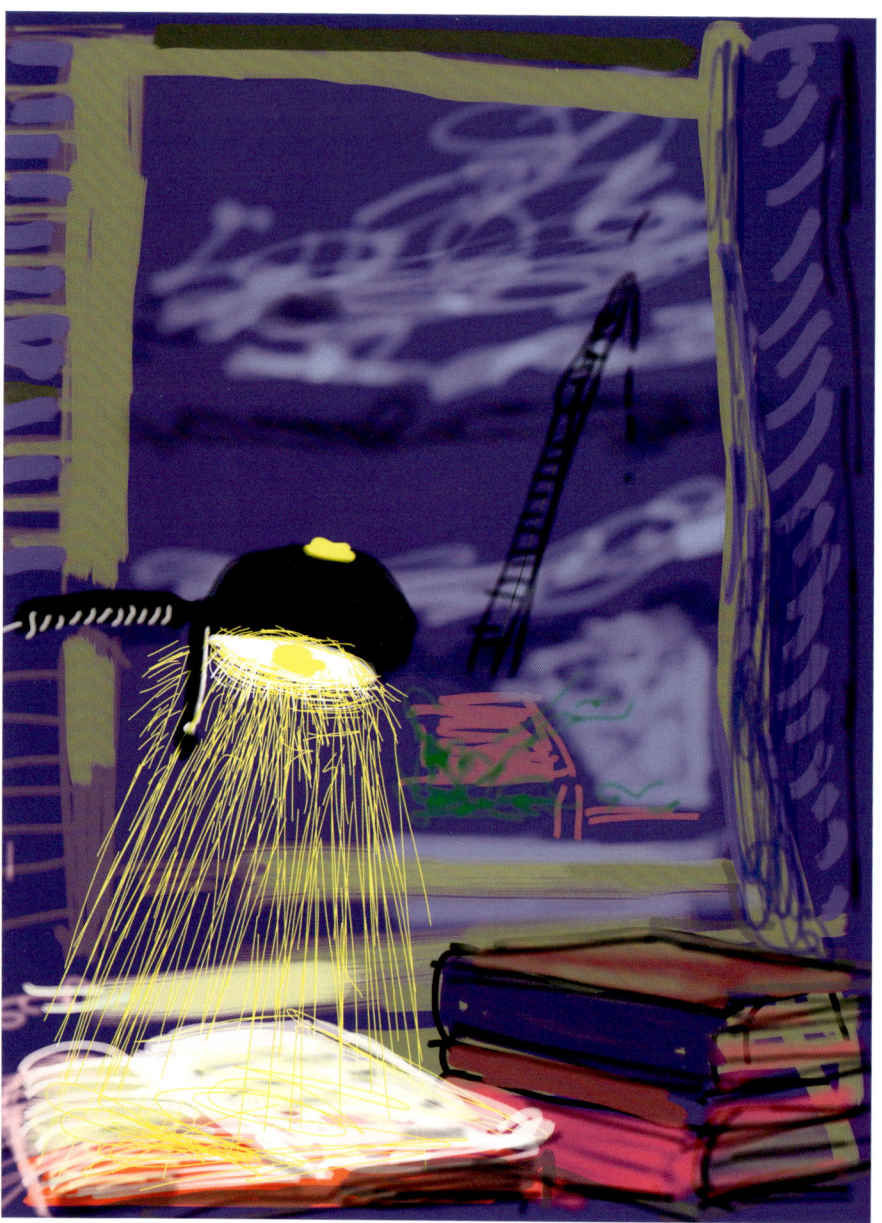

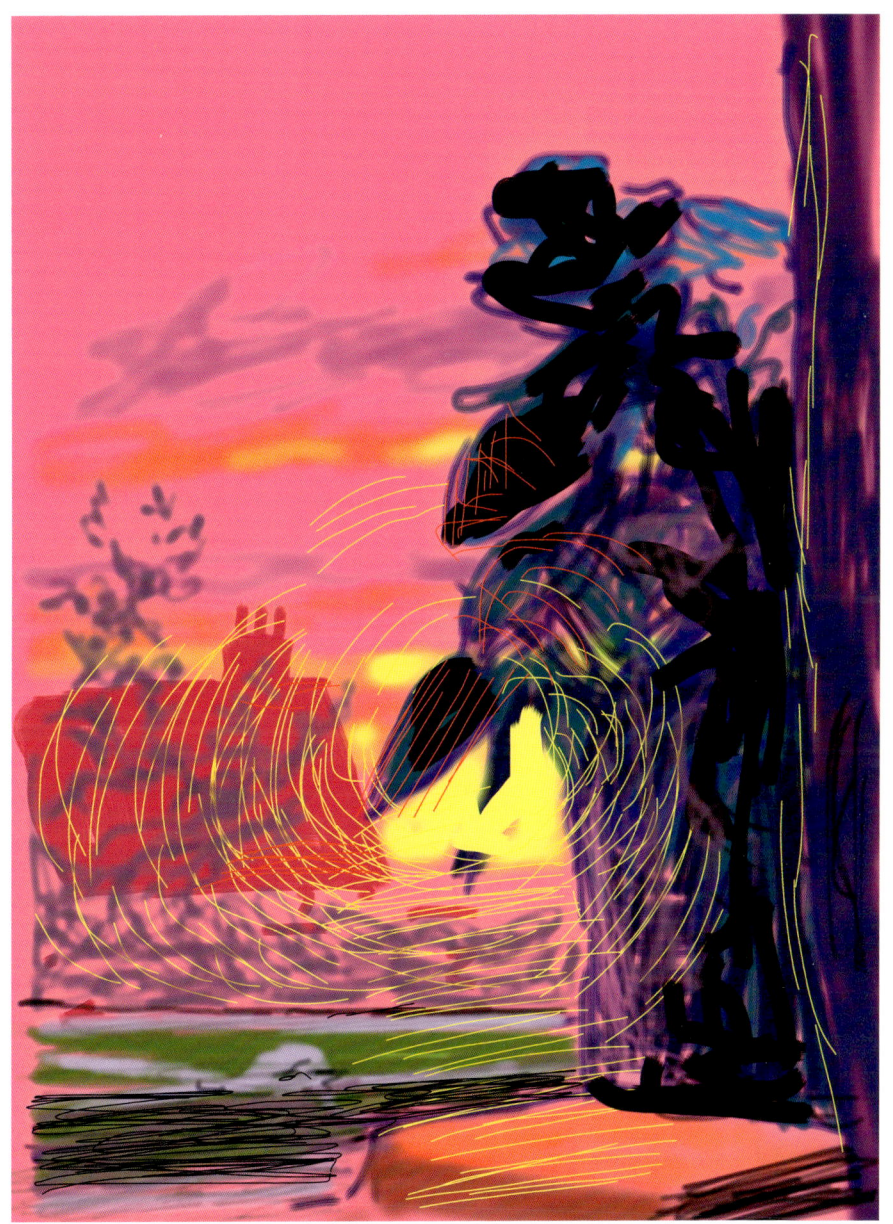

97

'No. 137', 1st June 2010, iPad drawing

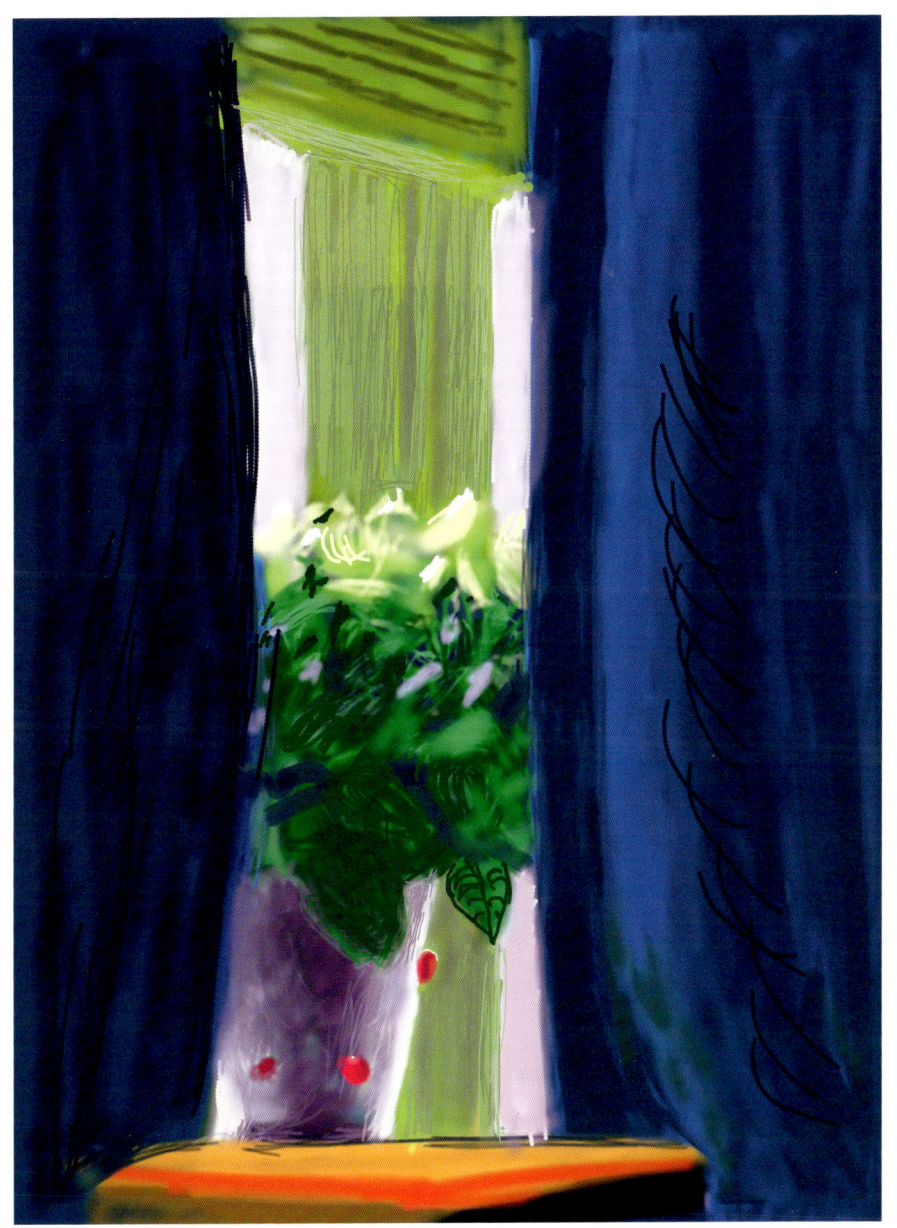

'No. 147', 1st June 2010, iPad drawing

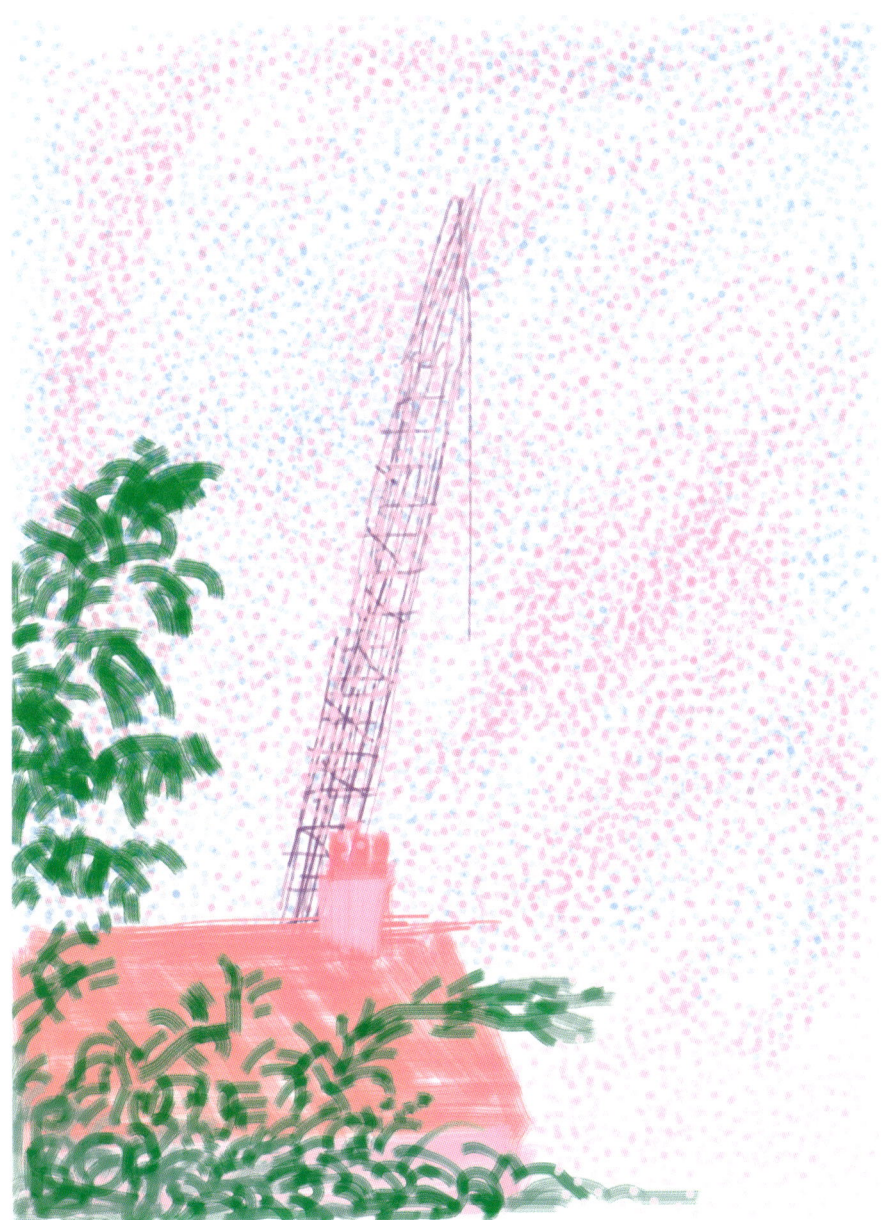

'No. 158', 9th June 2010, iPad drawing

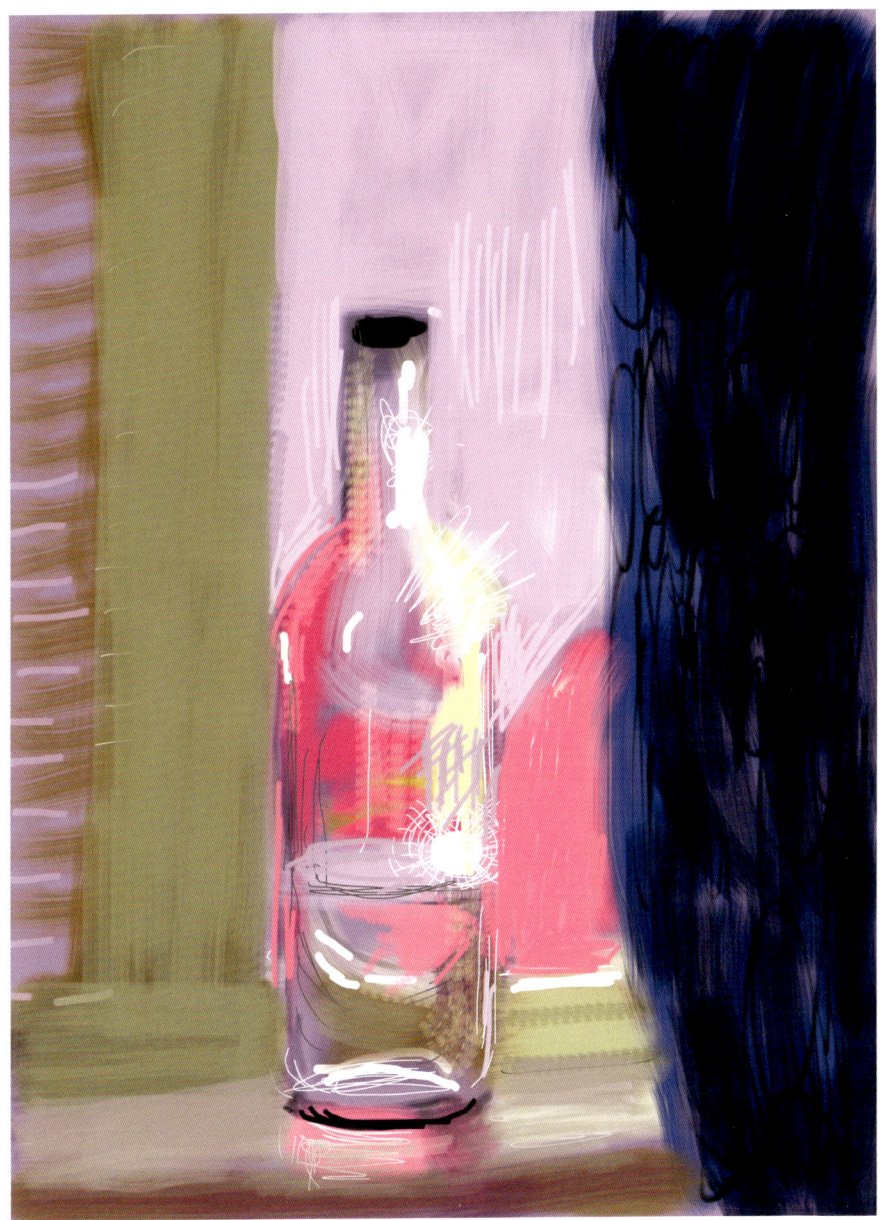

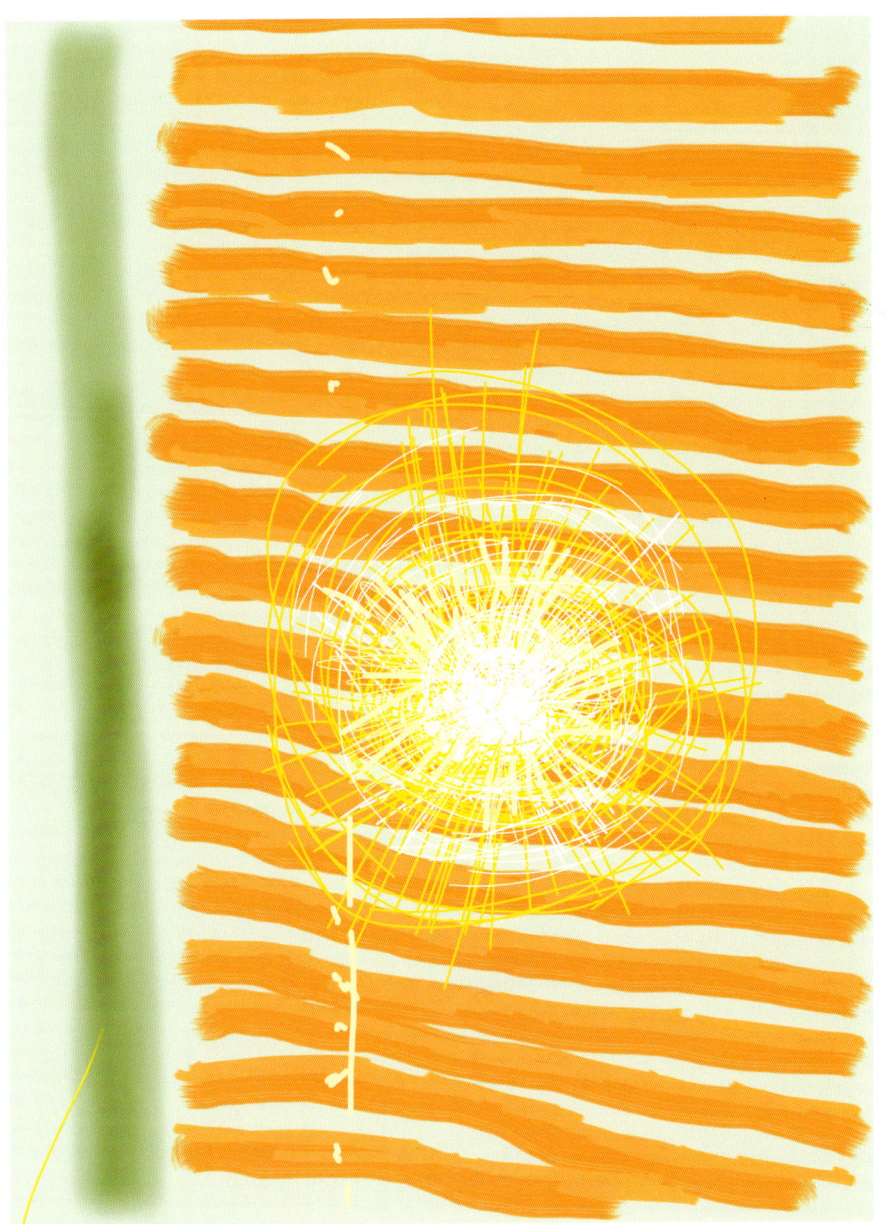

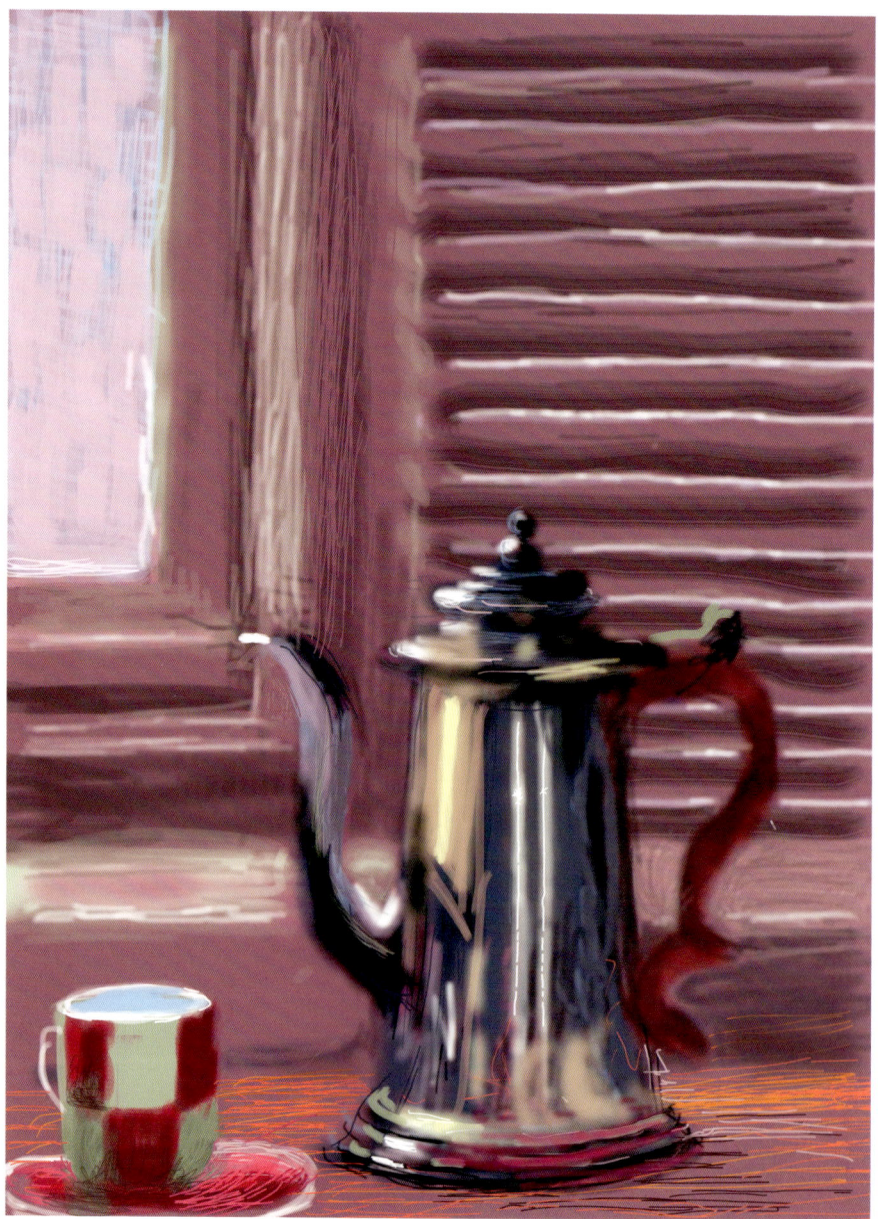

106

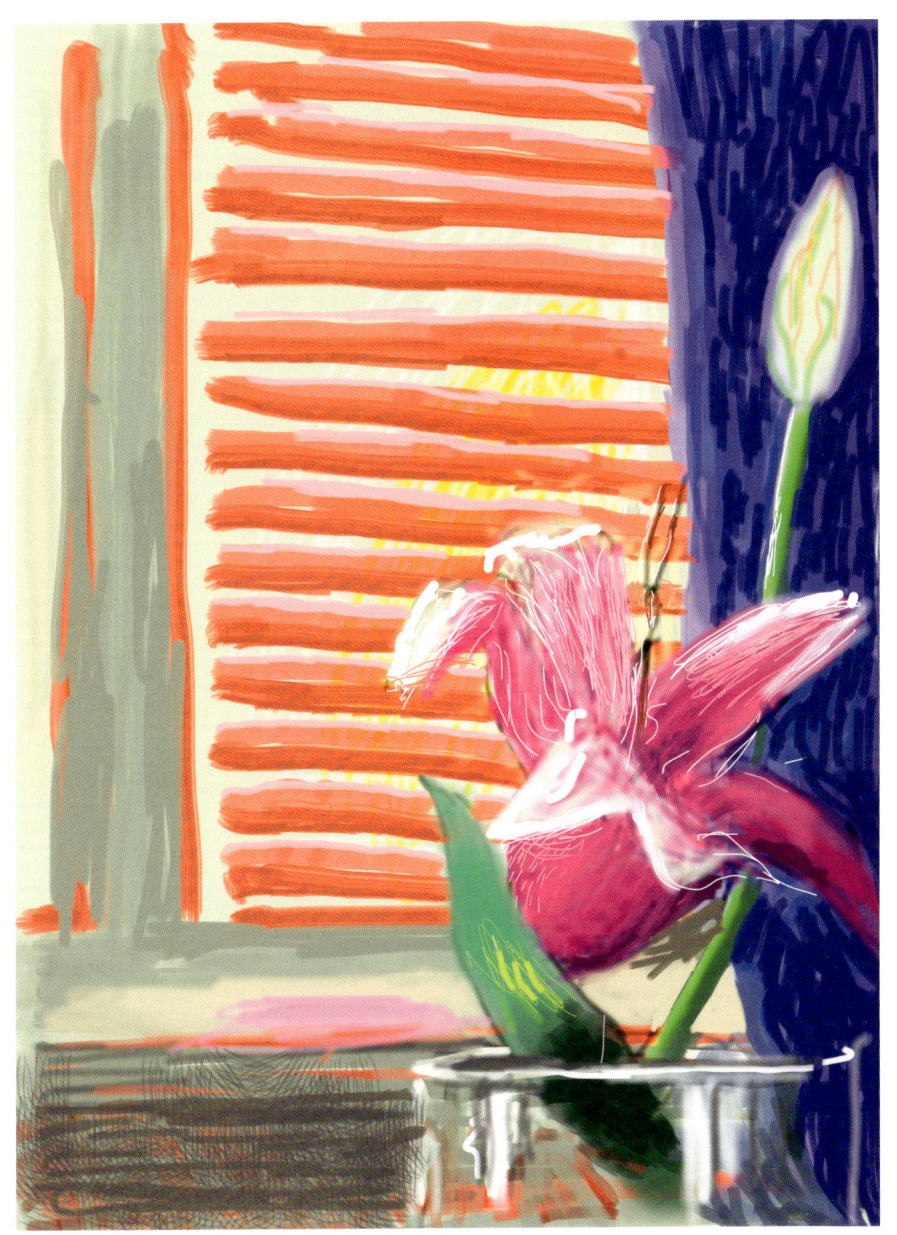

107

'No. 187', 17th June 2010, iPad drawing

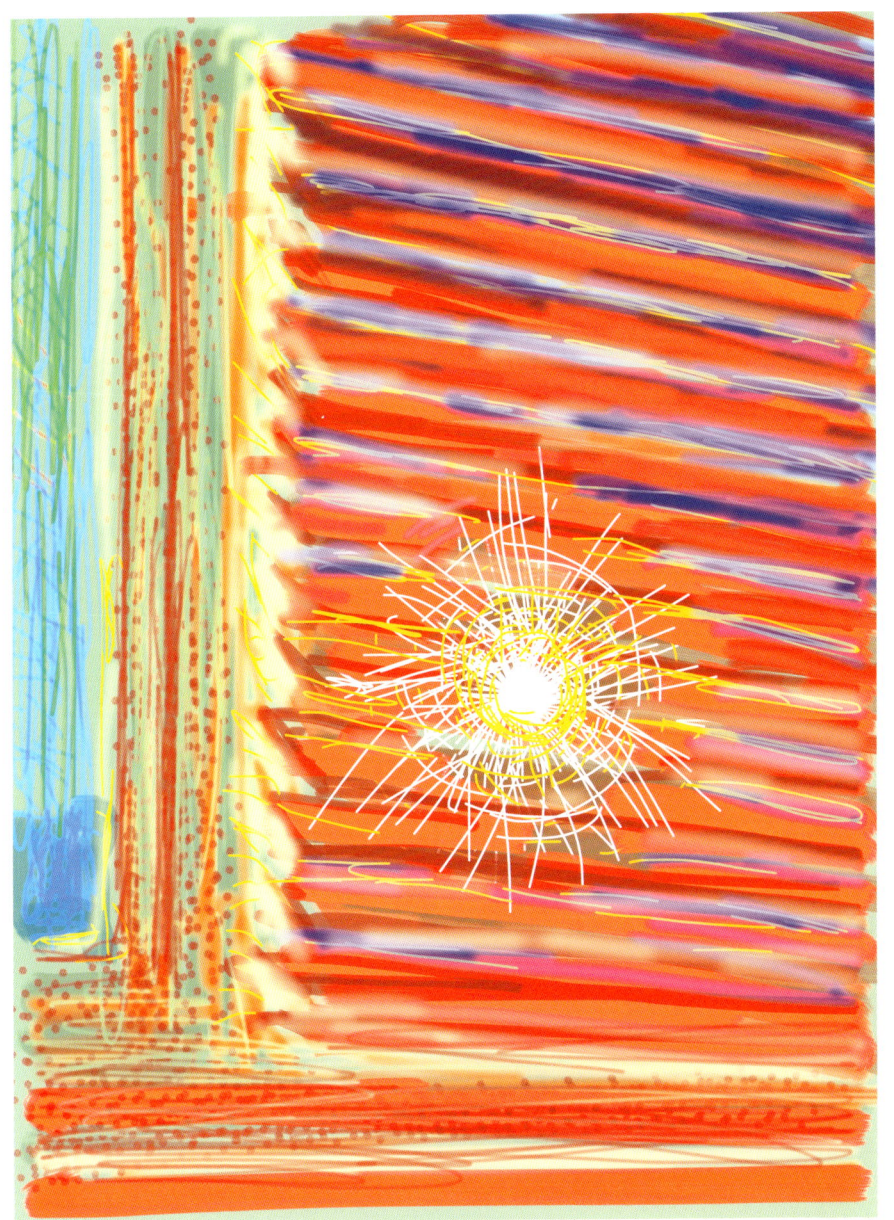

'No. 188', 20th June 2010, iPad drawing

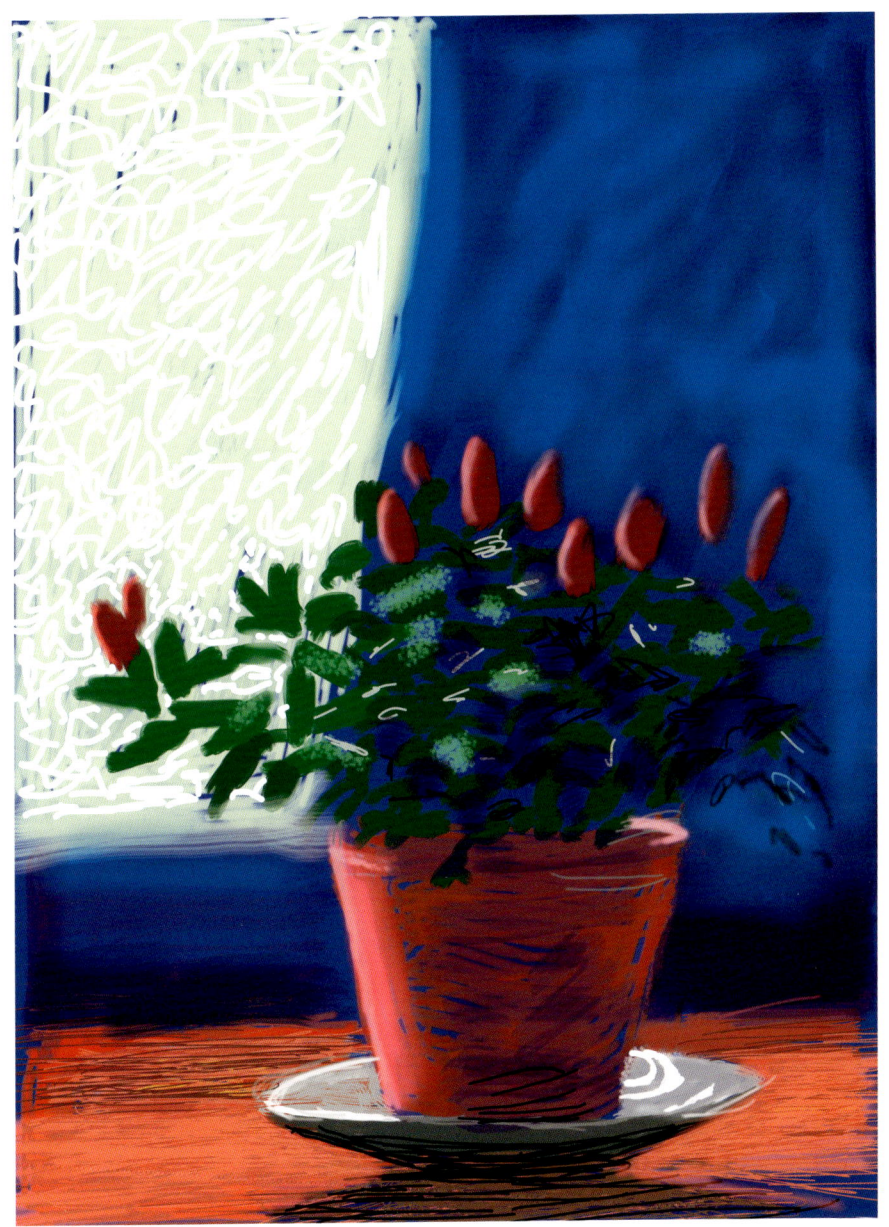

'No. 210', 1st July 2010, iPad drawing
Page 114: 'No. 250', 12th July 2010, iPad drawing;
Page 115: 'No. 268', 16th July 2010, iPad drawing

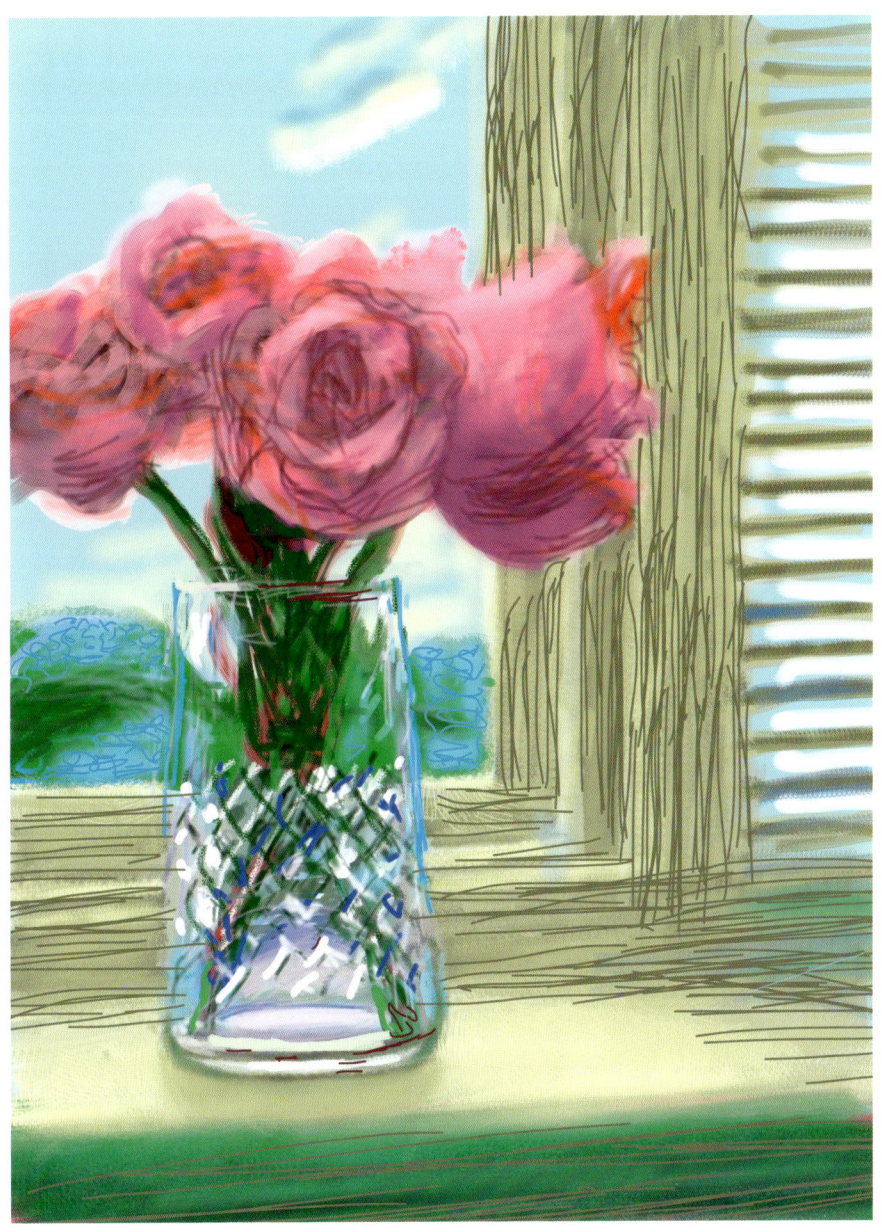

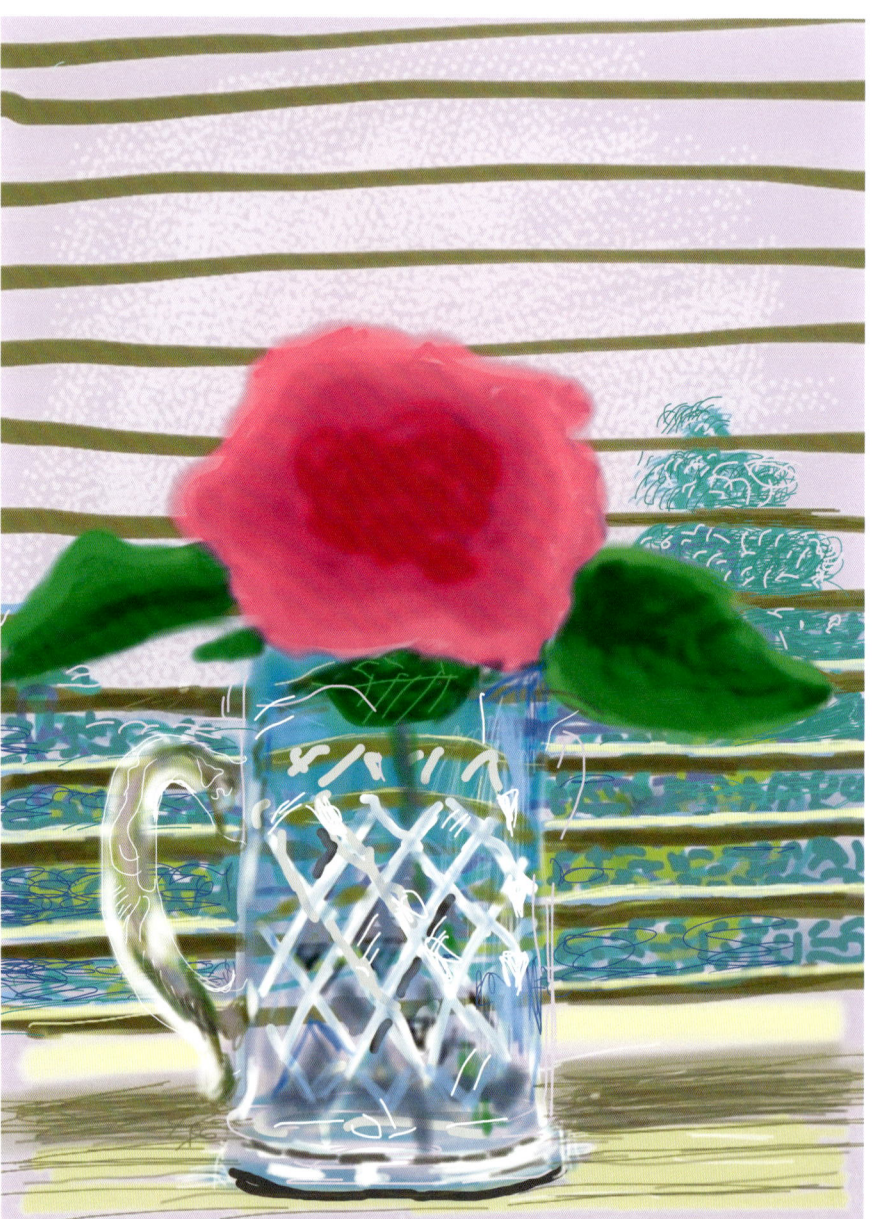

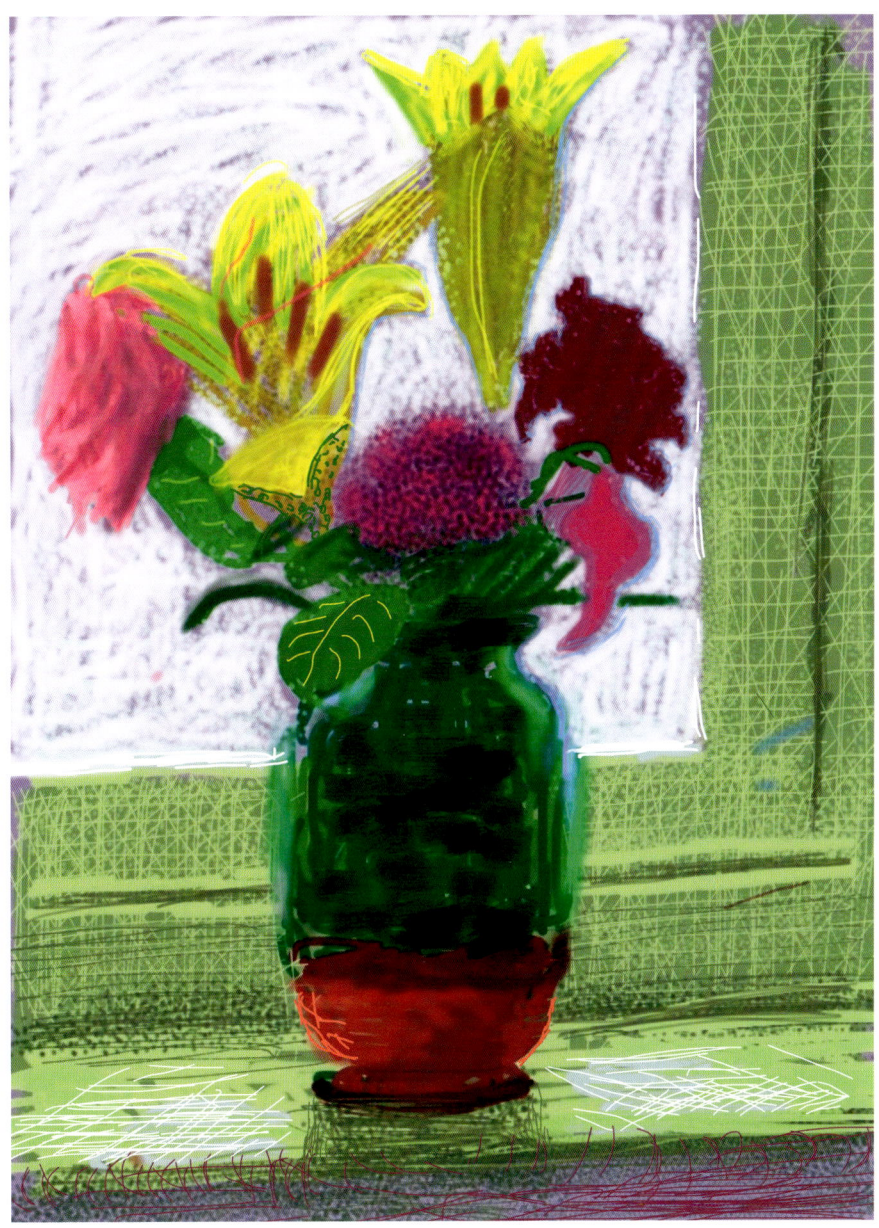

116   'No. 274', 21st July 2010, iPad drawing

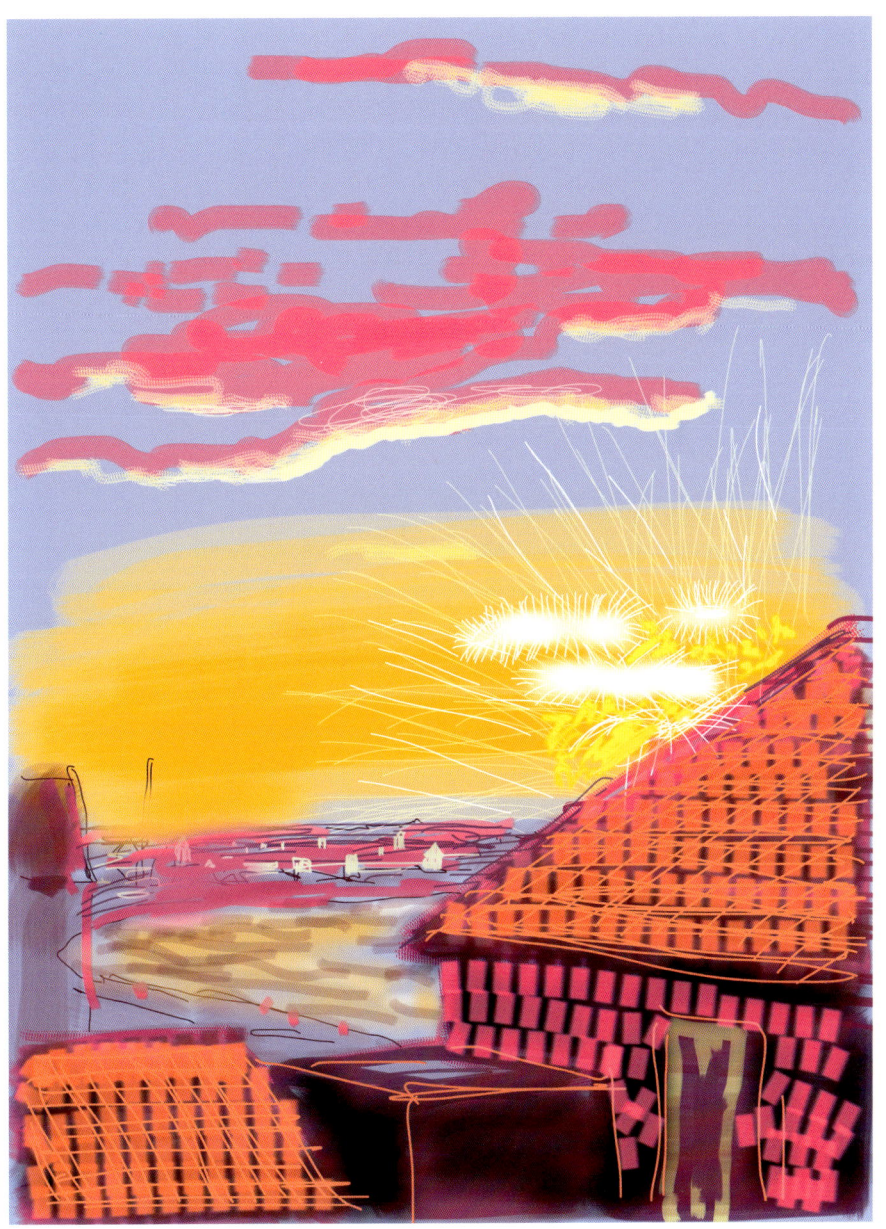

'No. 281', 23rd July 2010, iPad drawing
Page 120: 'No. 318', 3rd August 2010, iPad drawing;

Page 121: 'No. 578', 25th November 2010, iPad drawing

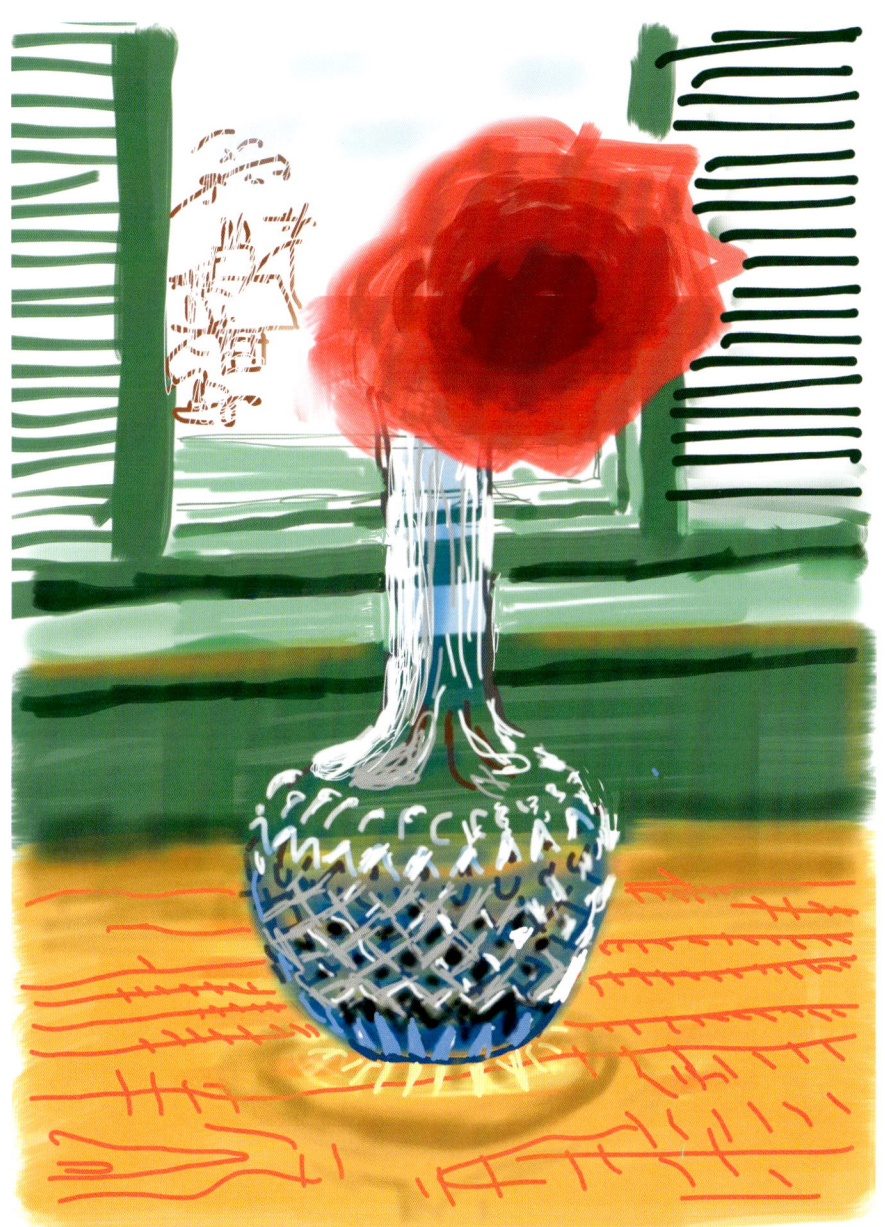

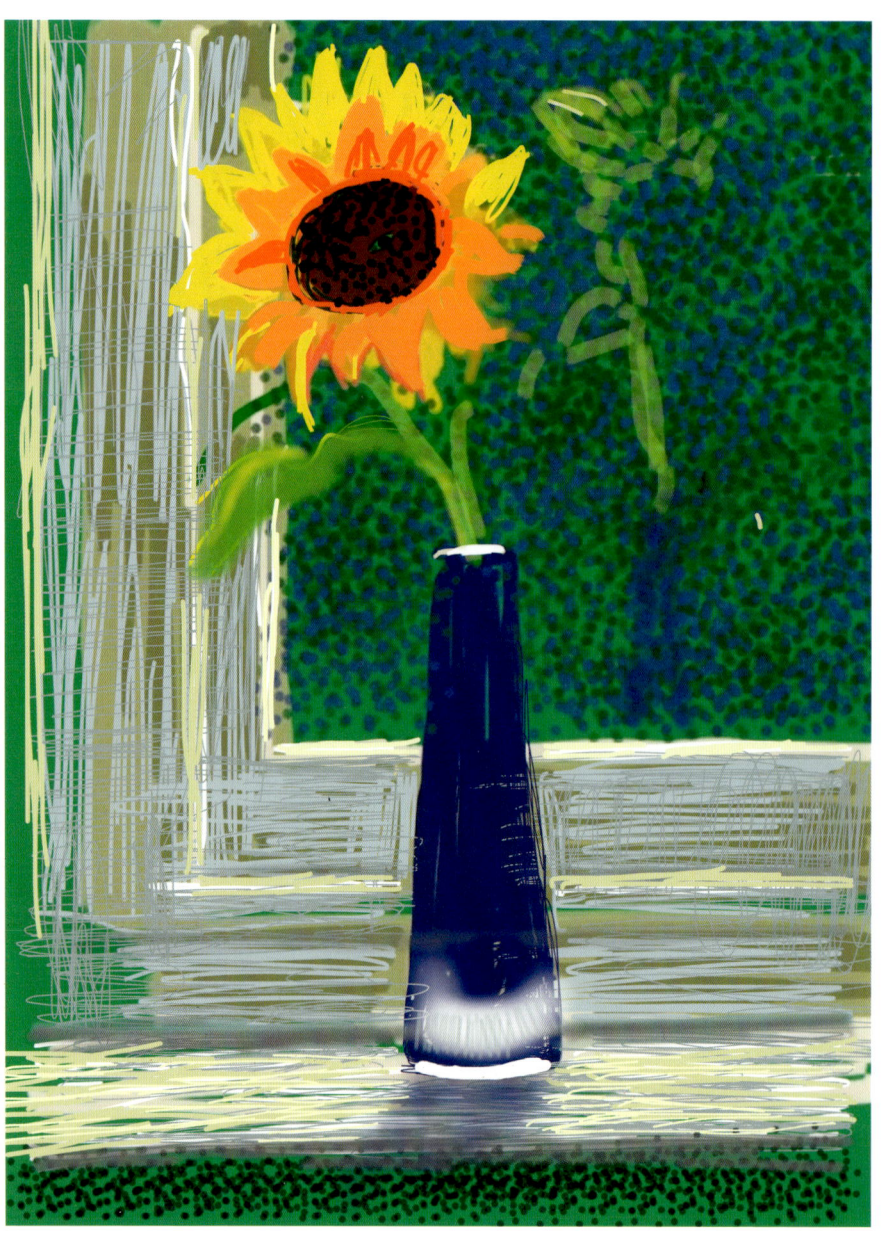

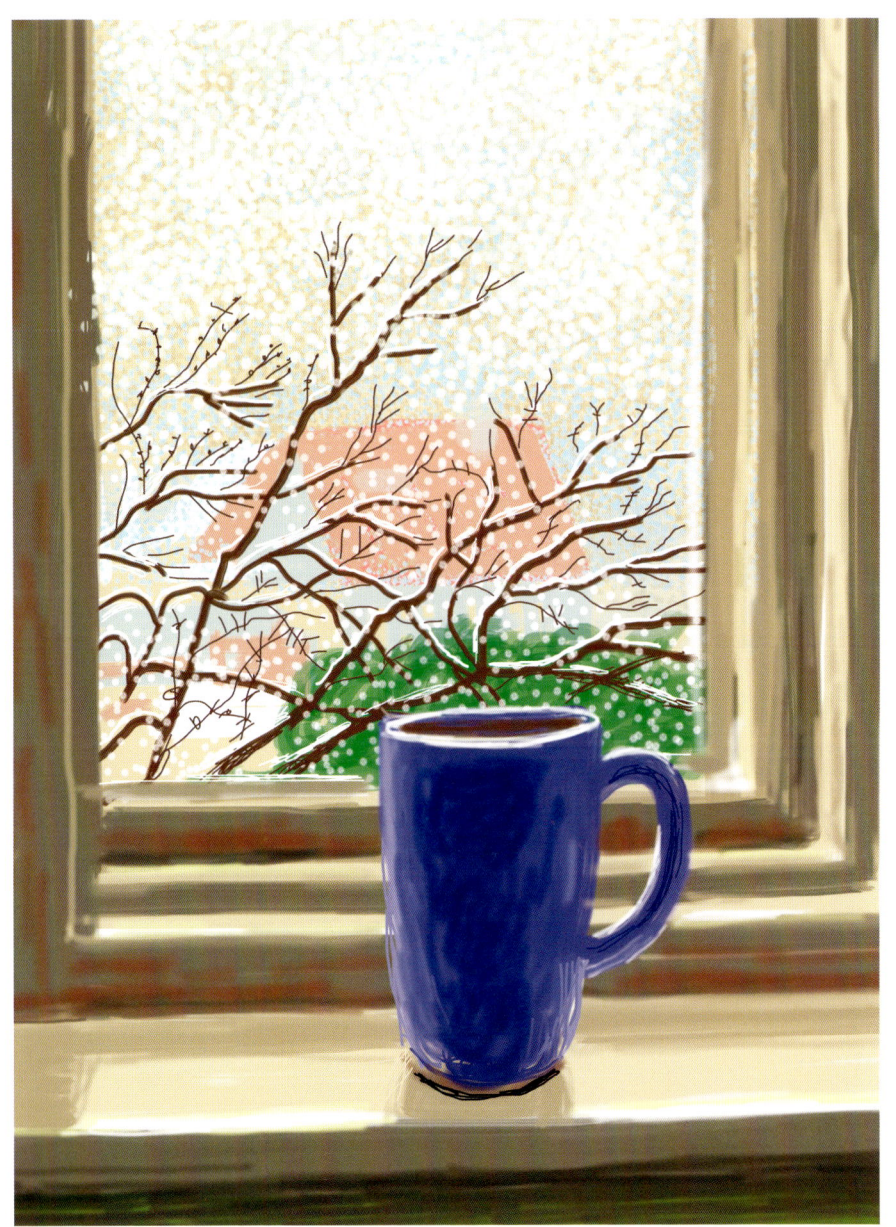

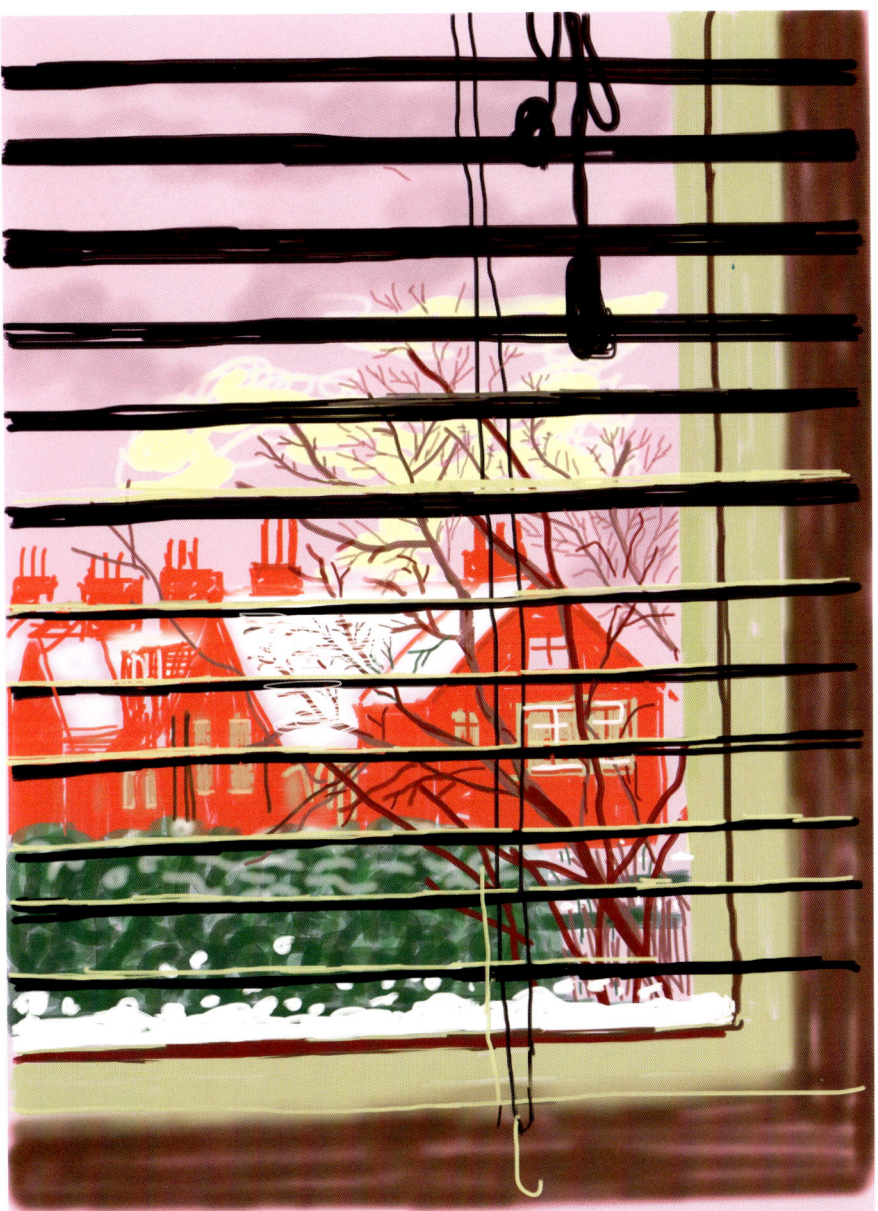

123

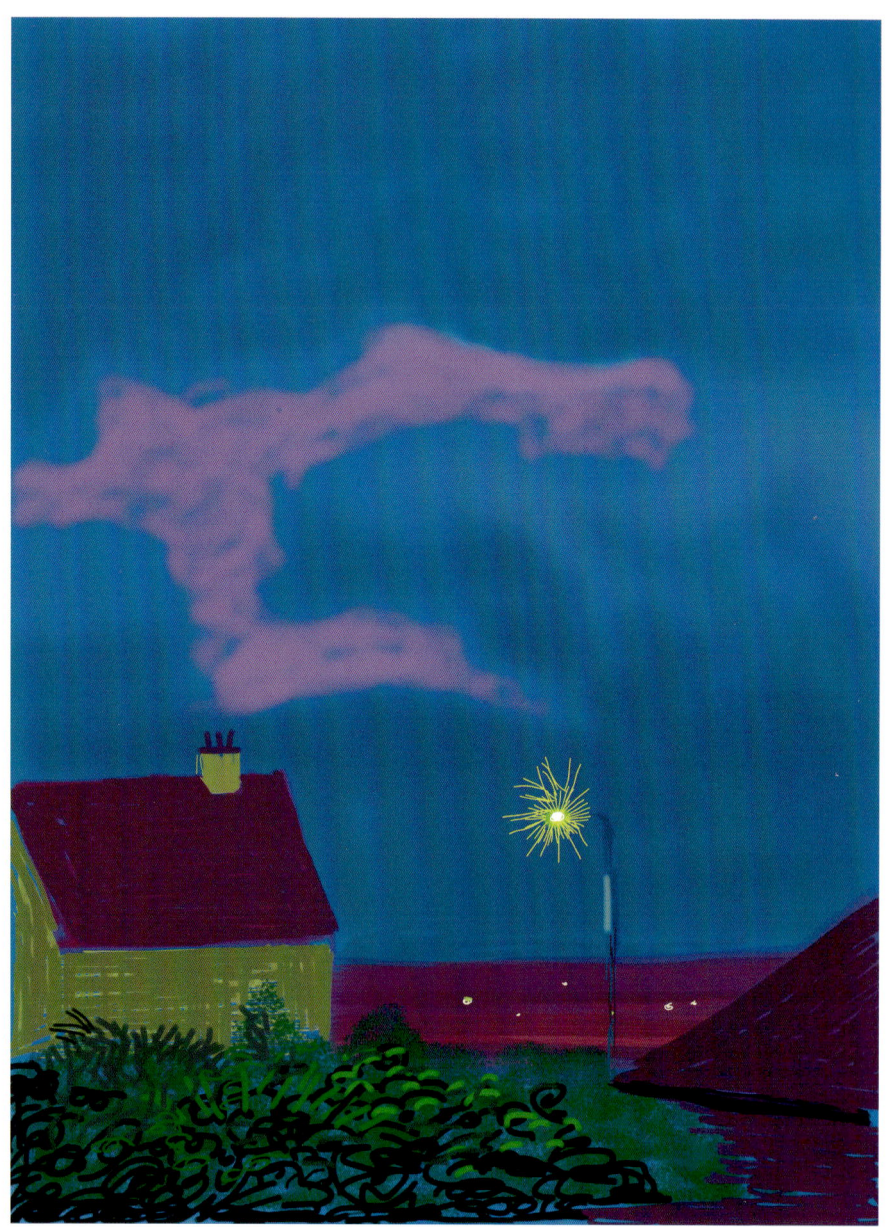

124

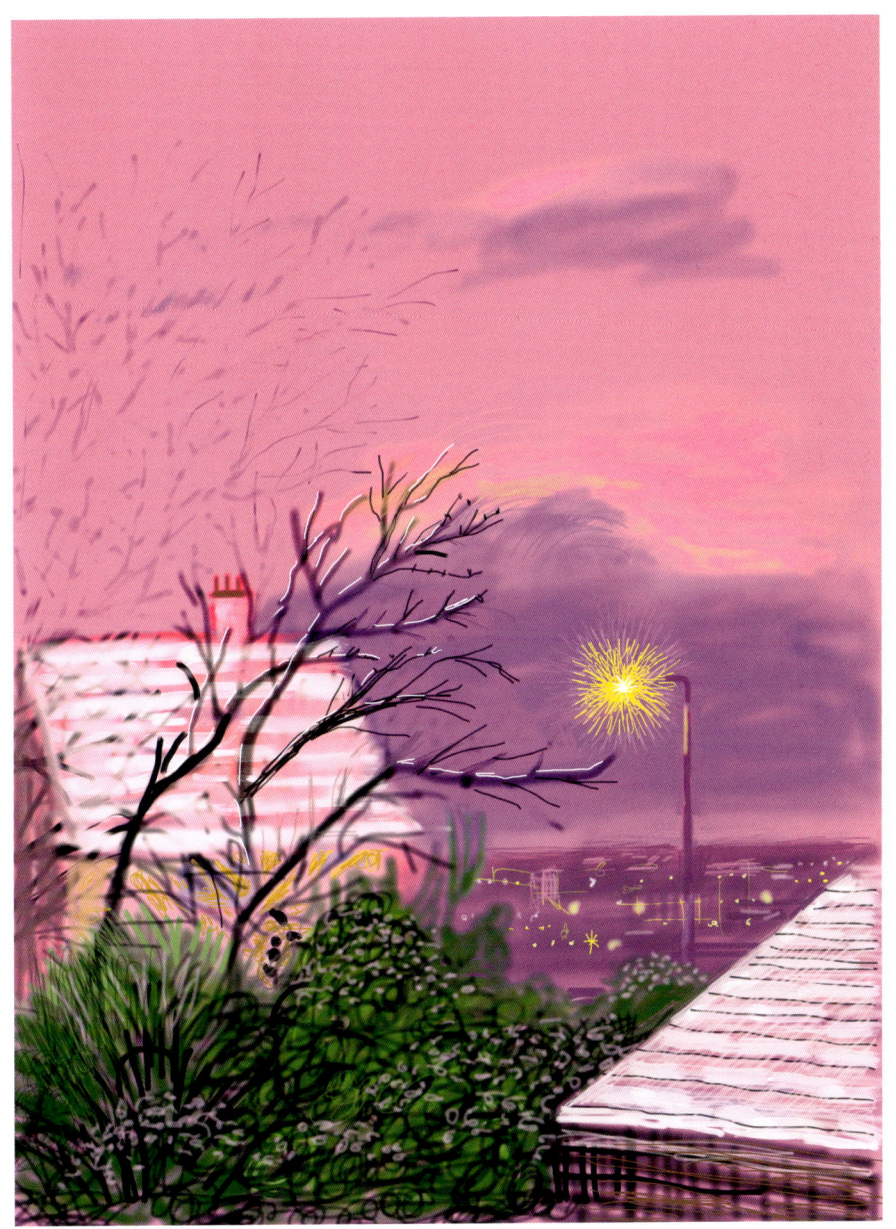

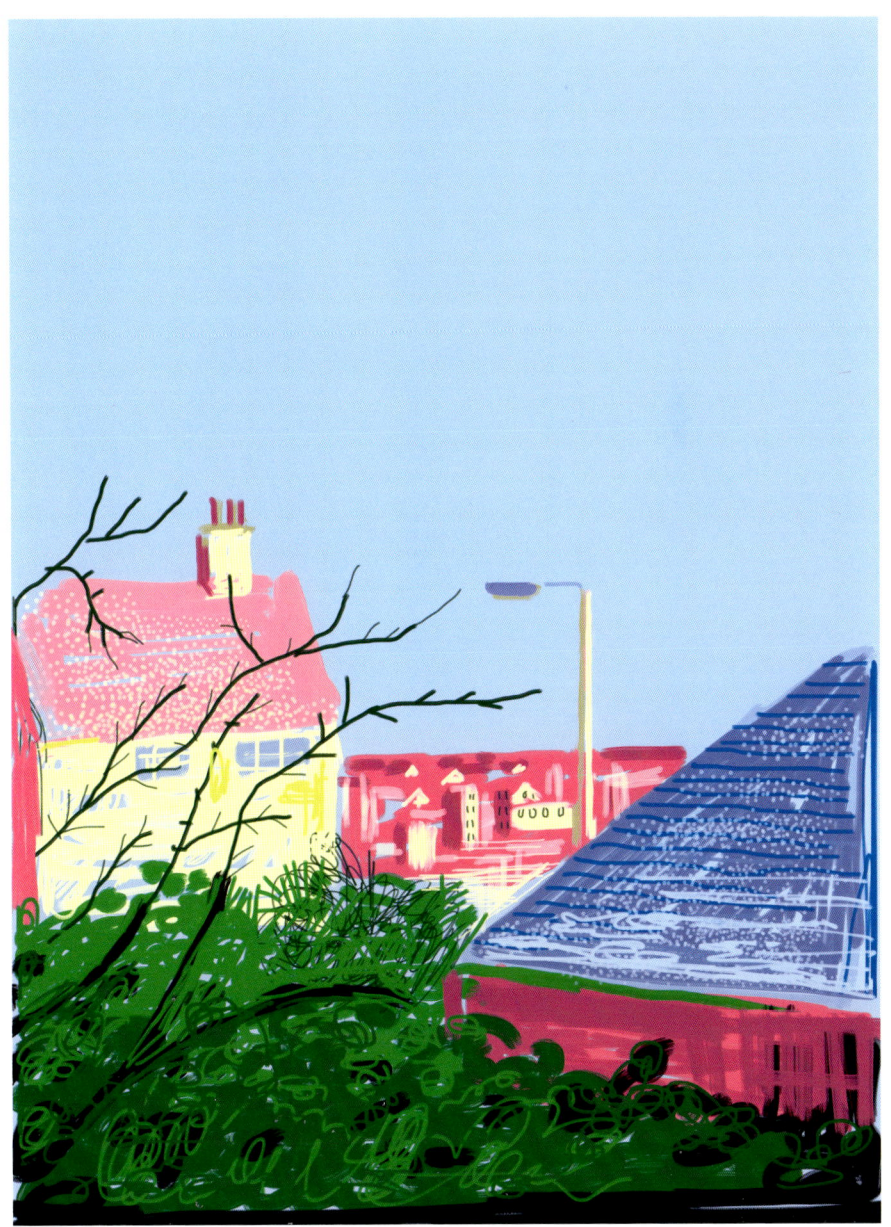

127

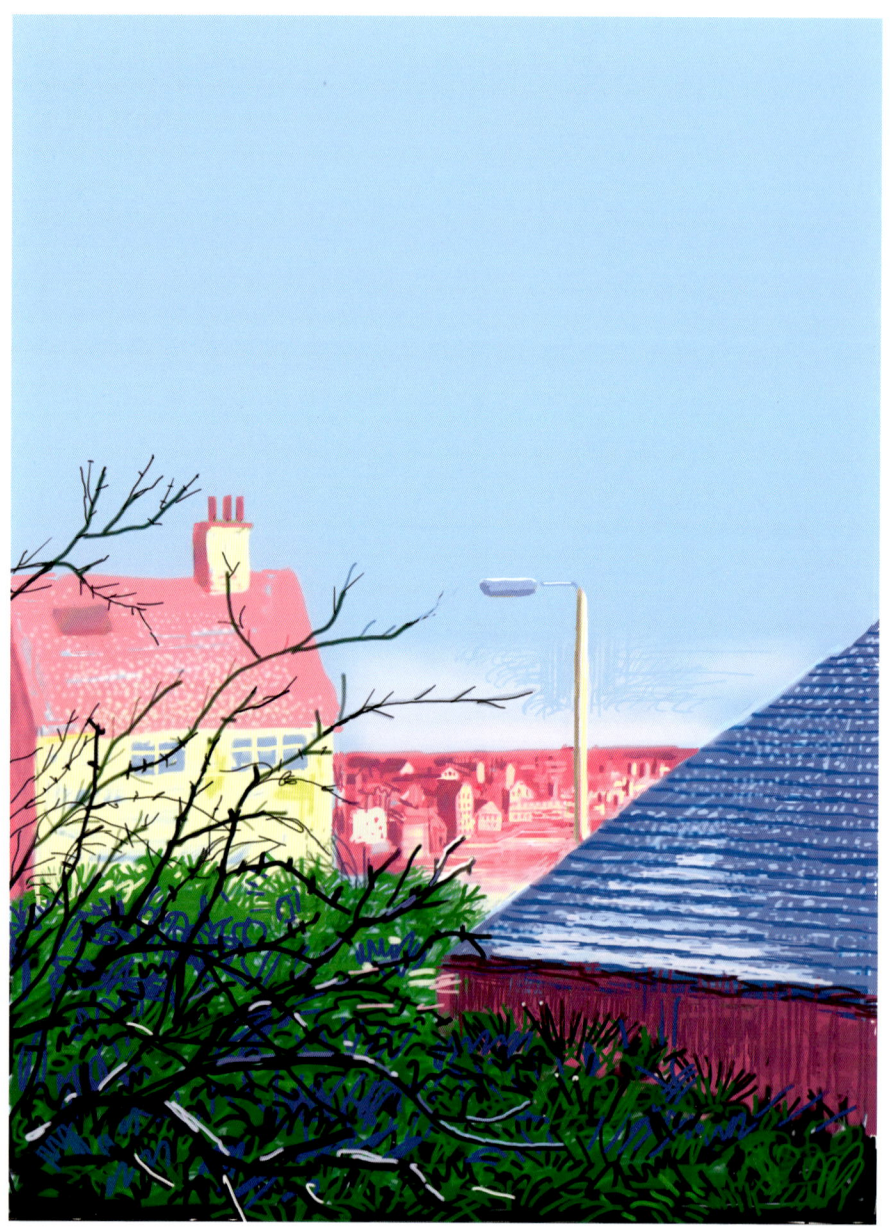

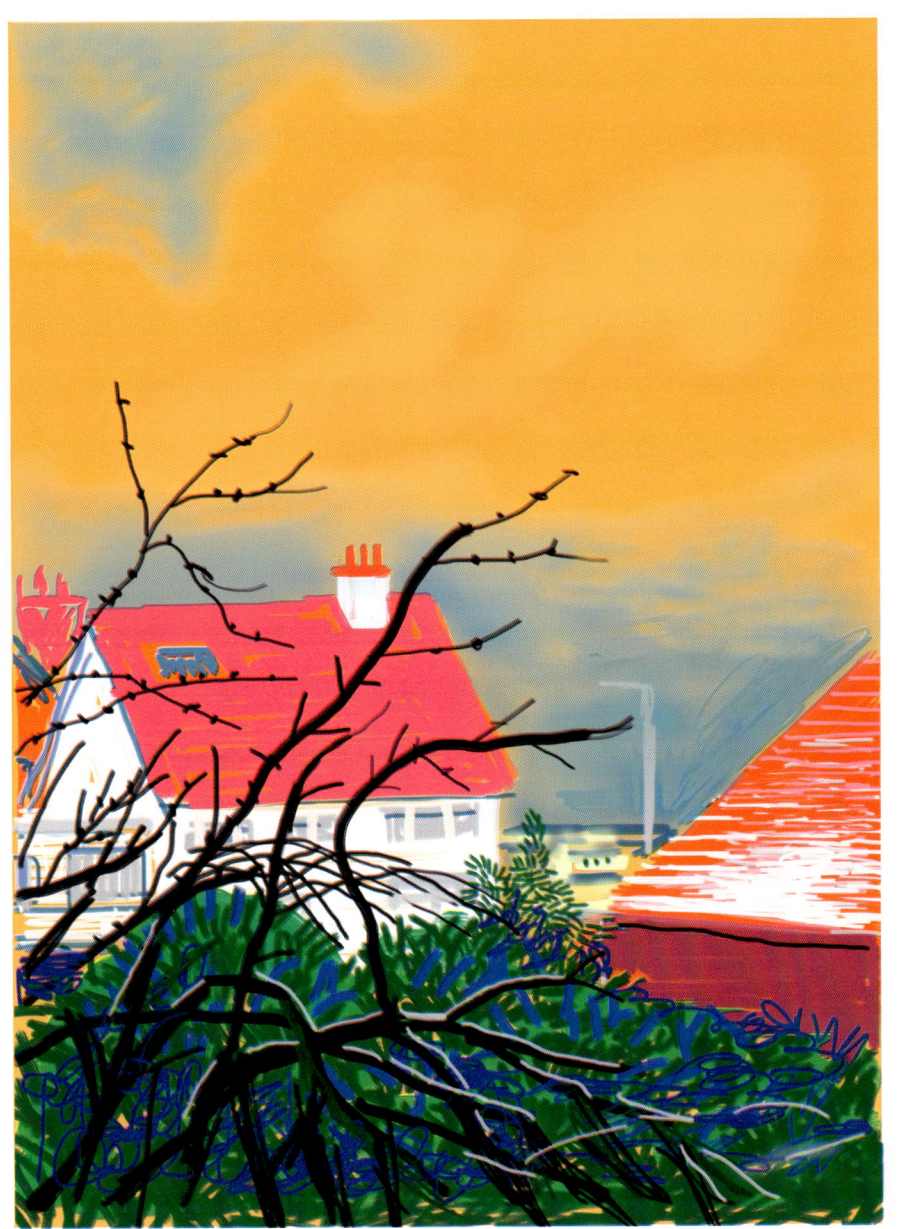

'No. 610', 23rd December 2010, iPad drawing

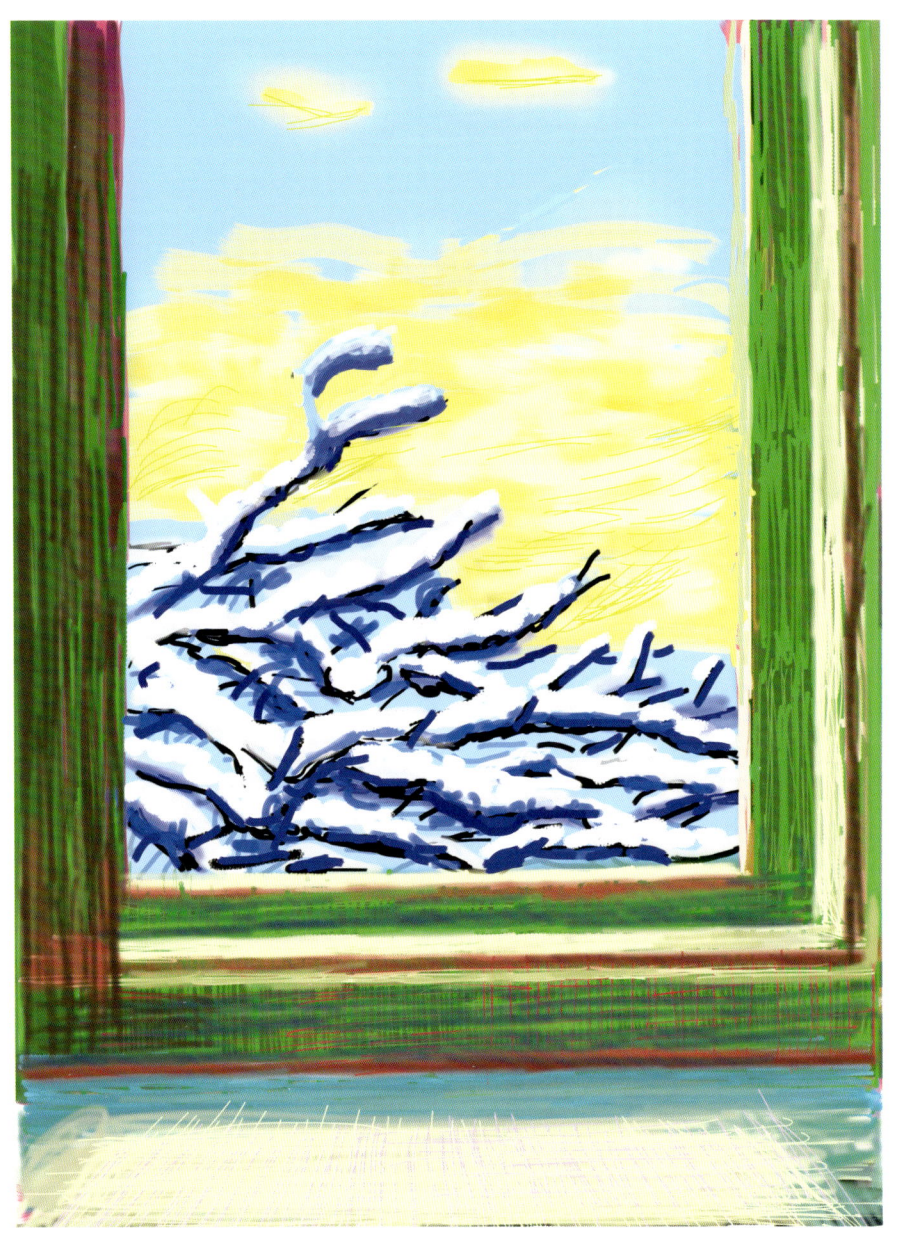

131

'No. 611', 23rd December 2010, iPad drawing

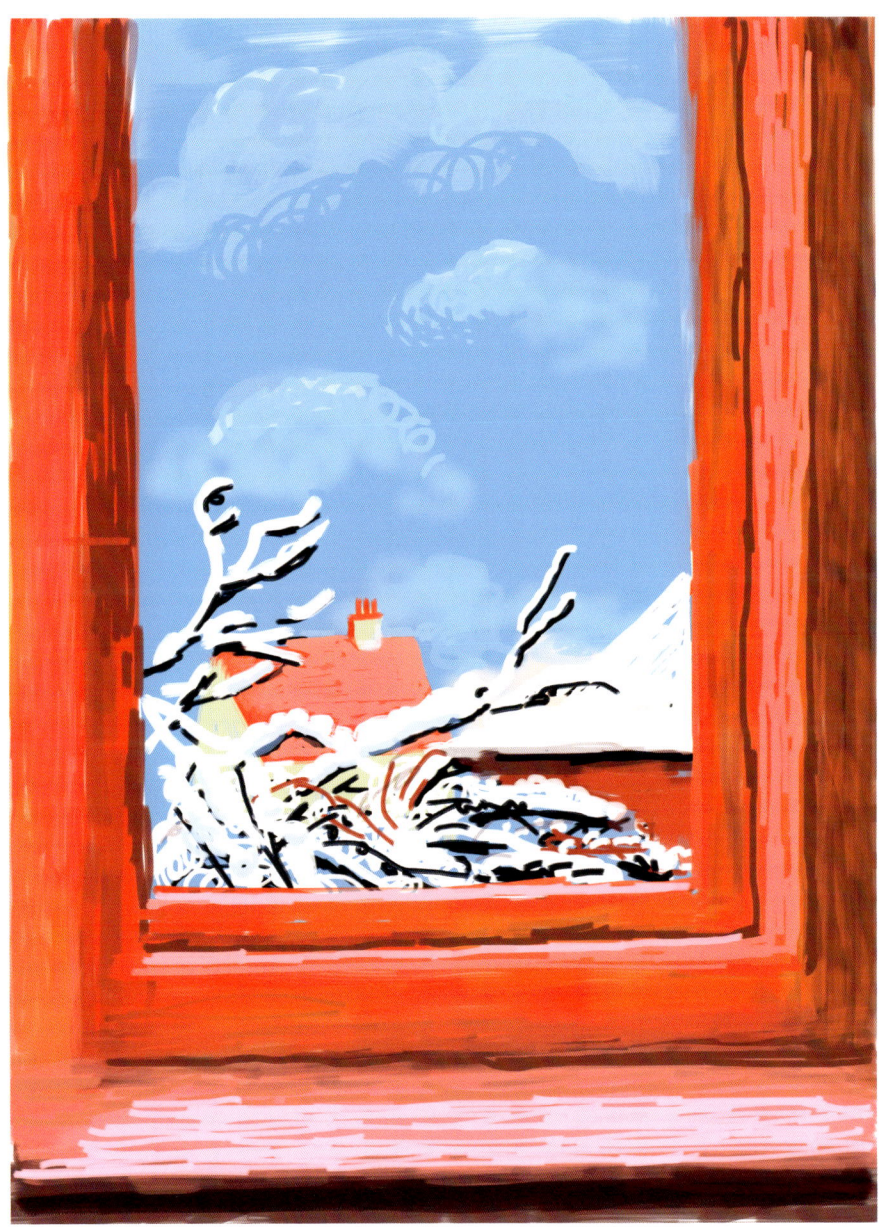

133

'No. 613', 25th December 2010, iPad drawing
Page 136: 'No. 617', 29th December 2010, iPad drawing;
134 Page 137: 'No. 620', 31st December 2010, iPad drawing

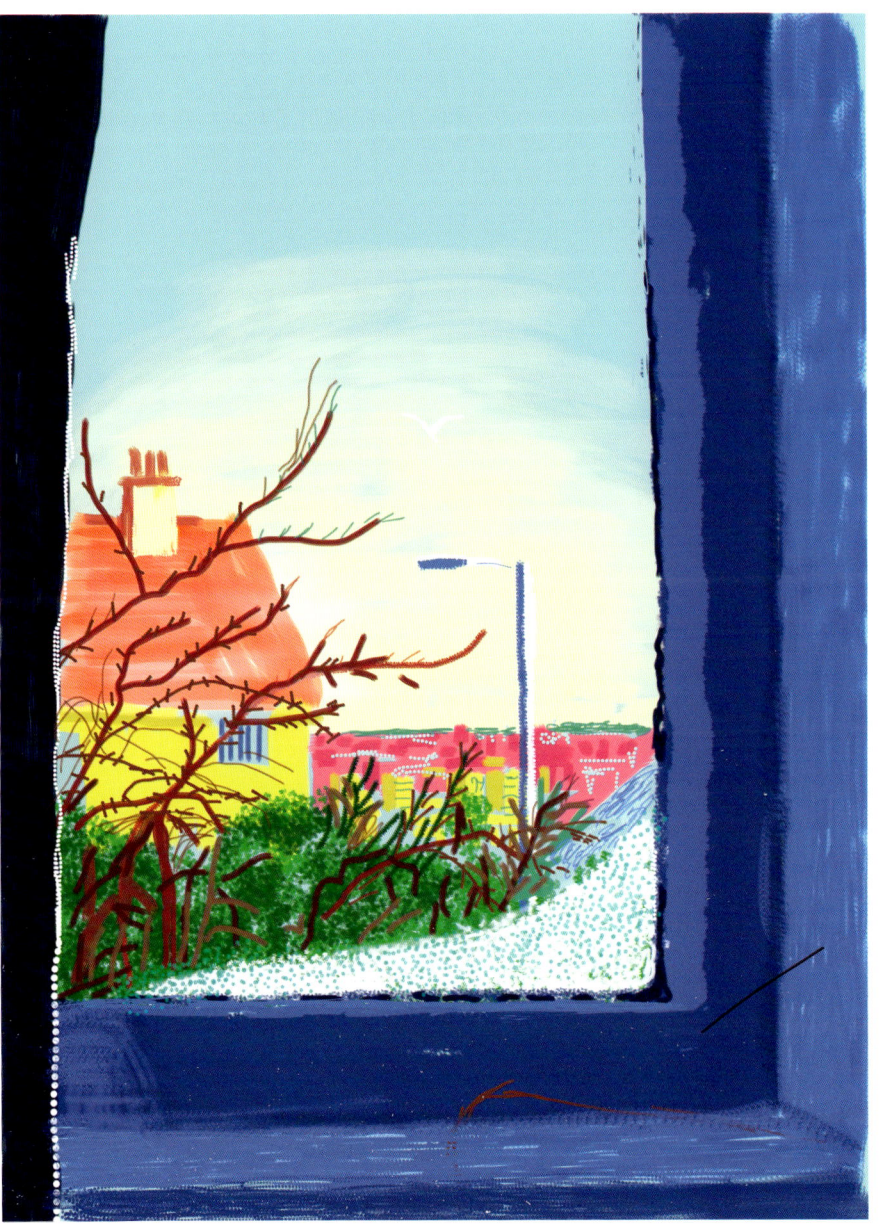

135

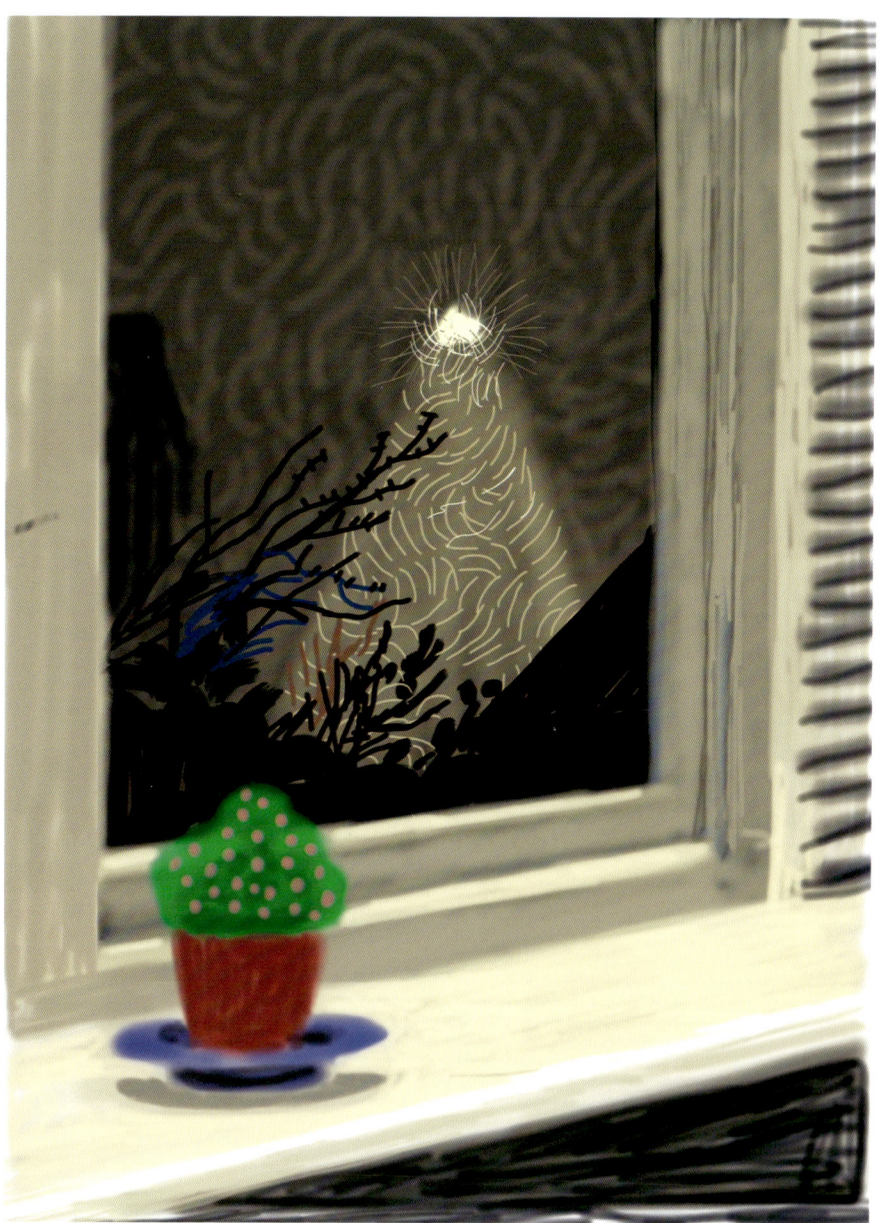

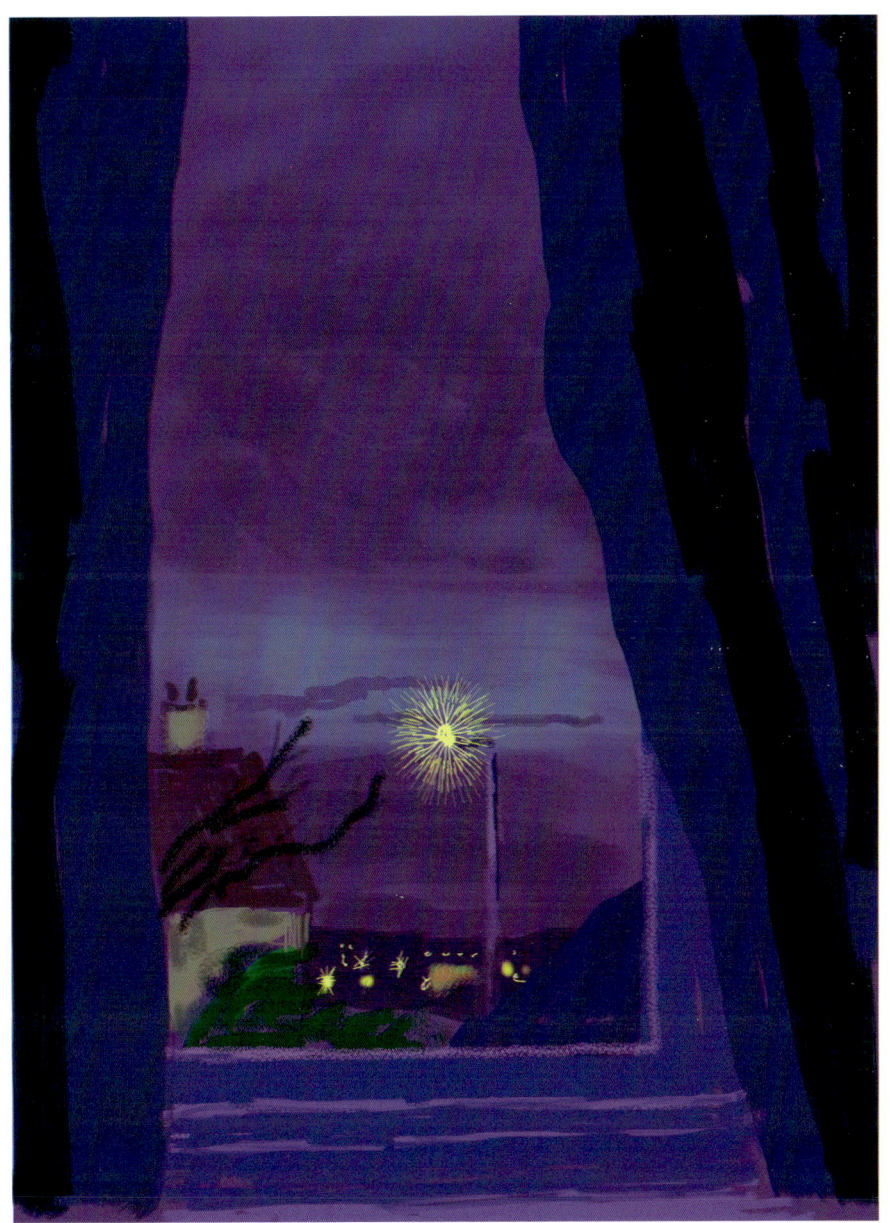

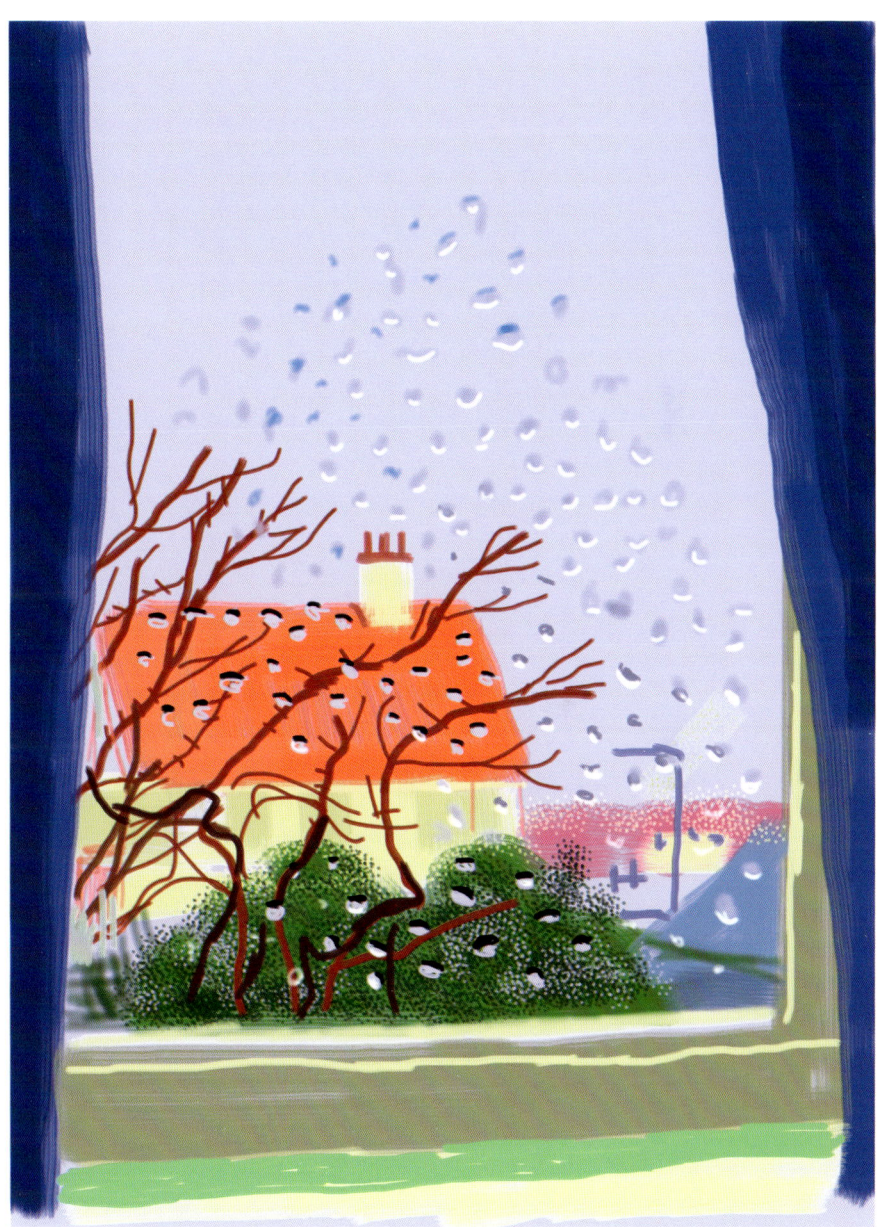

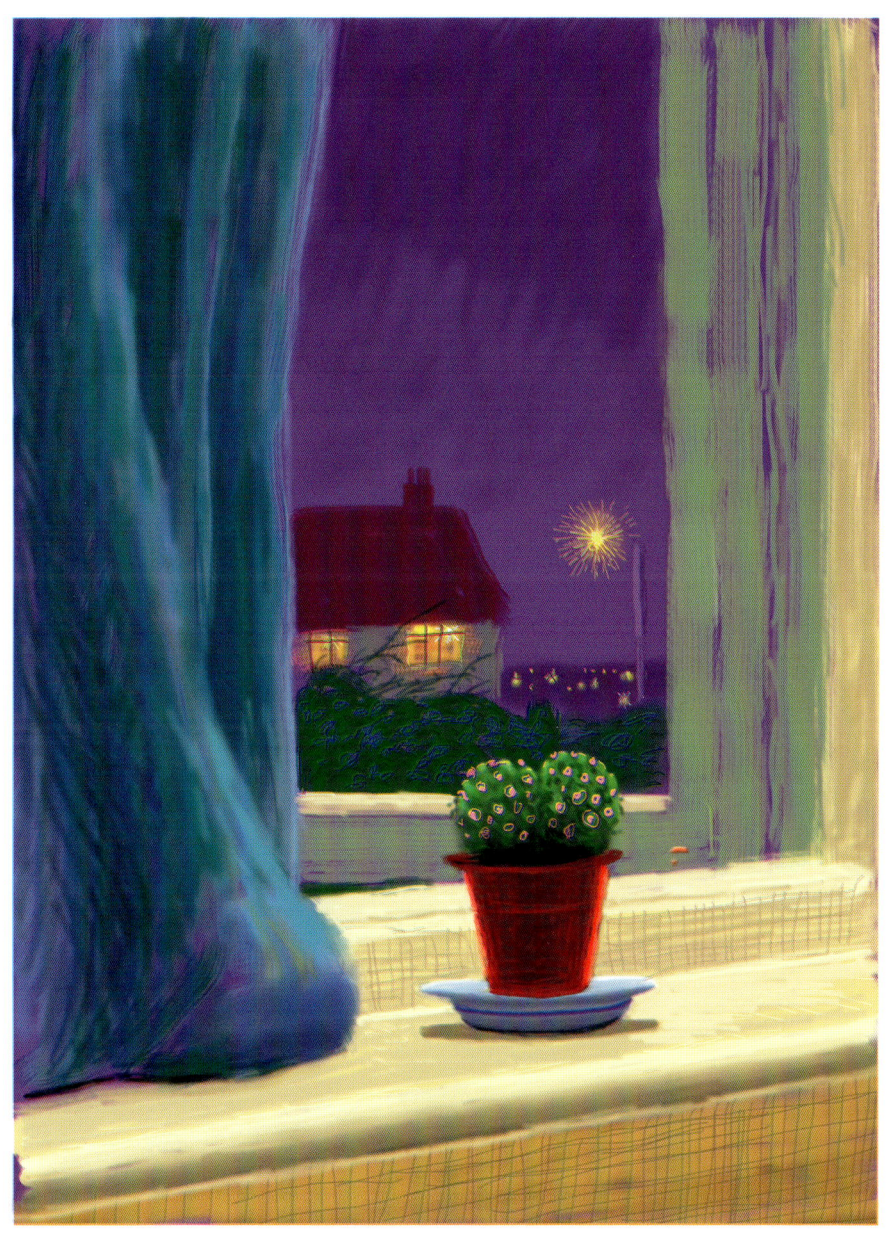

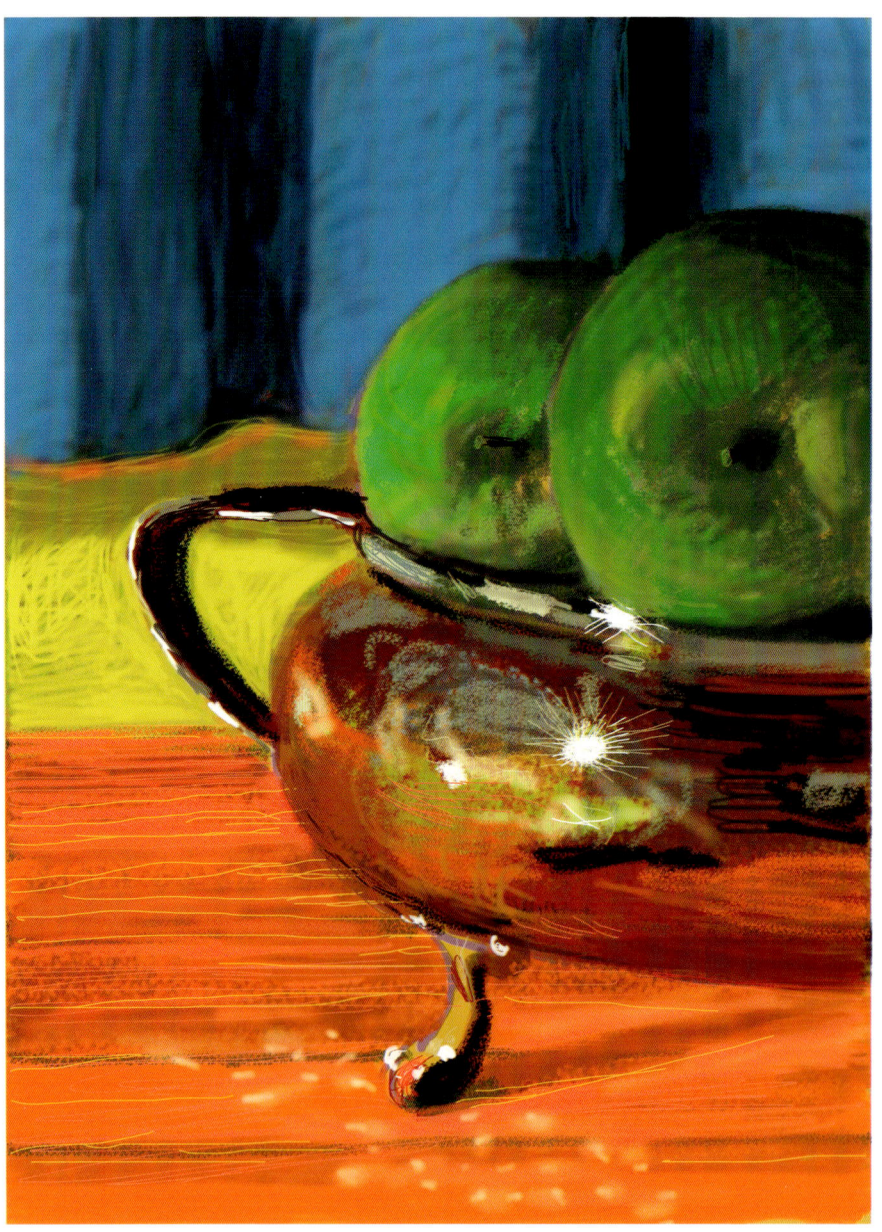

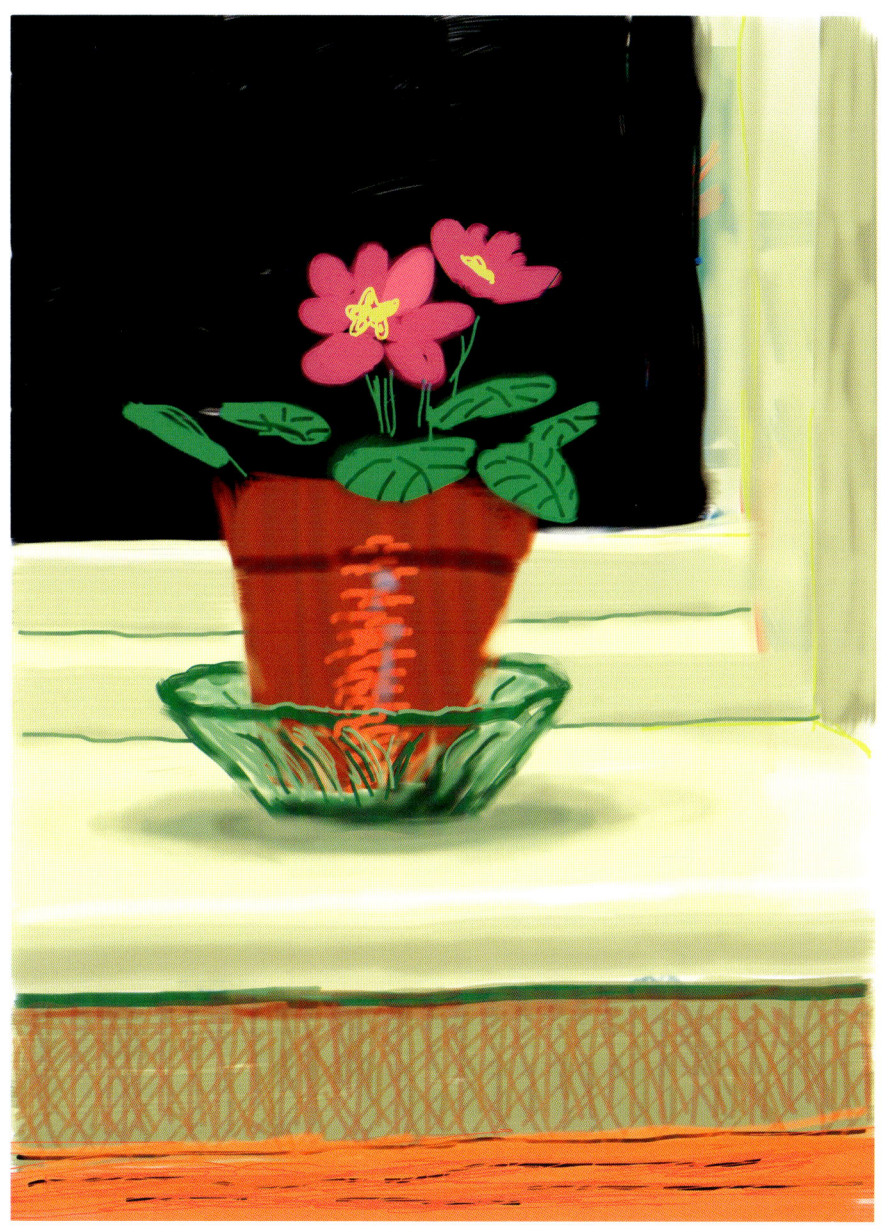

143

'No. 712', 7th March 2011, iPad drawing
Page 146: 'No. 733', 20th March 2011, iPad drawing;
144   Page 147: 'No. 739', 23rd March 2011, iPad drawing

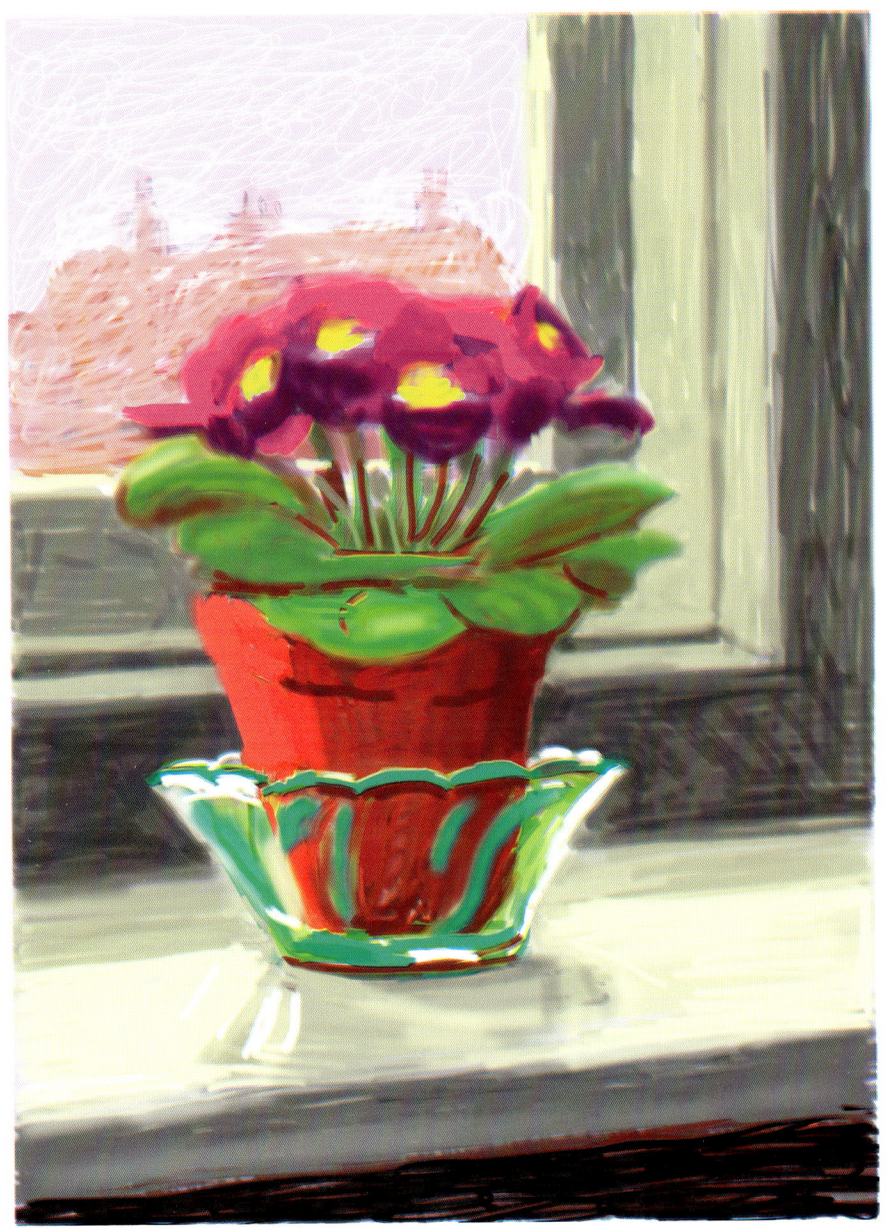

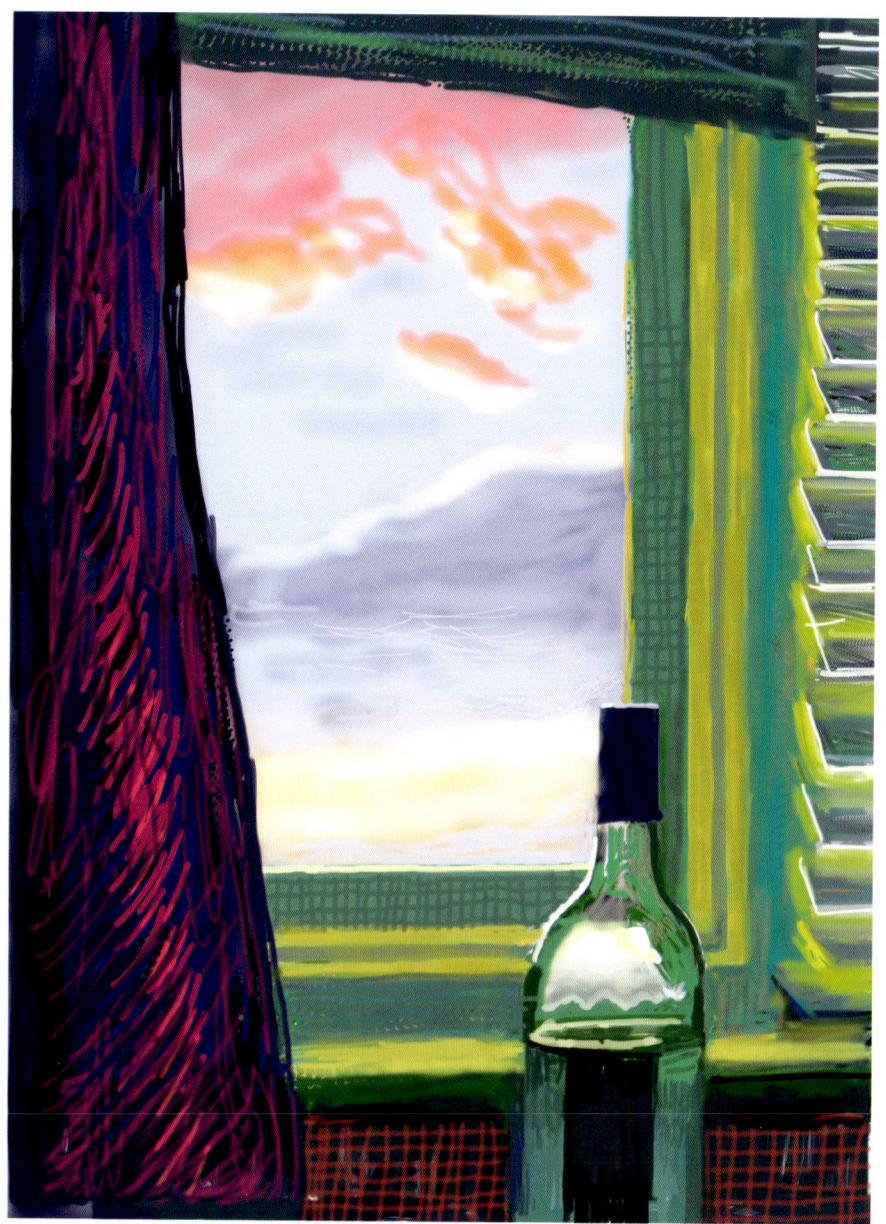

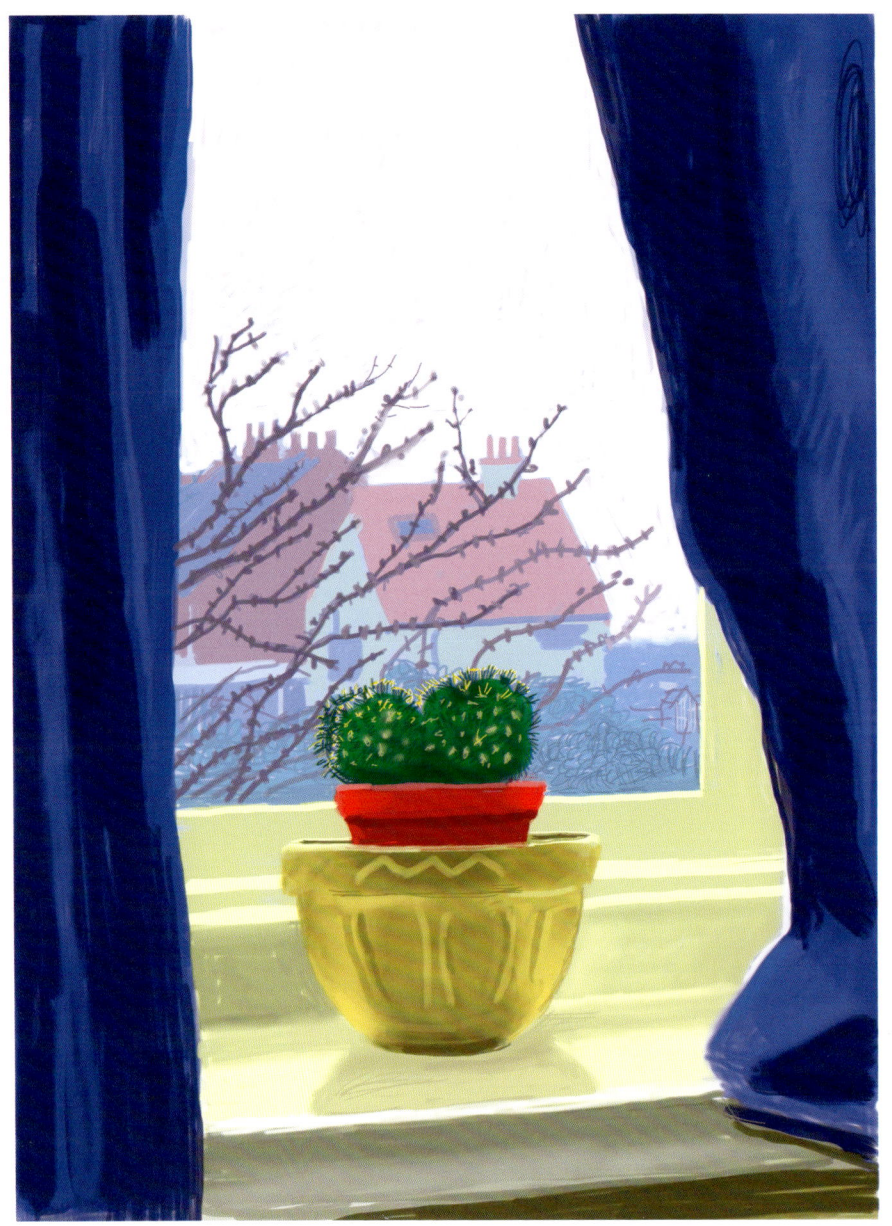

147

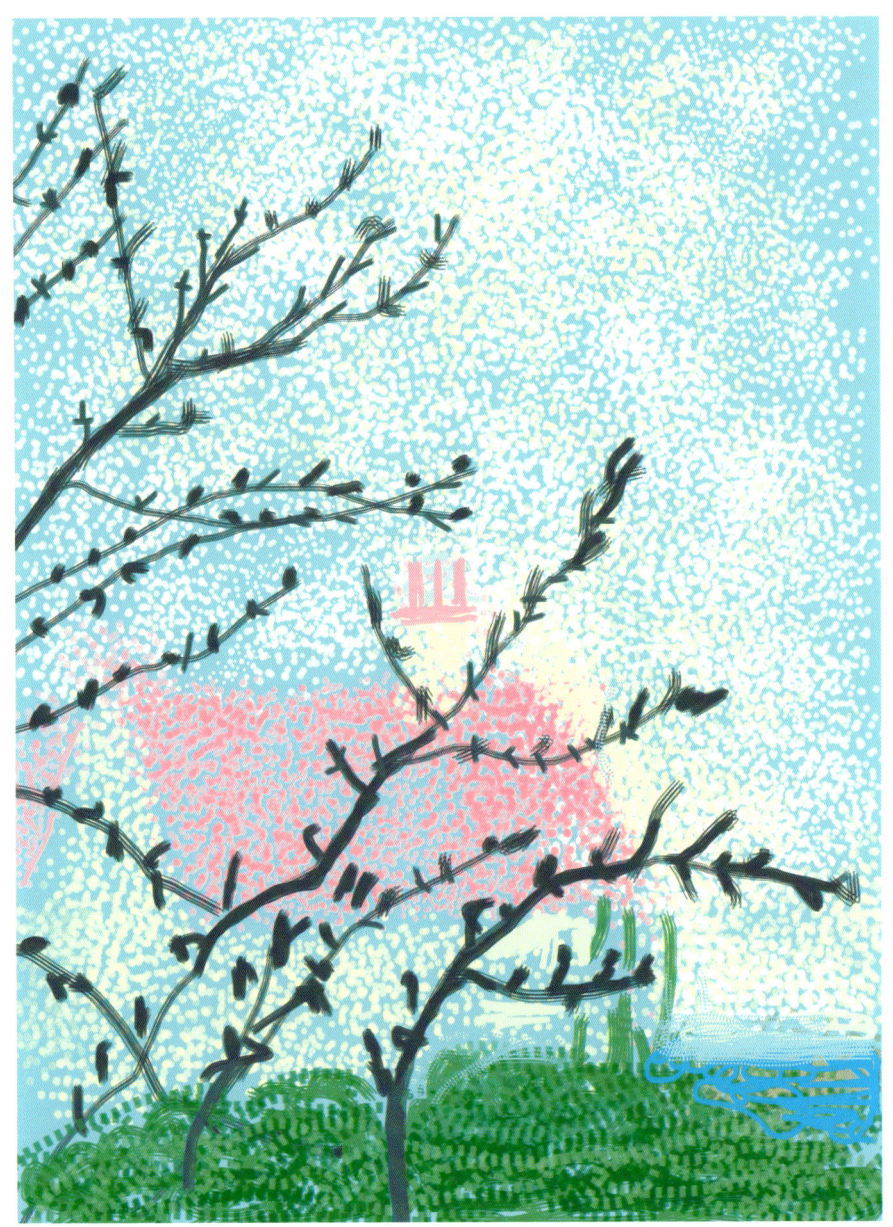

'No. 744', 31st March 2011, iPad drawing
Page 152: 'No. 749', 5th April 2011, iPad drawing;
Page 153: 'No. 764', 13th April 2011, iPad drawing

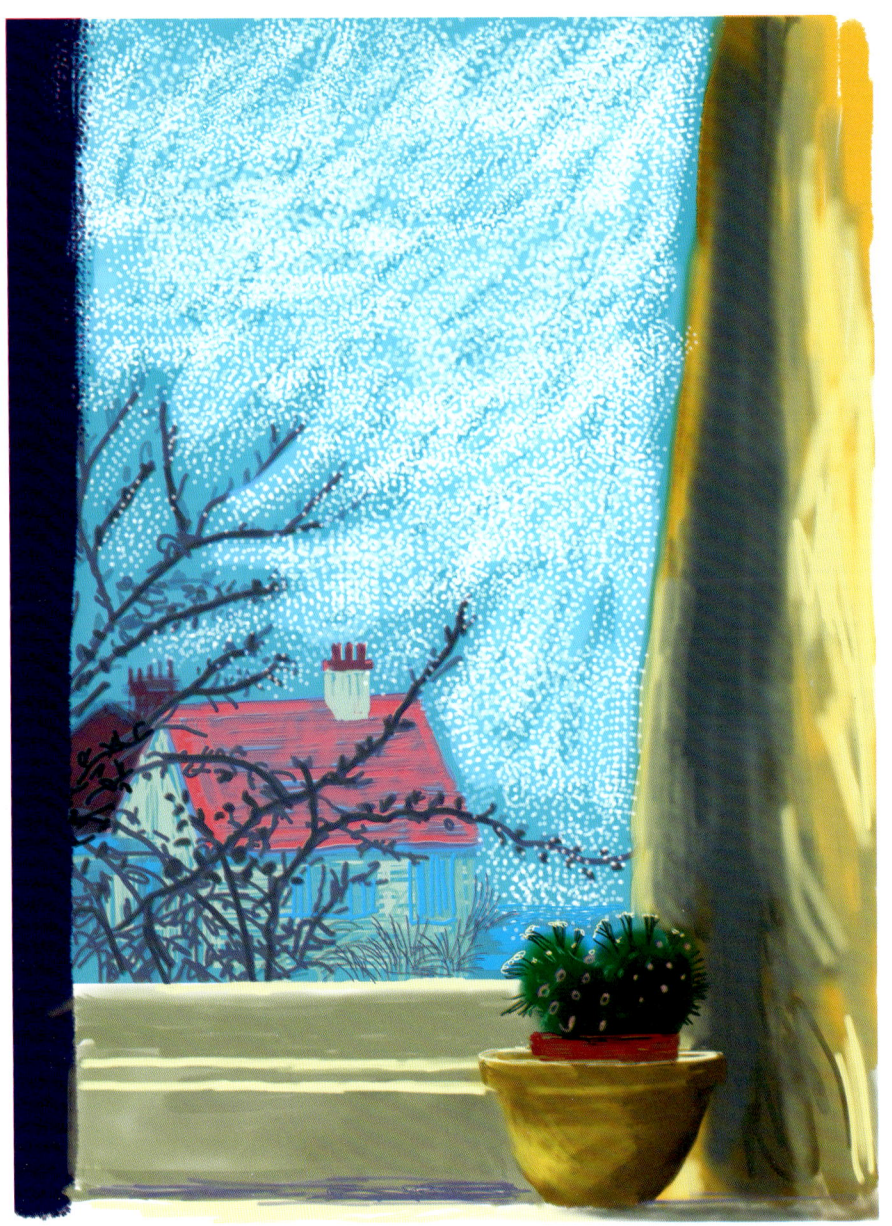

151

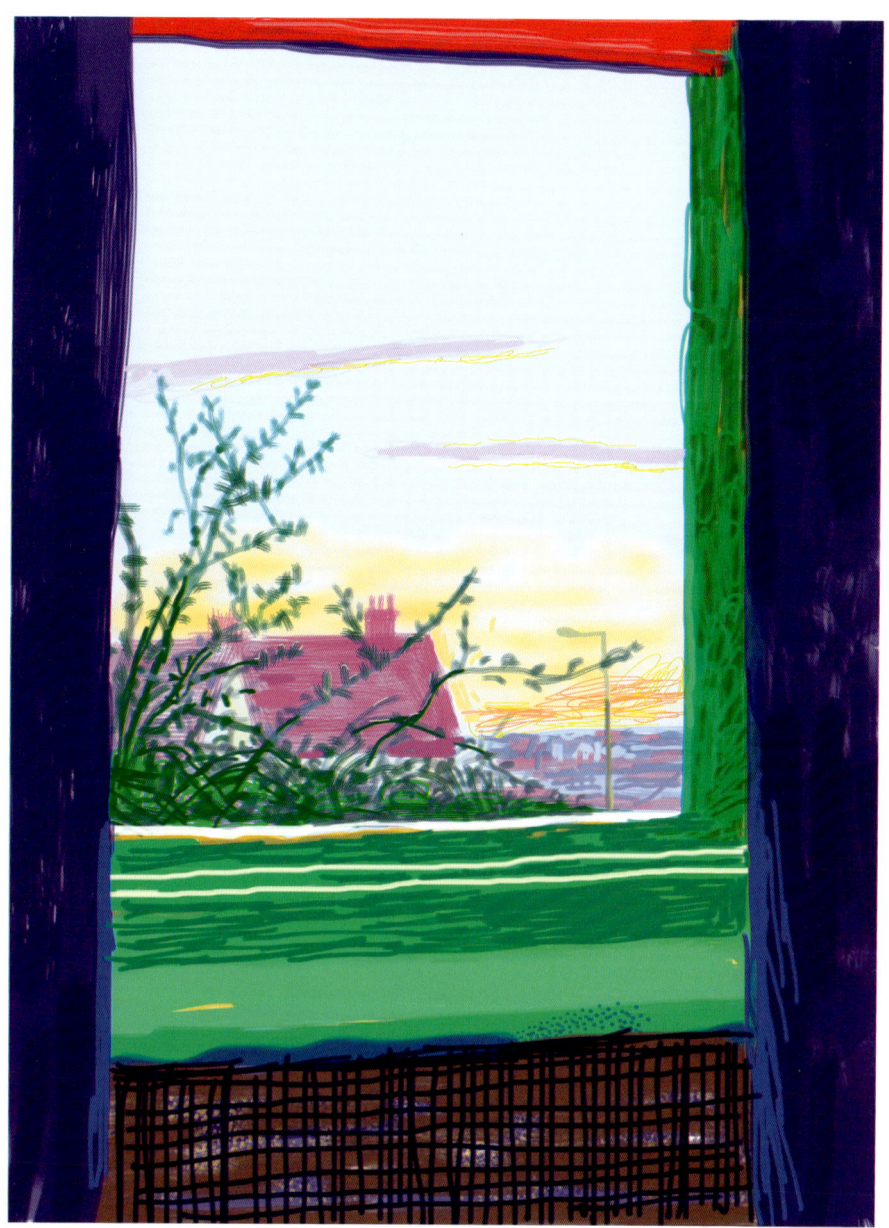

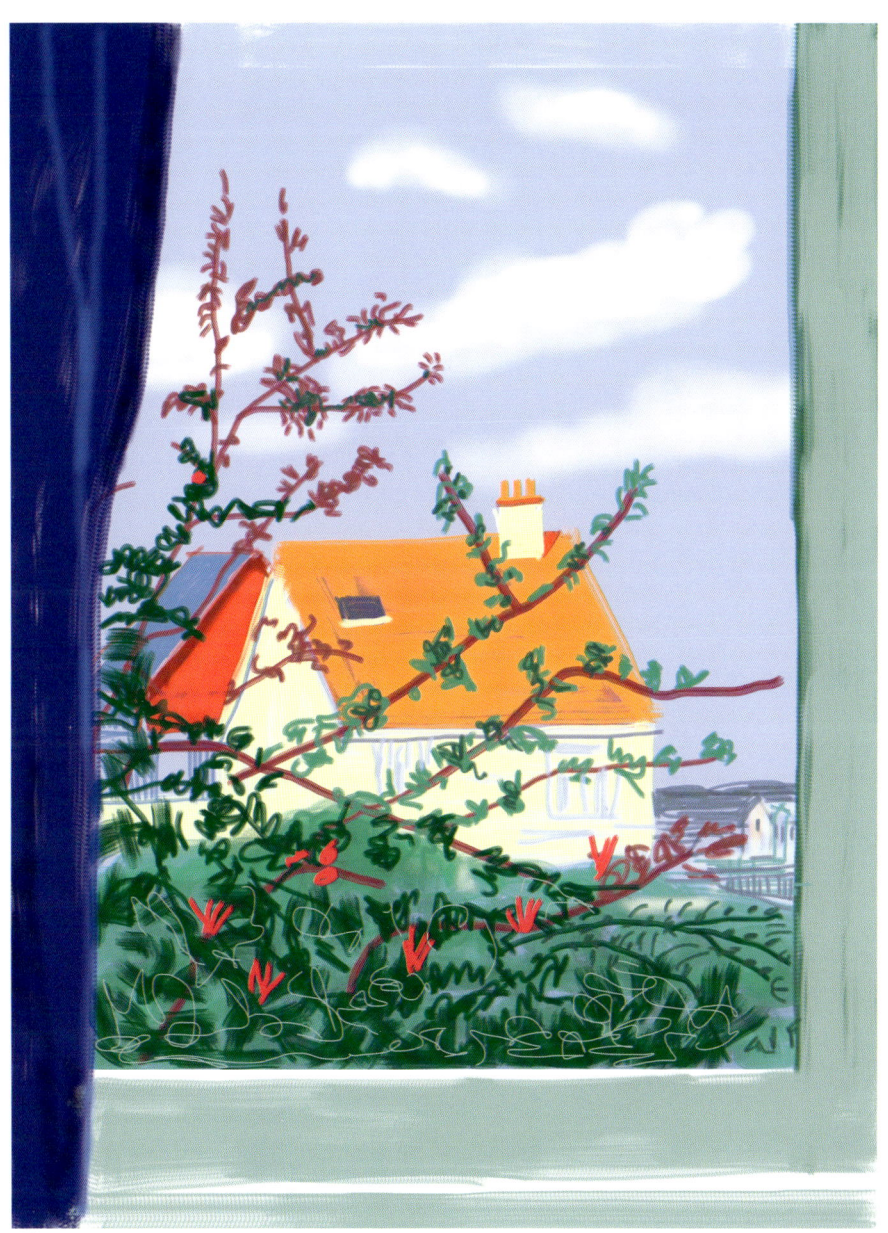

'No. 772', 16th April 2011, iPad drawing

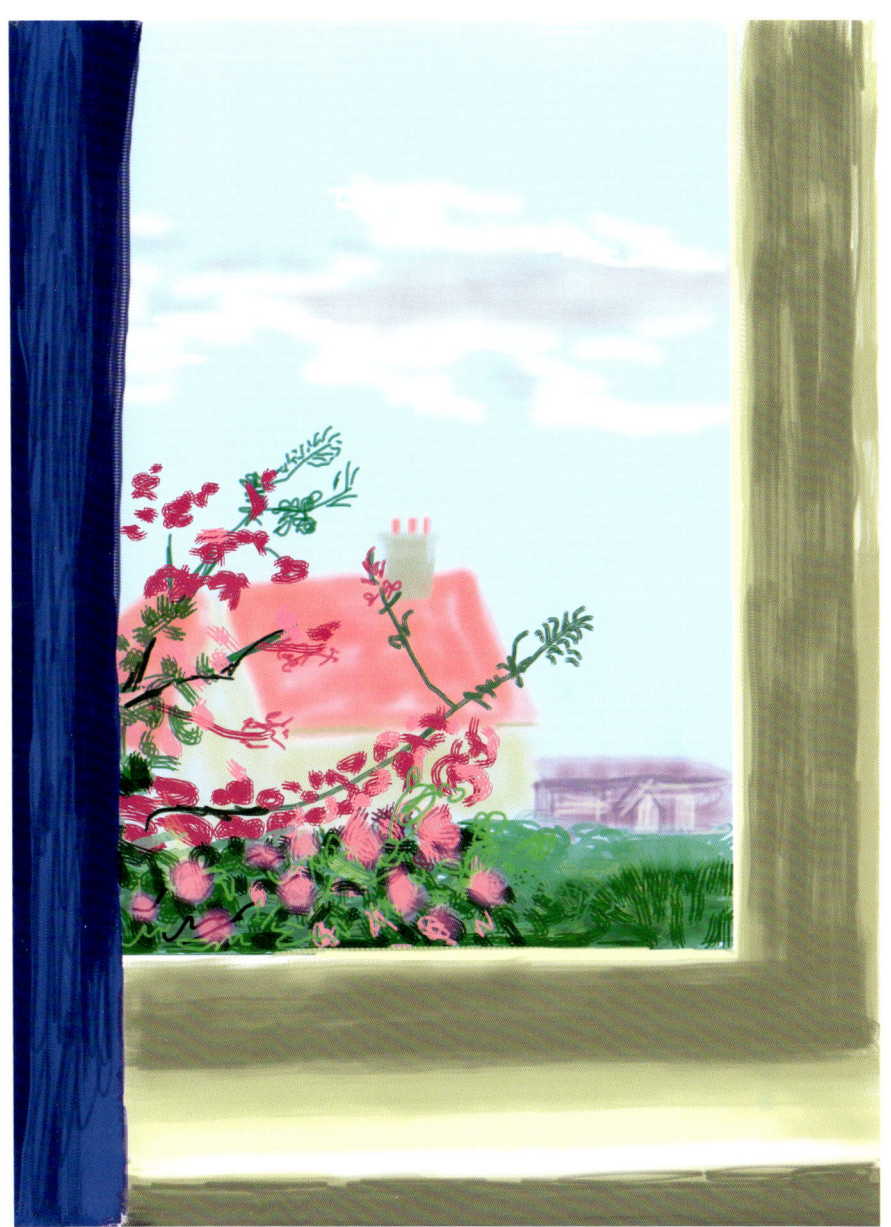

'No. 778', 17th April 2011, iPad drawing

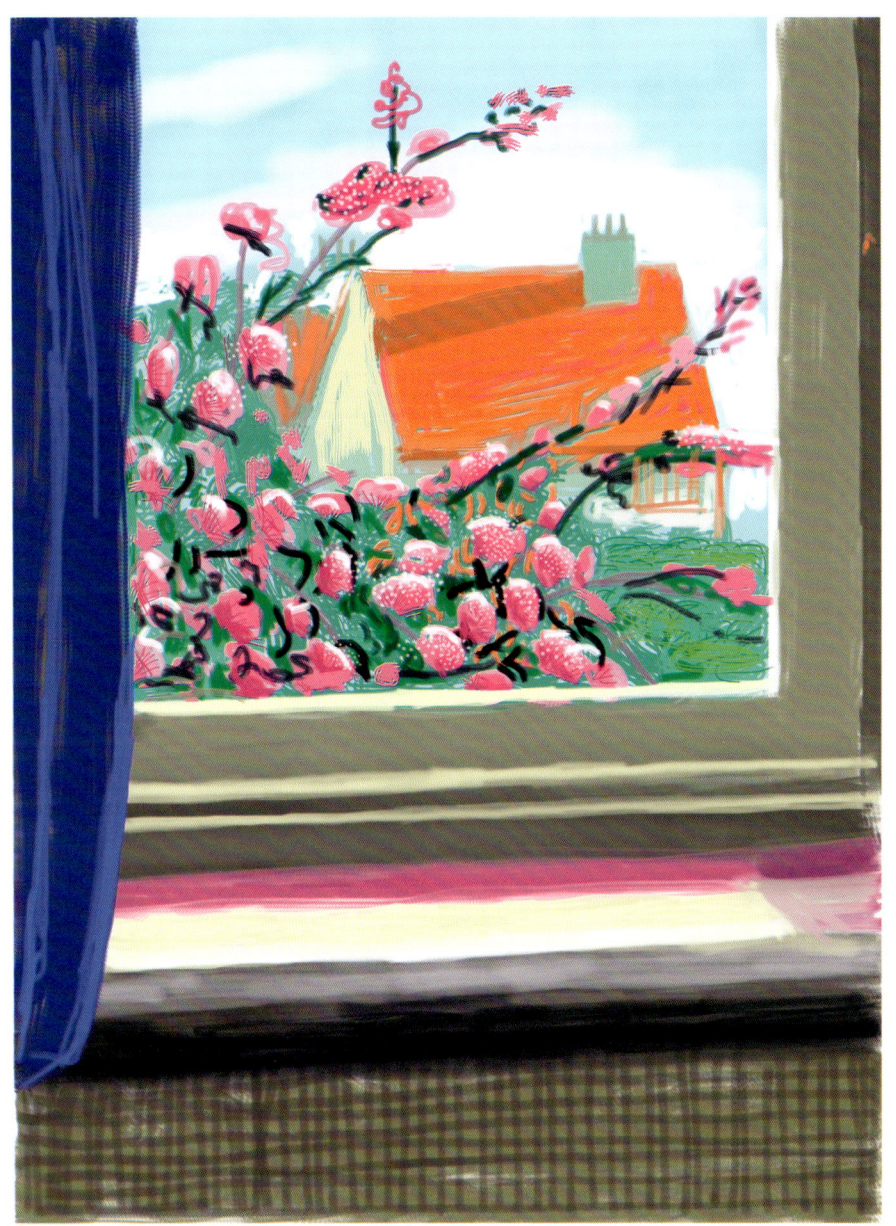

157

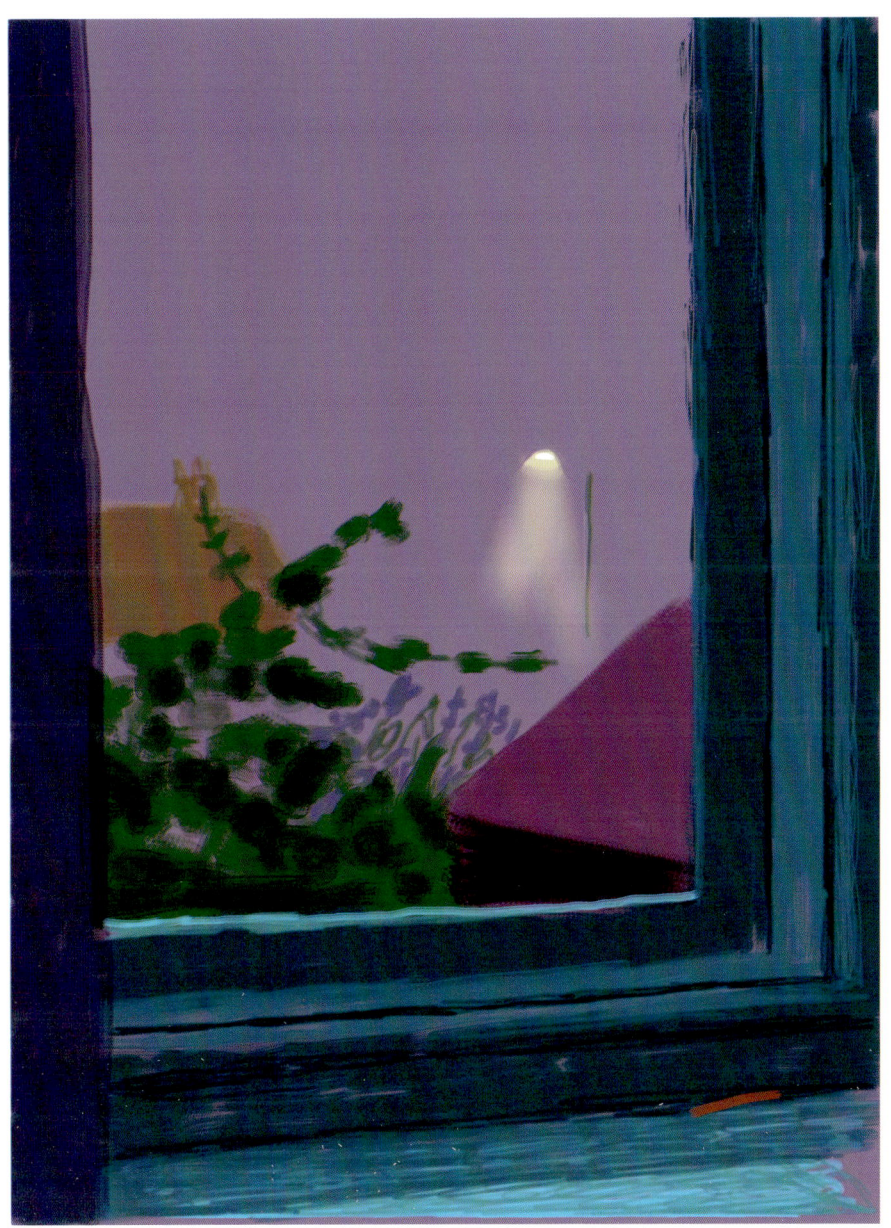

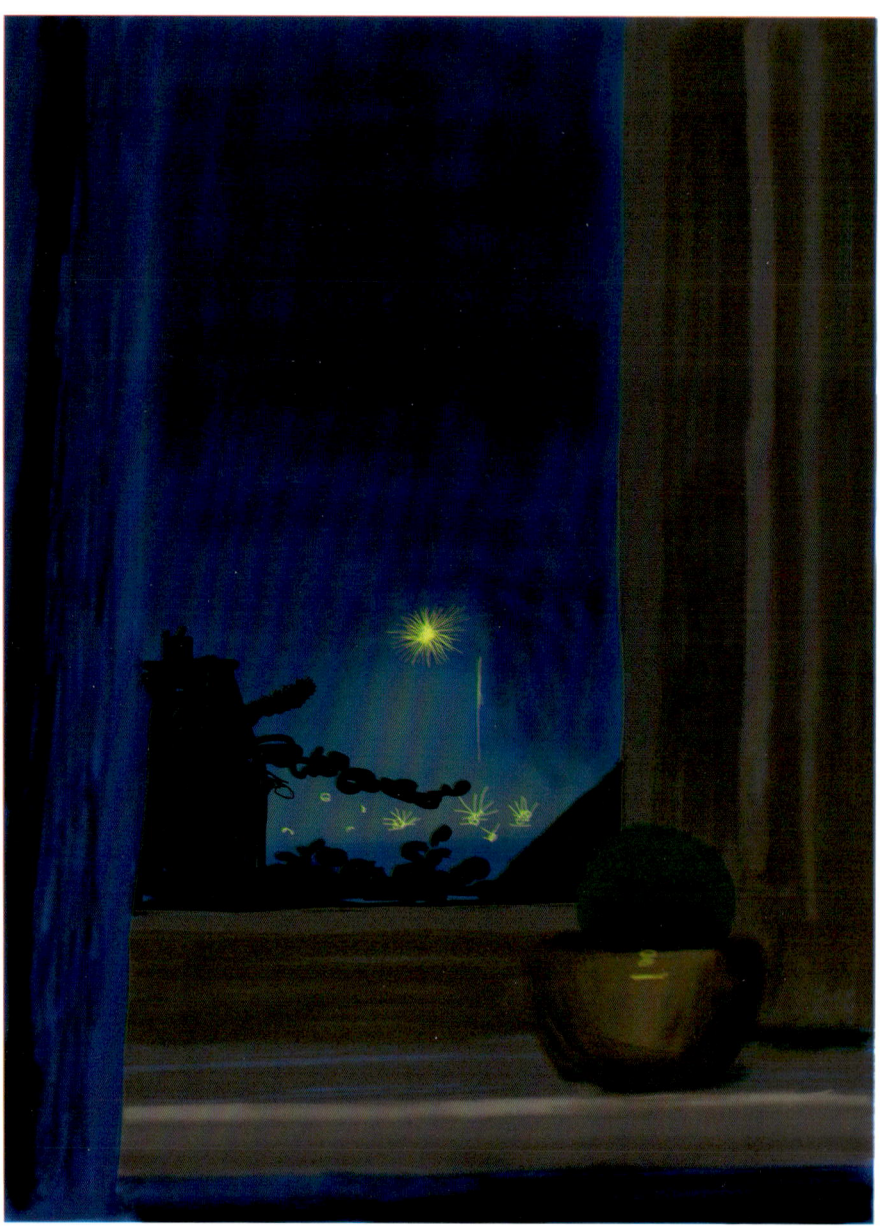

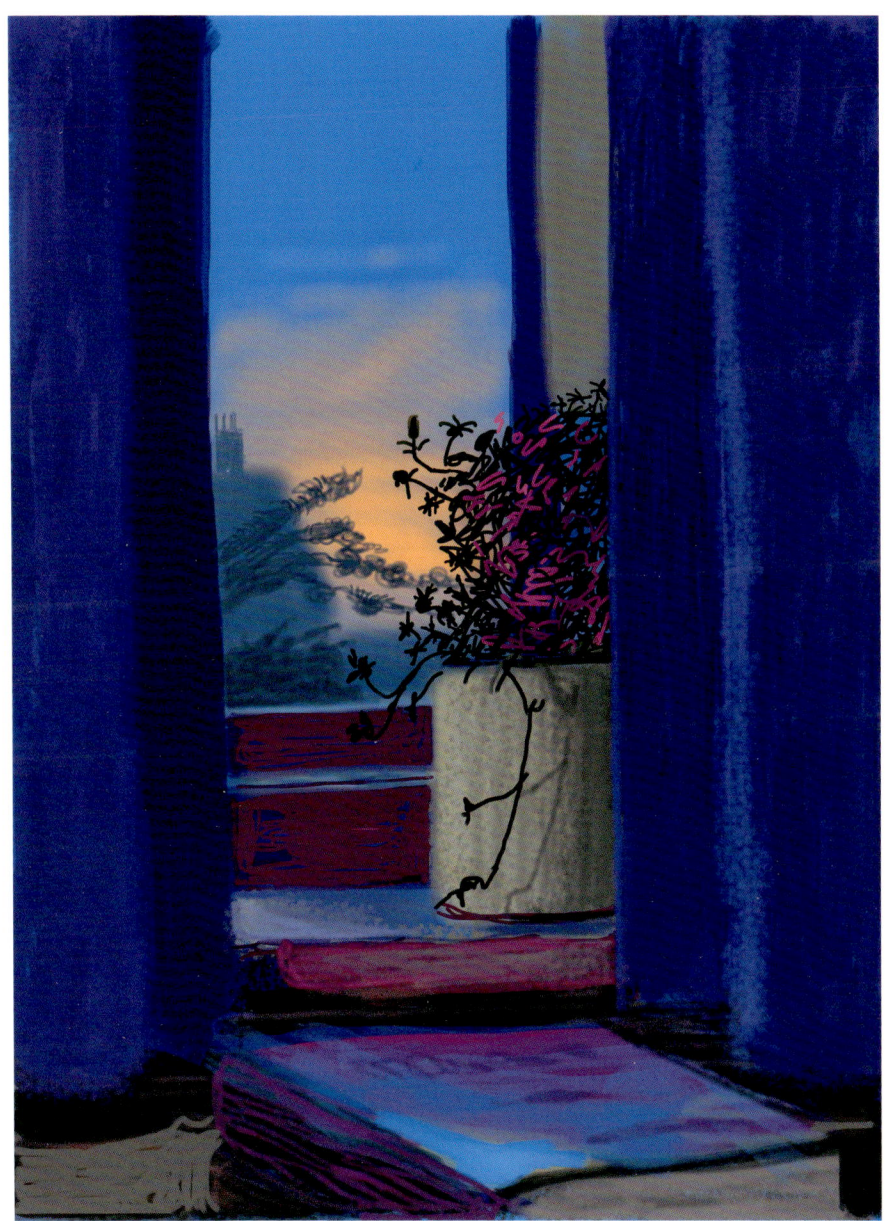

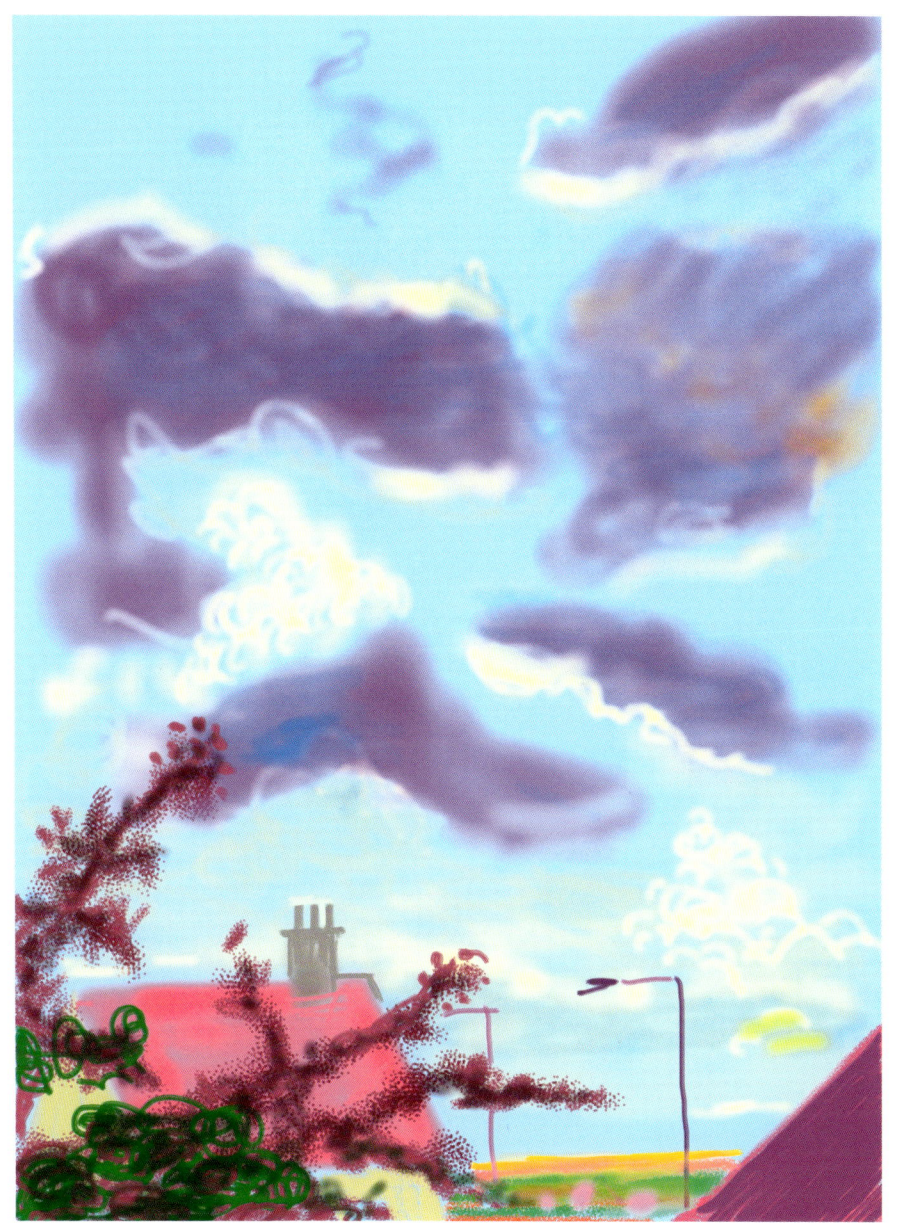

163

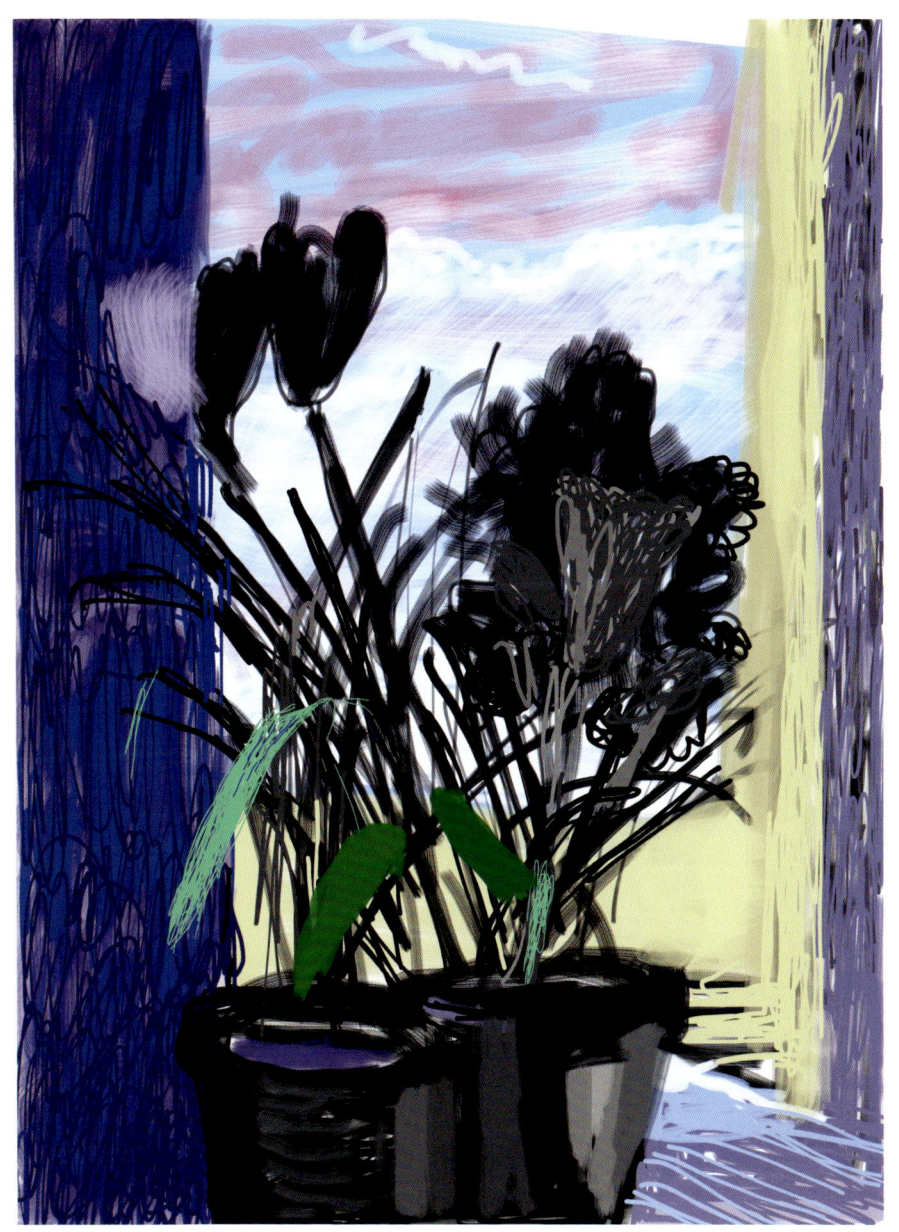

'No. 846', 7th May 2011, iPad drawing
Page 168: 'No. 869', 16th May 2011, iPad drawing;
Page 169: 'No. 883', 22nd May 2011, iPad drawing

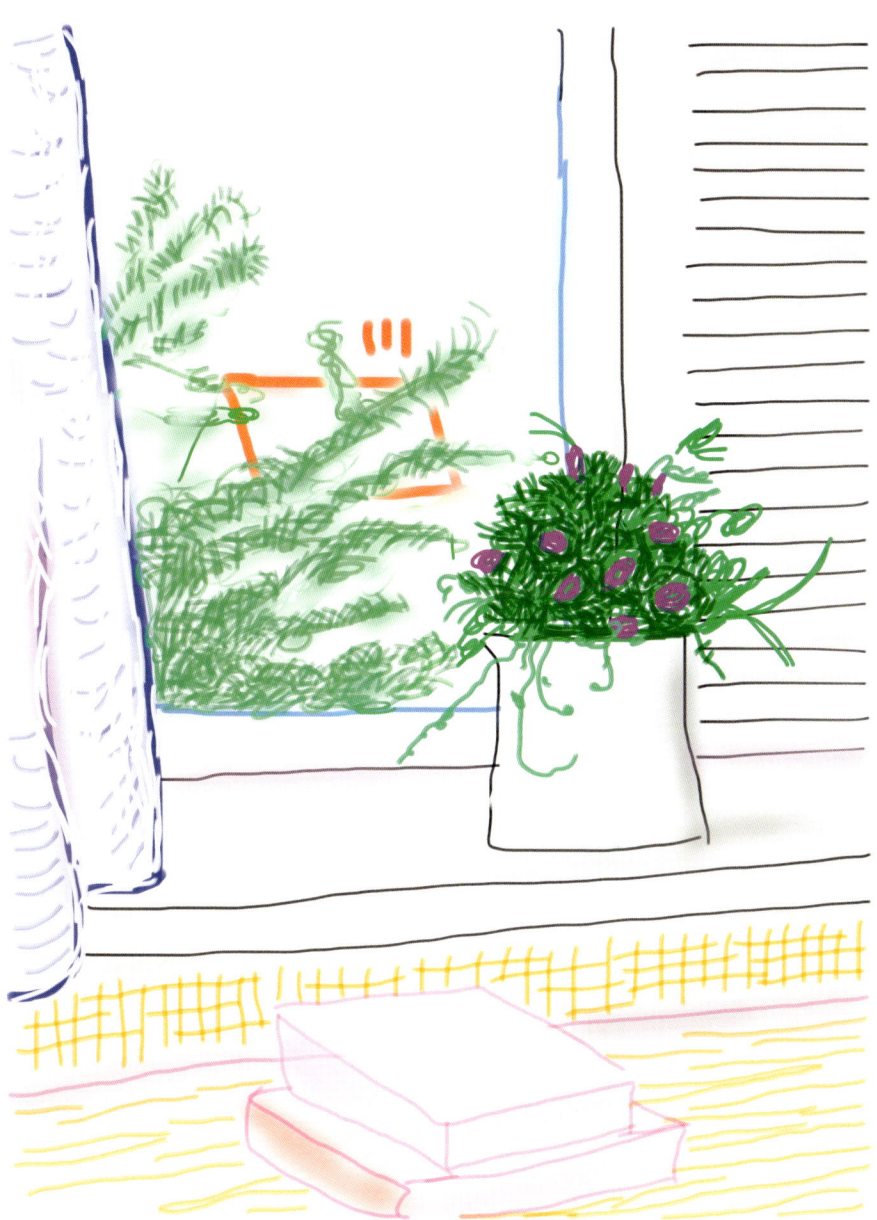

167

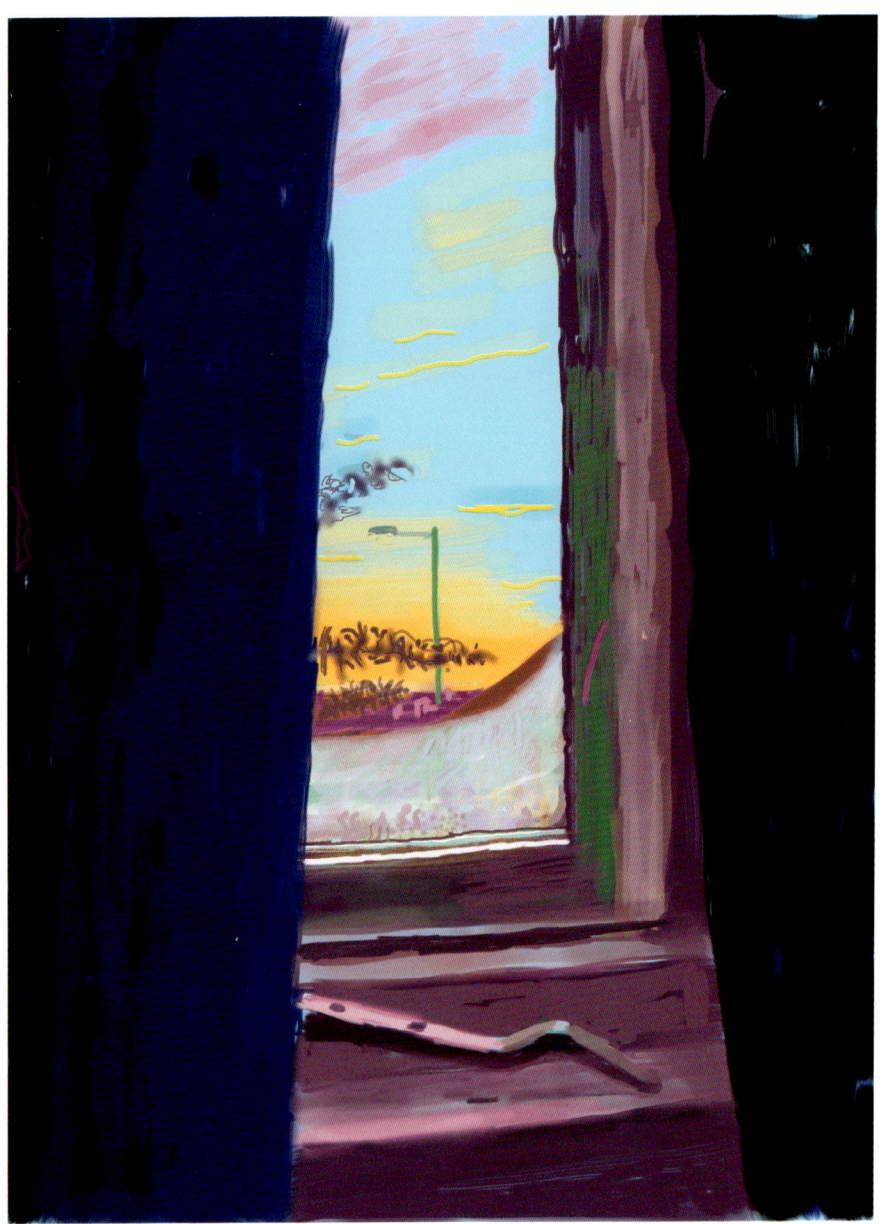

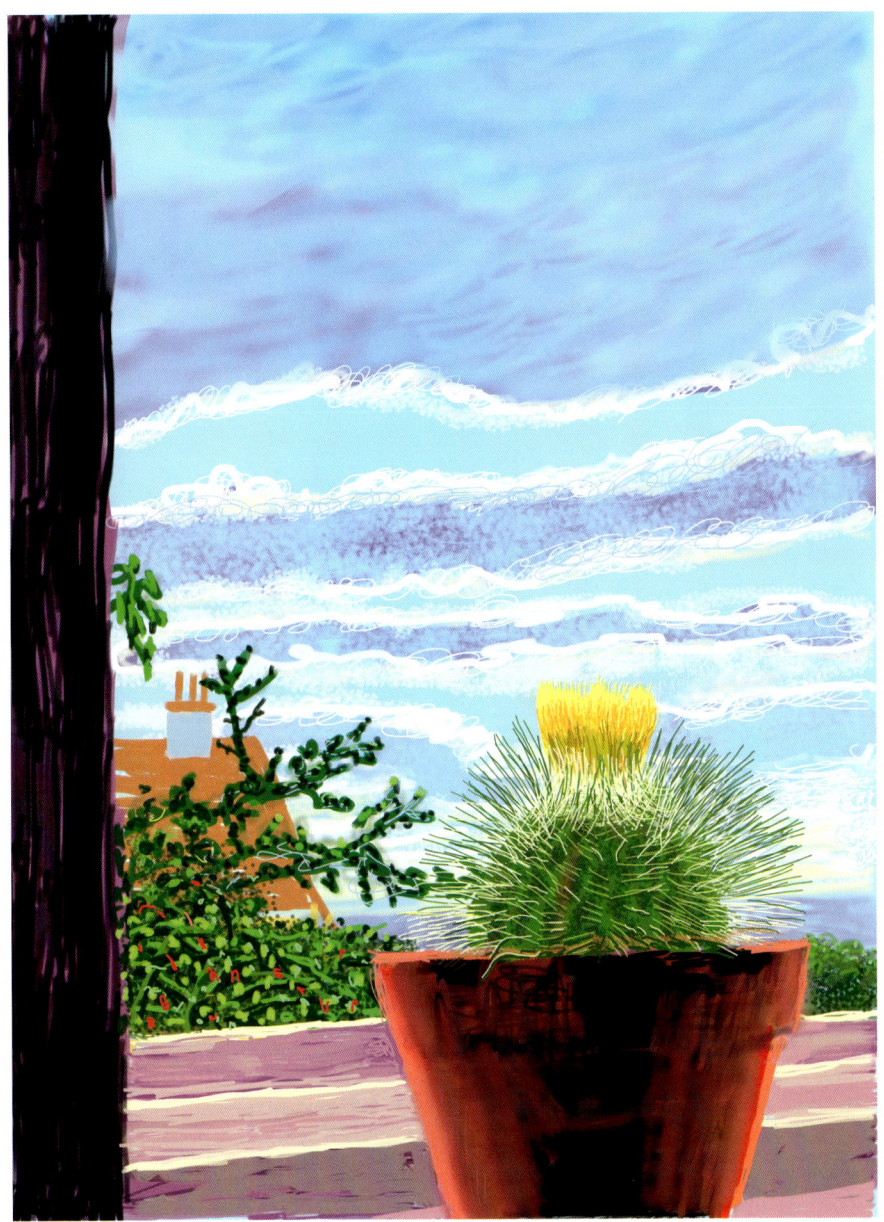

169

'No. 887', 24th May 2011, iPad drawing

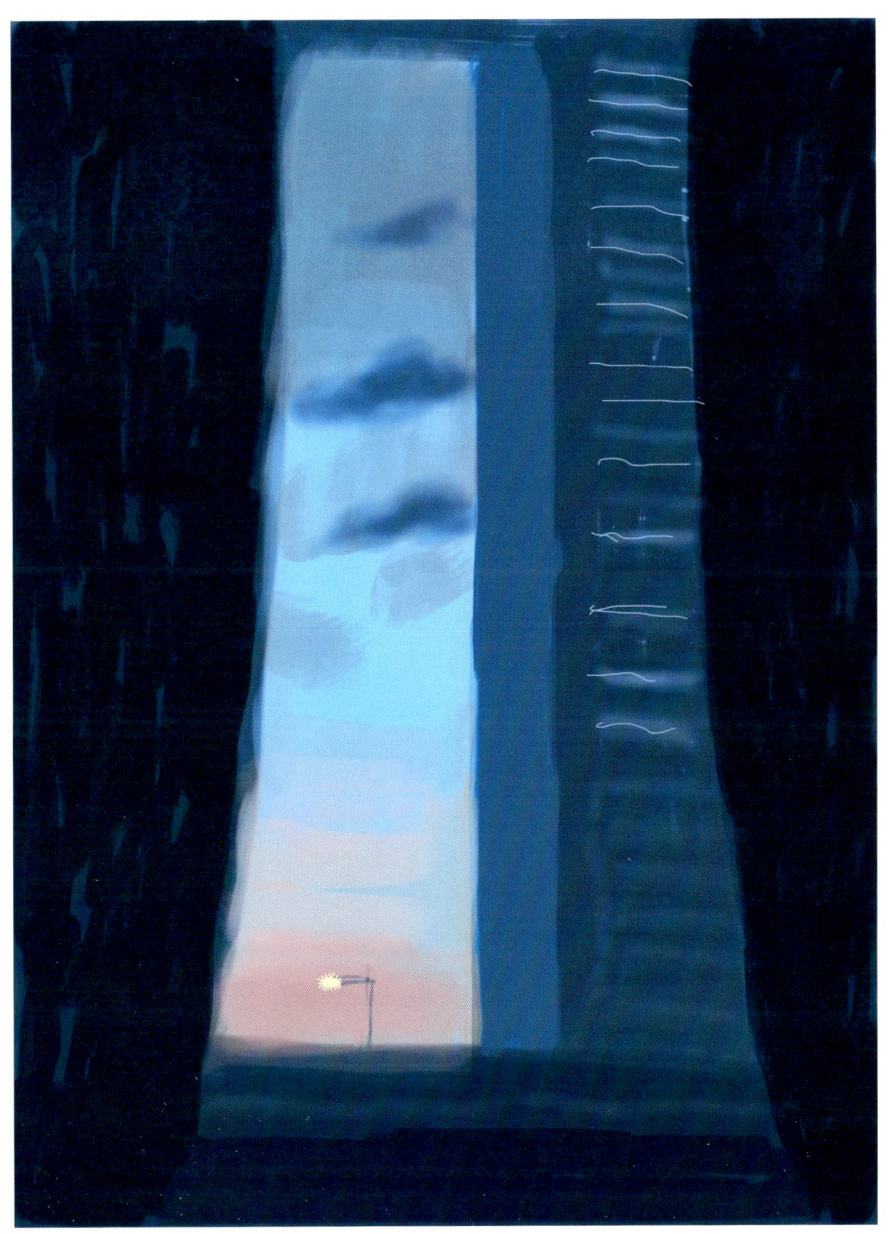

'No. 904', 9th June 2011, iPad drawing

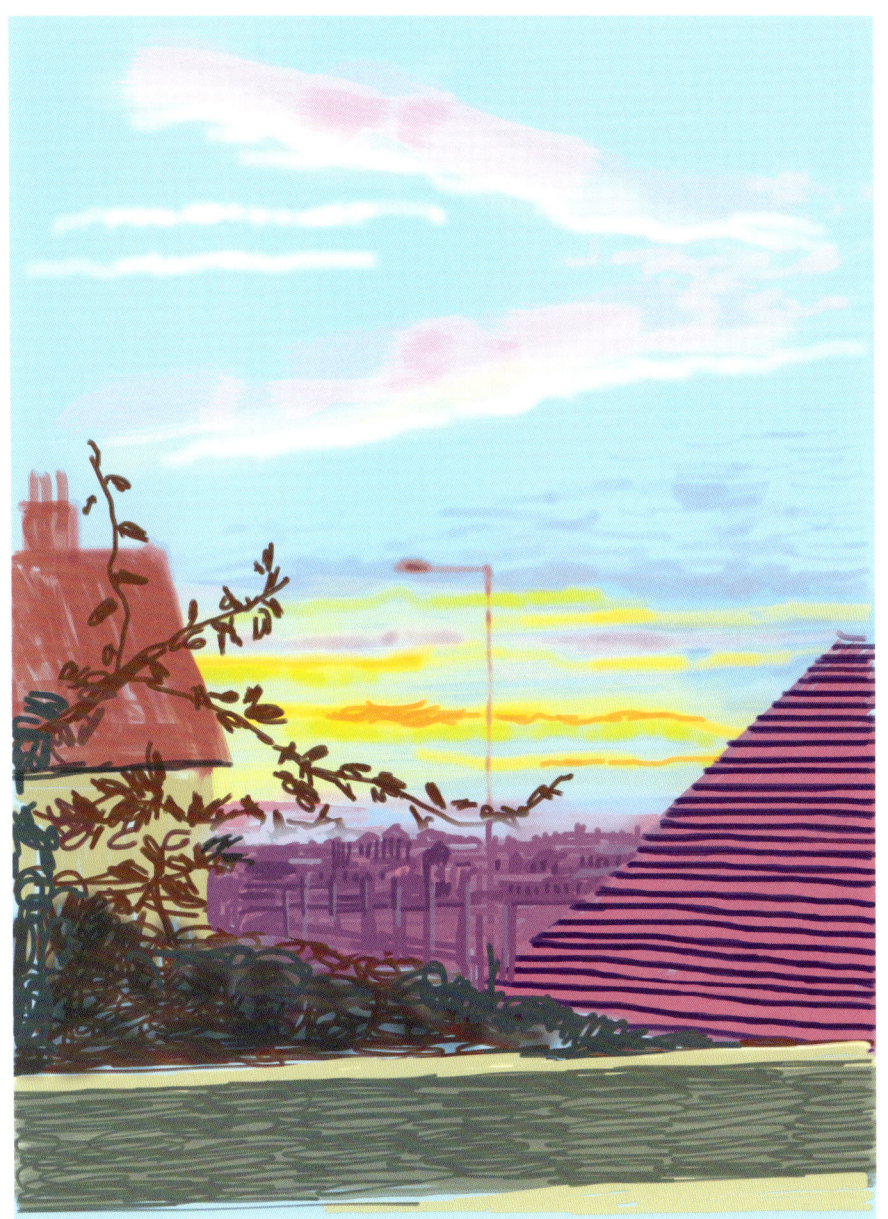

173

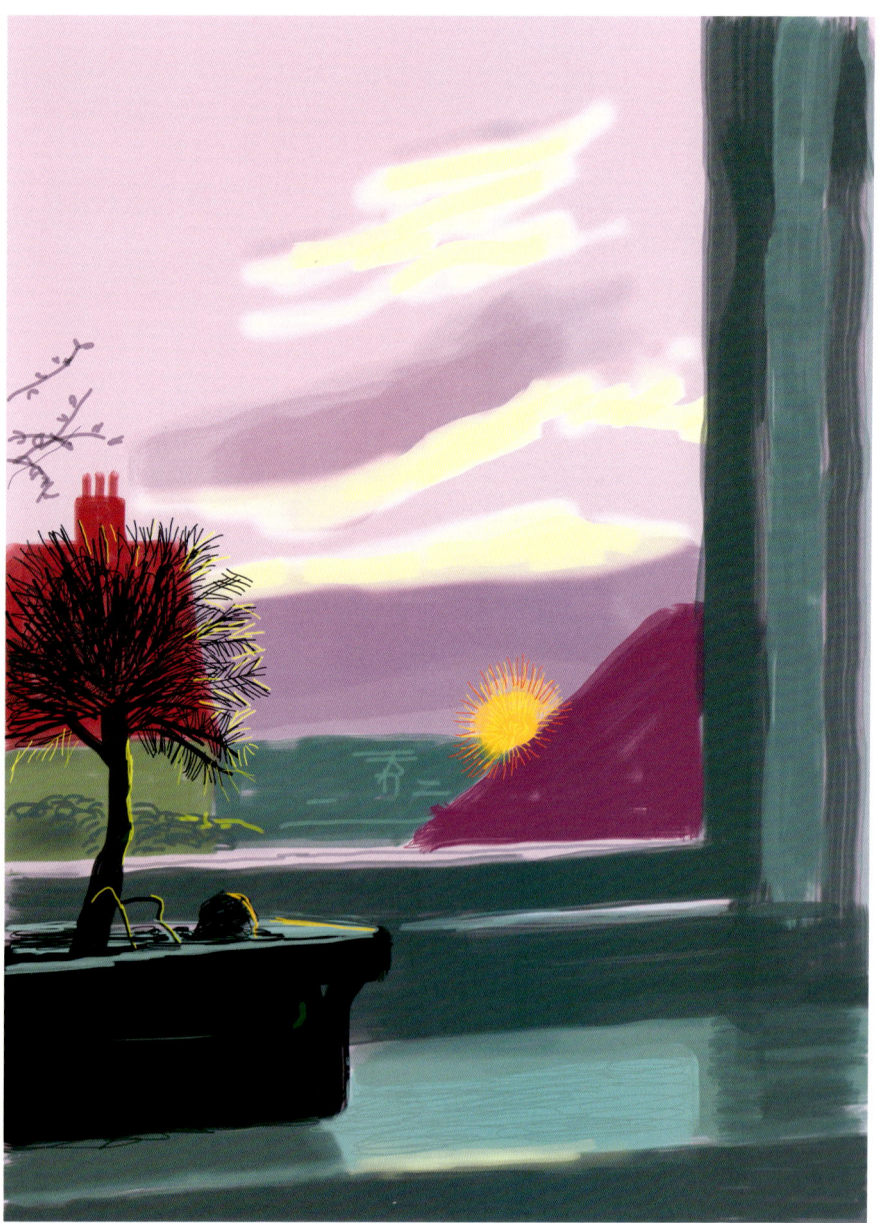

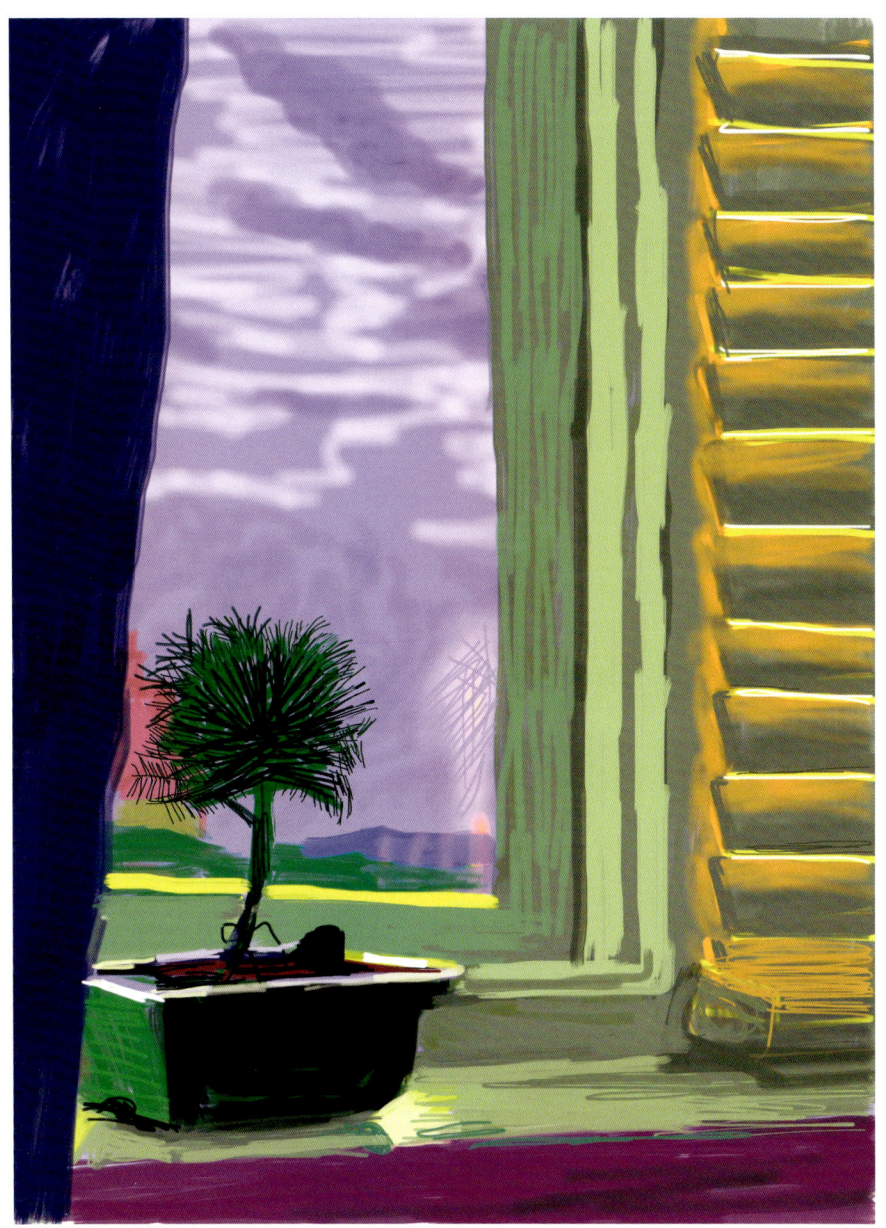

'No. 926', 20th June 2011, iPad drawing

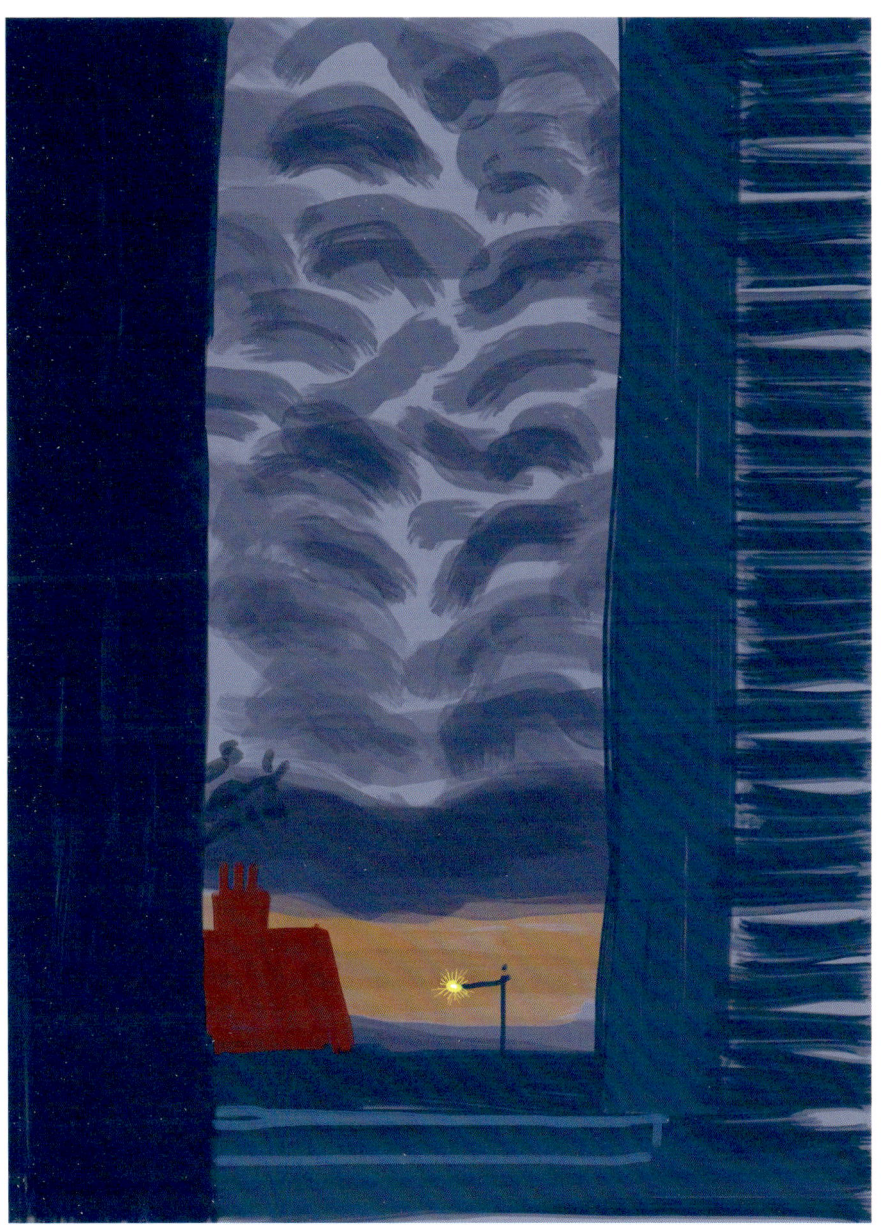

178 'No. 938', 27th June 2011, iPad drawing

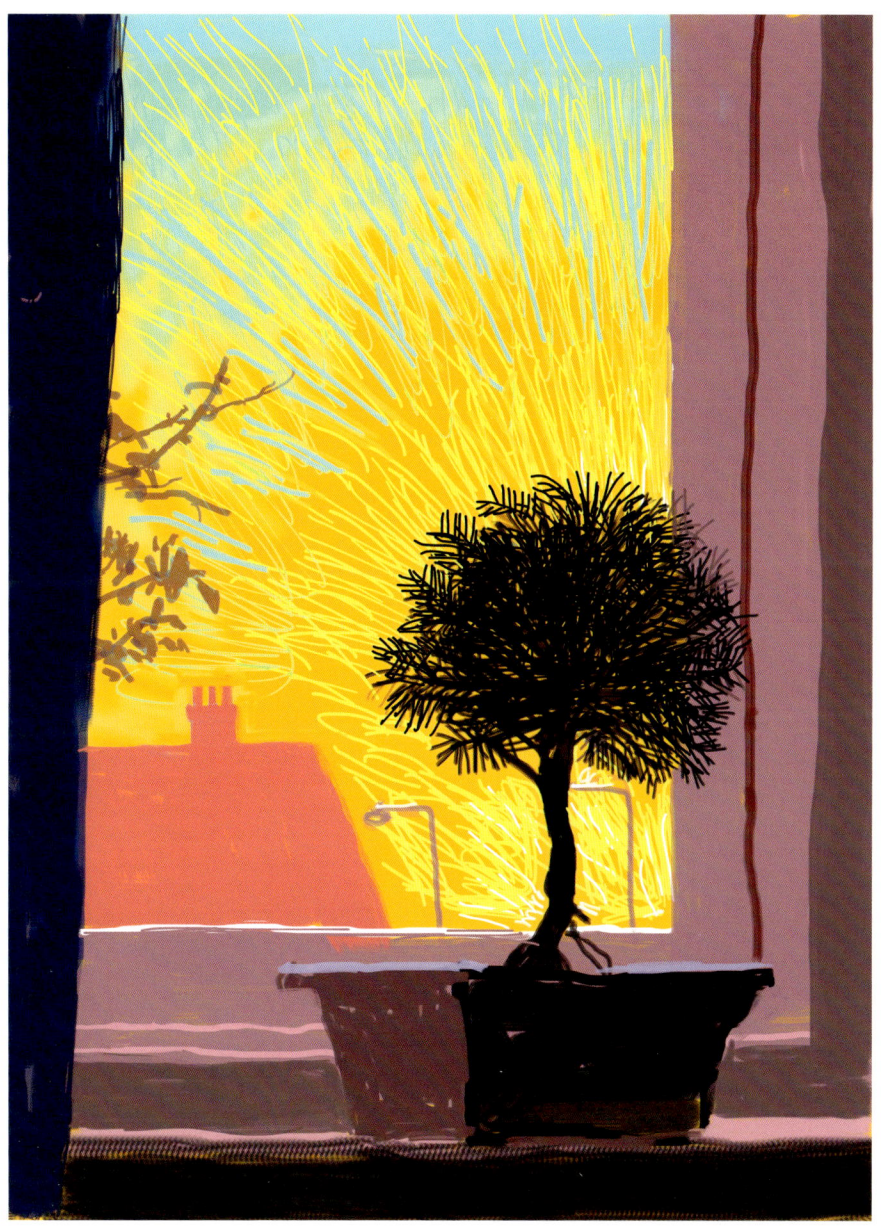

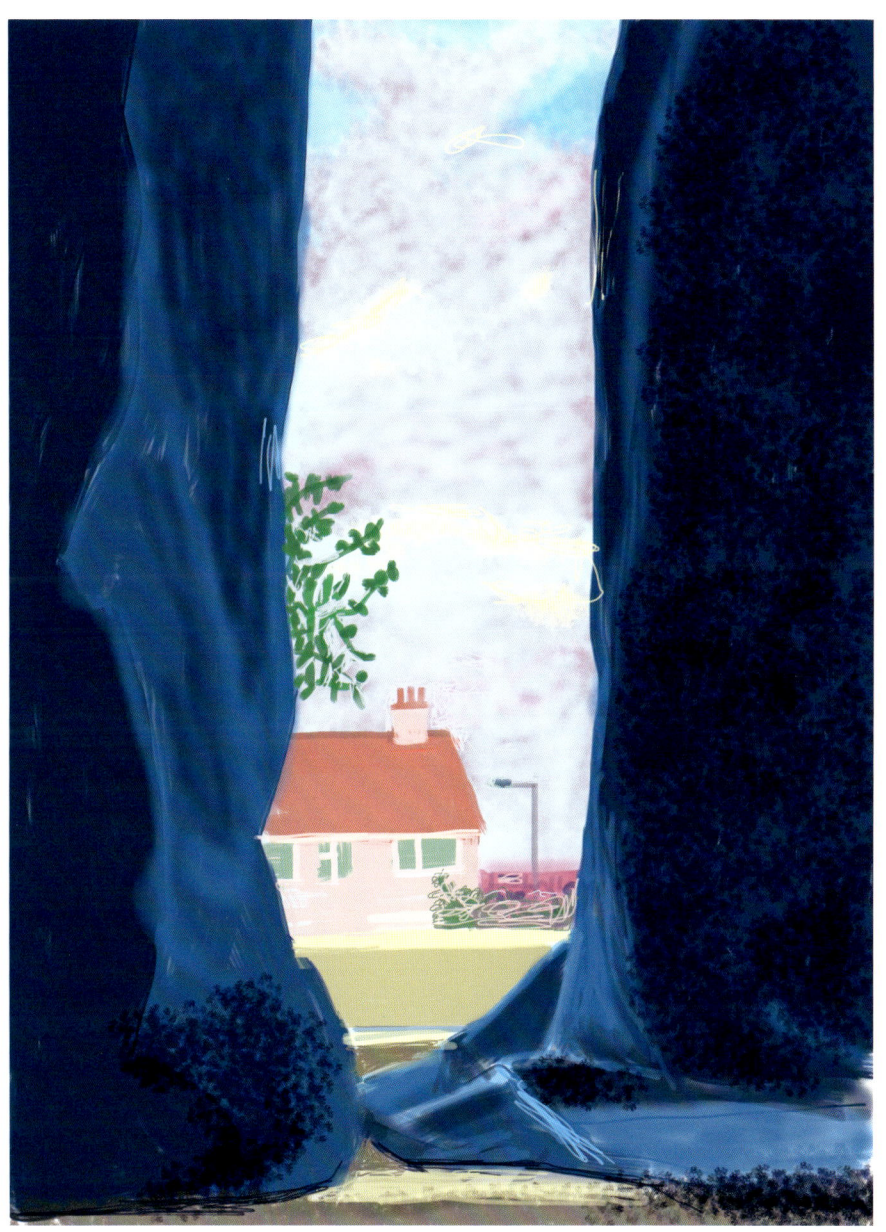

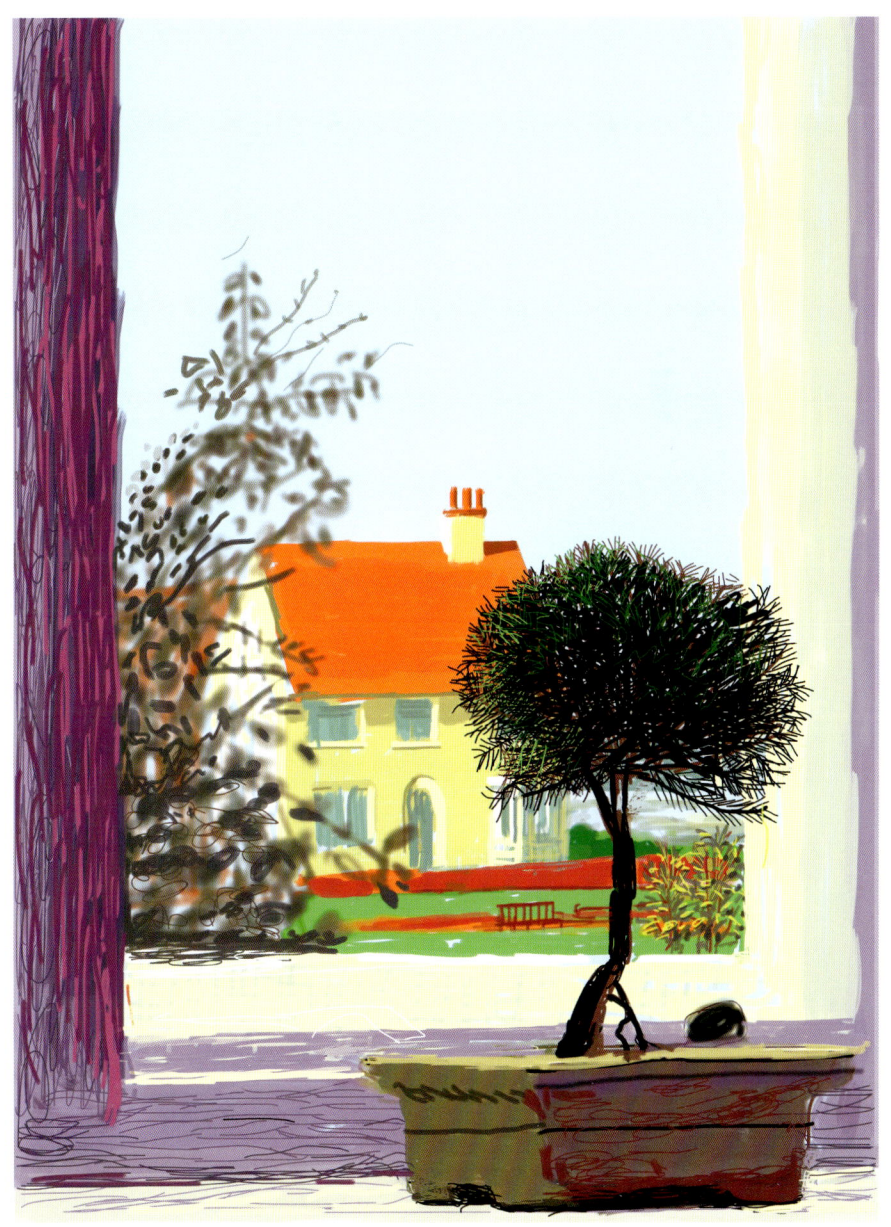

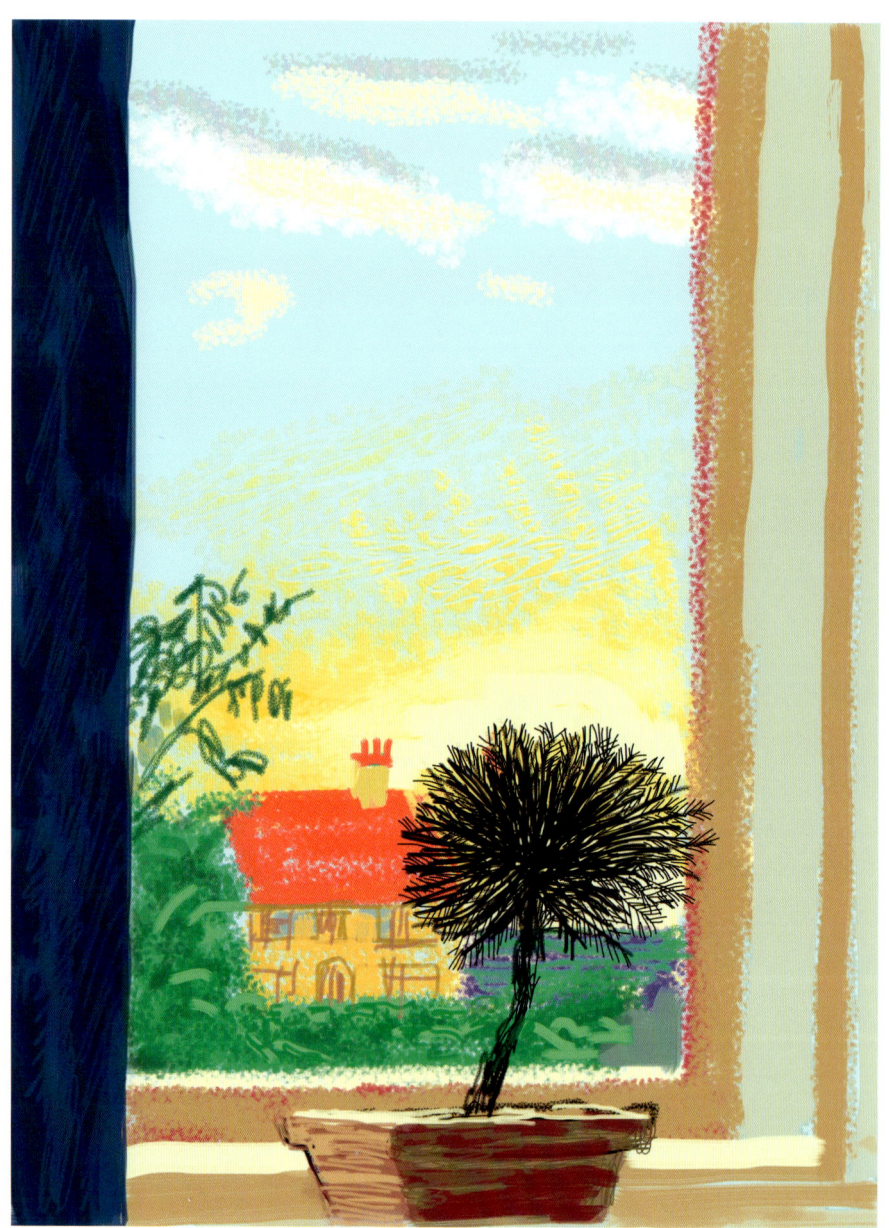

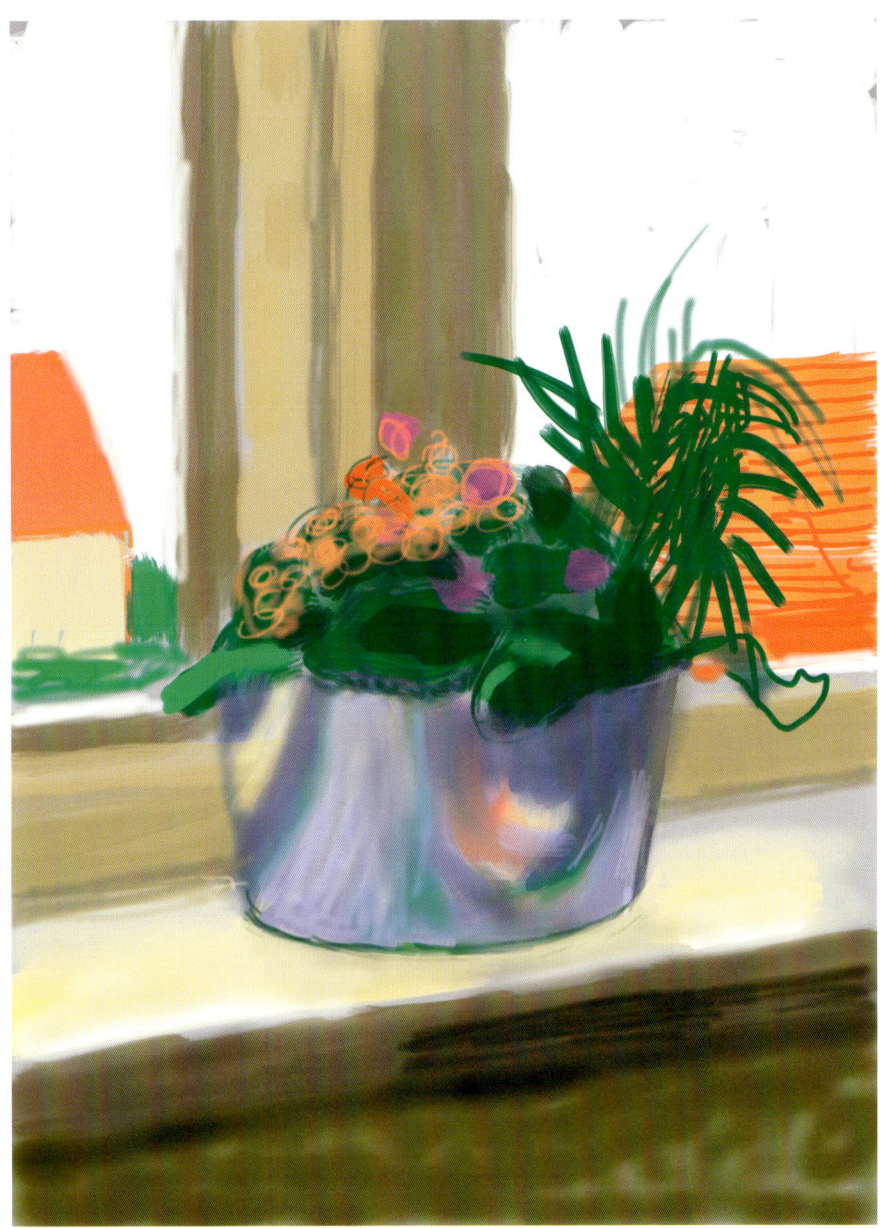

'No. 1061', 10th November 2011, iPad drawing

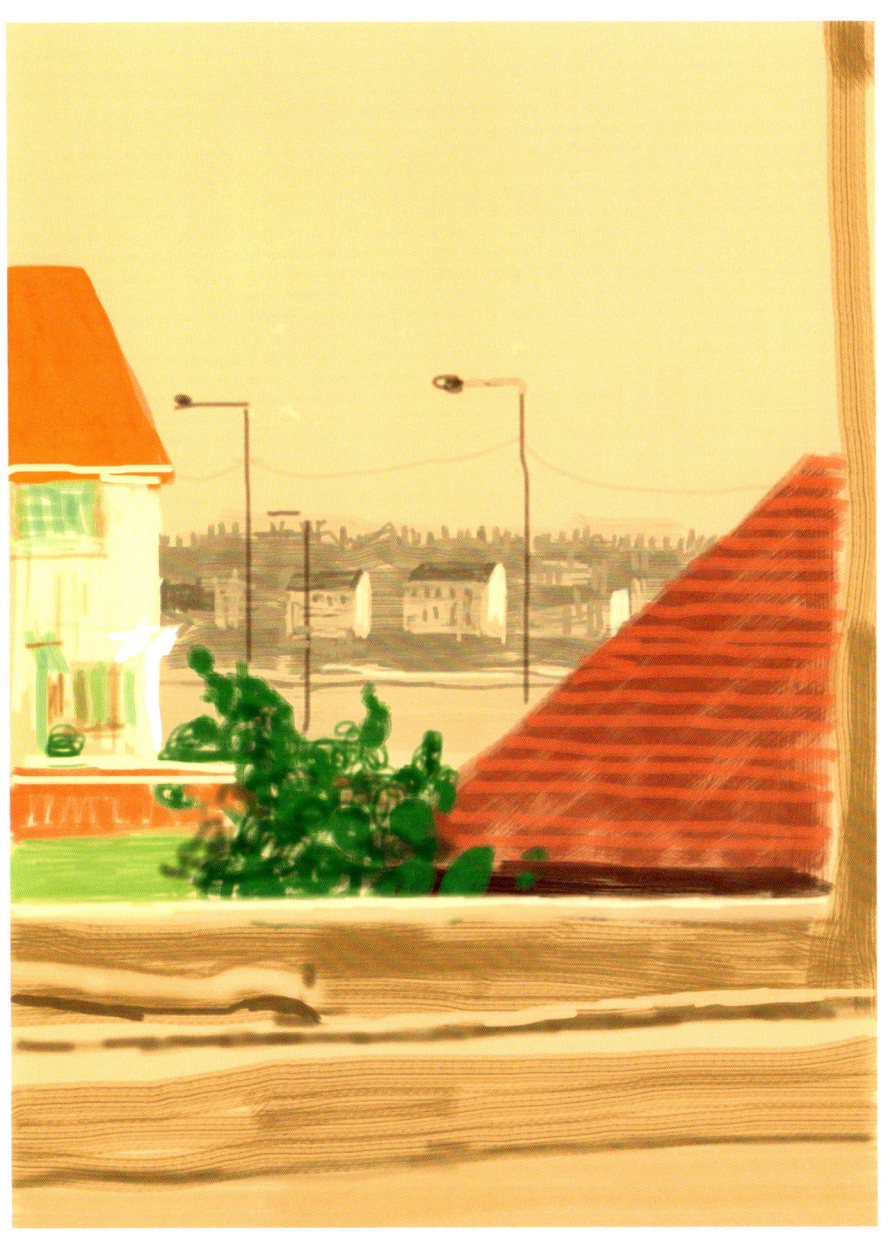

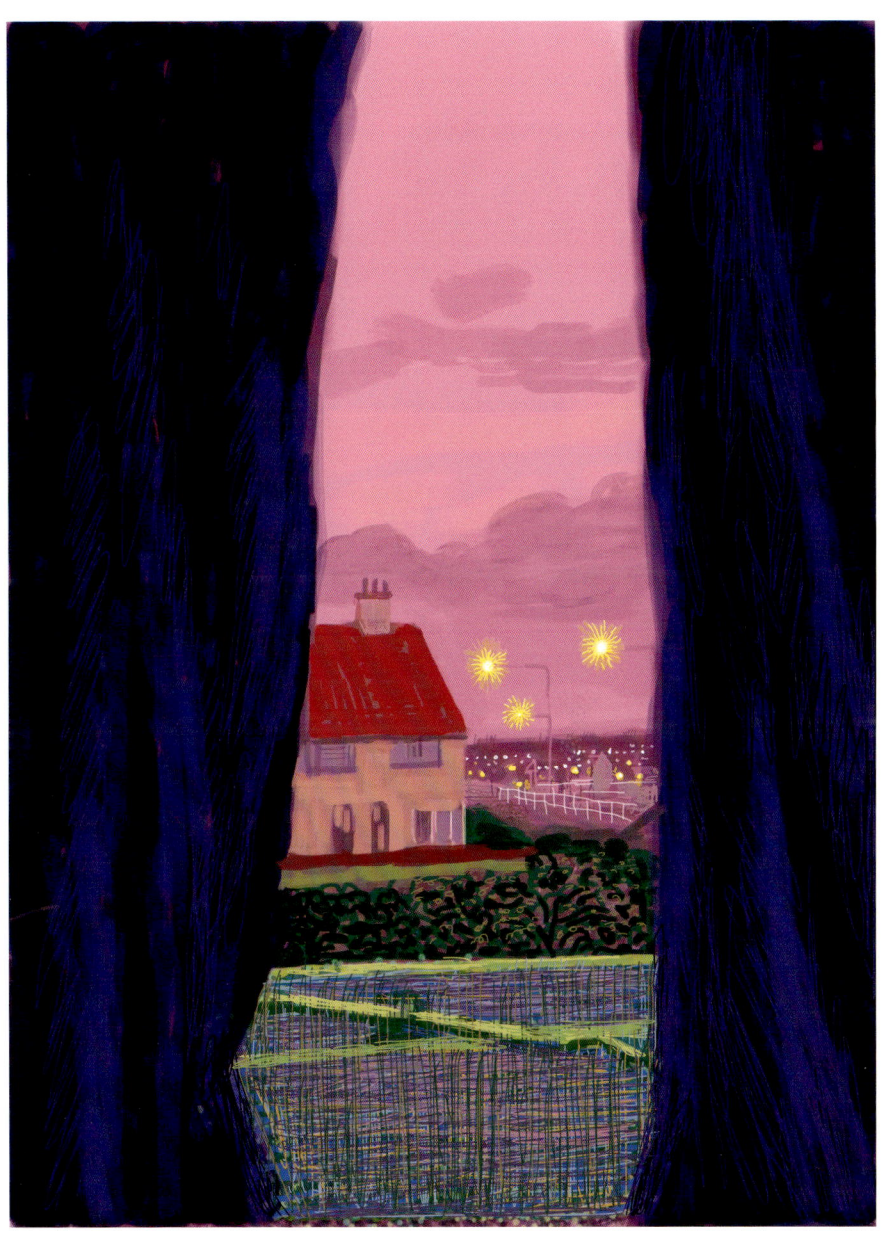

'No. 1283', 3rd July 2012, iPad drawing

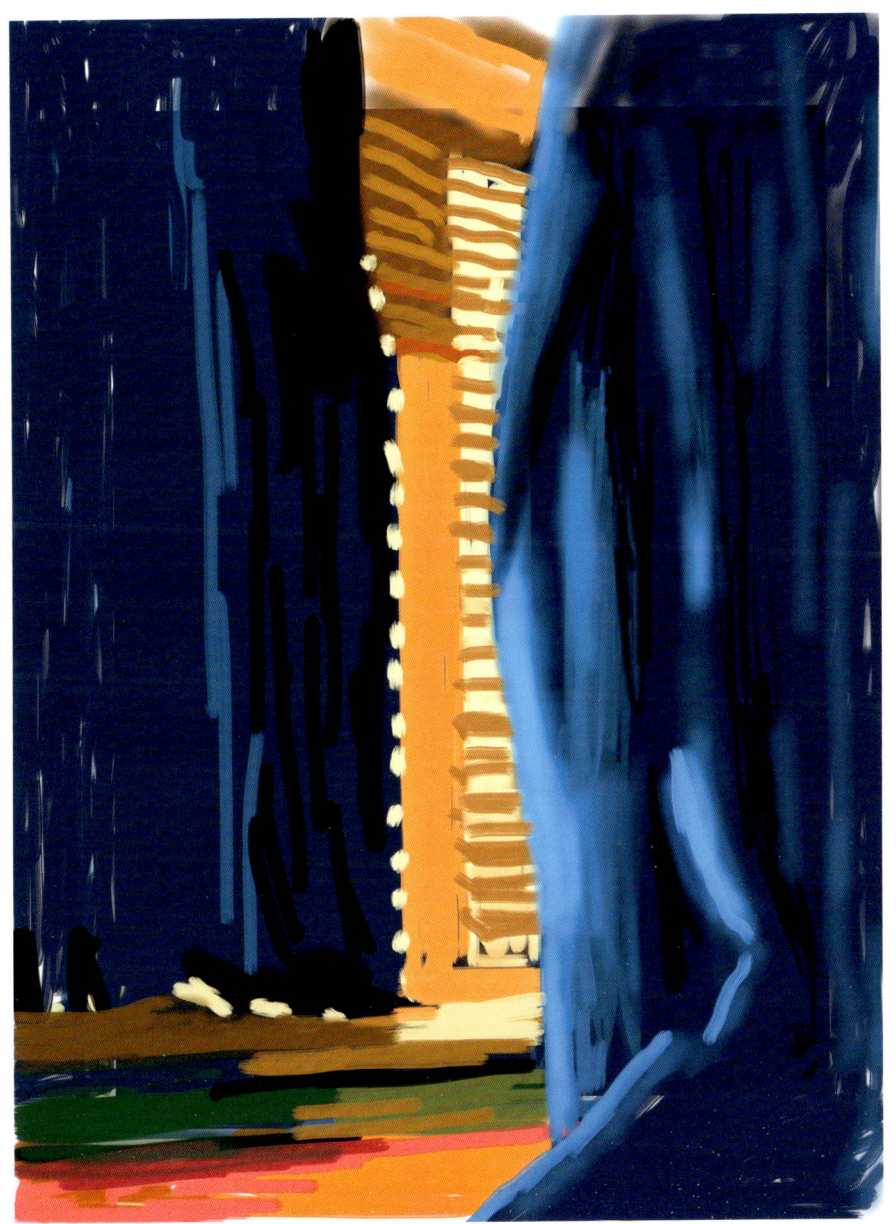

David Hockney—My Window

EACH AND EVERY TASCHEN BOOK PLANTS A SEED!
Each year, we offset our annual carbon emissions with carbon credits
at the Instituto Terra, a reforestation program in Minas Gerais, Brazil, founded
by Lélia and Sebastião Salgado. To find out more about this ecological
partnership, please check: www.taschen.com/institutoterra.
Inspiration: unlimited. Carbon footprint: (almost) zero.

Want to see more? Visit taschen.com to view our current publications,
browse our latest magazine, and subscribe to our newsletter.

Edited and designed by David Hockney and Hans Werner Holzwarth,
with Jean-Pierre Gonçalves de Lima and Jonathan Wilkinson
Cover by David Hockney
Cover: 'No. 846', 7th May 2011, iPad drawing (detail)
Back cover: 'No. 281', 23rd July 2010, iPad drawing (detail)
All works and text by David Hockney © David Hockney, 2025

© 2025 TASCHEN GmbH
Hohenzollernring 53, 50672 Köln, Germany, www.taschen.com
Printed in Italy
ISBN 978-3-8365-9796-8